IN LEVIATHAN'S BELLY

Borgo Press Books by DARKO SUVIN

In Leviathan's Belly: Essays for a Counter-Revolutionary Time

IN LEVIATHAN'S BELLY

ESSAYS FOR A COUNTER-REVOLUTIONARY TIME

DARKO SUVIN

THE BORGO PRESS

MMXII

Stokvis Studies in Historical
Chronology and Thought
ISSN 0270-5338
Number Eighteen

FIRST EDITION

Published by Wildside Press LLC

www.wildsidebooks.com

DEDICATION

This book is dedicated to the teachers of my formative years at the university or at its margins: **Petar Guberina** (Zagreb), **L. C. Knights** (Bristol), **Lucien Goldmann** (Paris). They are not posed in the volume but presupposed.

The essays would not exist without my lifelong fascination with and learning from **Karl Marx** and **Bert Brecht**, who took the best from the German language and tradition, and revolted against the powers ruling their country;

Nor without **Nena**: all of us exiles and émigrés.

CONTENTS

ACKNOWLEDGMENTS

"Introduction 2012: The Winter of the World" is published here for the first time. Copyright © 2012 by Darko Suvin.

"On Stance, Agency, and Emotions in Brecht" was originally published in different form in several journals of the 1990s, but appears here in this form for the first time. Copyright © 2012 by Darko Suvin.

"Two Cheers for Essentialism and Totality" was first published in *Rethinking Marxism* 10.1 (1998). Copyright © 1998, 2012 by Darko Suvin.

"Capitalism Means/Needs War" was first published in *Socialism & Democracy* 16.2 (2002). Copyright © 2002, 2012 by Darko Suvin.

Brecht's poem *Das Manifest* is from: Bertolt Brecht, *Werke*, Grosse kommentierte Berliner und Frankfurter Ausgabe, Band 15: *Gedichte* 5. © Bertolt-Brecht-Erben / Suhrkamp Verlag 1993. My commentary, "Brecht's Manifesto and Us," was first published in *Socialism & Democracy* 16.1 (2002); an abbreviated version of its second part, the commentary on the translation, is available in German at www.linksnet.de/ Copyright © 2002, 2012 by Darko Suvin.

"To Laputa and Back" was presented as a keynote speech to the Italian Anglistic Association; it was first published in shorter form in *Atti del Convegno AIA 2003* (2005), and in full in *Critical Quarterly* 47.1-2 (2005) : 142-64. Copyright © 2005, 2012 by Darko Suvin.

"Immigration in Europe Today" was first published n *Critical*

I thank all the editors involved, and especially my helpful colleagues Victor Wallis and Colin MacCabe, for their friendly permission to use these, often more or less changed, texts in this book. My thanks also go to W. F. Haug for the insights arising from the discussions of various Inkrit annual meetings and through the process of German translation for some of them in *Das Argument*, and to Srećko Horvat for those arising out of Croatian translations of Essays 8 and 9 in *Up & Underground* (Zagreb). I also owe a great debt of gratitude to many people with whom various drafts were discussed throught the years, the most directly concerned of whom are mentioned in notes to the essays.

INTRODUCTION 2012: THE WINTER OF THE WORLD

If I had a hammer/ I'd hammer in the morning/ I'd hammer in the evening/ All over this land/ I'd hammer out danger/ I'd hammer out love between my brothers and my sisters/ All over this land//...// Well I've got a hammer/ And I've got a bell/ And I've got a song to sing/ All over this land/ It's the hammer of justice/ It's the bell of freedom/ It's the song of love between my brothers and my sisters/ All over this land

The Hammer Song, by Lee Hays and Pete Seeger, 1958

And Jesus said unto him, No man, having put his hand to the plow, and looking back, is fit for the Kingdom of God.

Luke, 9.62

1. What Are We At?

Je voy encore du païs au delà, mais d'une vue trouble et en nuage, que je ne puis desmeler. (I still see a country beyond, but uncertainly and darkly, which I cannot recognize.)

Montaigne, *Essais* I.xxvi

In 1956, in the dead-end of the Cold War, Horkheimer and Adorno embarked on recorded discussions in view of a new version of the *Communist Manifesto* for the new times (just as Brecht had in 1944 felt the need to renew it for the age of world wars and in hexameter form, see Essay 4). The Cold War was also the culmination of "military Keynesianism" with plentiful funding for social needs of people and an attention to them in capitalist countries in order to forestall the Soviet "communist" enemy. This led the two philosophers to state "that Europe and America are probably the best civilizations history has produced up to now as far as prosperity and justice are concerned. The key point now is to ensure the preservation of those gains. This can be achieved only if we remain ruthlessly critical of this civilization." While fiercely inimical to "Russian bureaucrats," they affirmed "a greater right [of the Russian Revolution] as opposed to Western culture. It is the fault of the West that [this] Revolution went the way it did." (41). My position is the same (though I'd update some terms).

A dozen years later, the great historian Eric Hobsbawm wrote an essay where he foresaw "a combination of social disintegration and economic breakdown...more explosive than anything that occurred between the [World W]ars," except in Nazi Germany (334). His then offbeat and outrageous forecast has been proved in spades and beyond anybody's imagination in that generation, certainly including my own. The classical "marxist case against capitalism, that it would not work, and against liberal bourgeois democracy, that it was ceasing to exist, being replaced by fascism" (158), has become embarrassingly clear in the utter cynicism of the stock-market fascists (as one would have to call them) who by now rule the whole world. The stockmarketeers are more elitist than the Nazi variety, but destroy the lives of labouring people and democracy from below if anything more efficiently than Hitler and the Japanese imperialists, with a global reach which those never managed: the number of hungry people has around 2009 reached the record figure of 1,250 million, near to one sixth of the world's population....

In the half century between Hobsbawm's lookout and today,

capitalism has become more powerful, unified, and speedy than ever before. It has not only found new niches by means of profit-oriented sciences from cybernetics and electronics to genetics and nano-technology (see Essay 8), it has also colonized in capillary ways culture and even naked life—say of the immigrants and other sub-proletarians who are by now a world majority. In the last two decades, capitalism has definitely forsaken its bourgeois industrial roots in favour of financial fantasies creating only shameful mass misery and shameless billionaires. What may be crucial: it has most efficiently used the degeneration of the communist idea in the USSR, and other States claiming to be such, to forestall any mass rethinking on a real Left—today almost nowhere visible on the political map, so that we have to enthuse over Chiapas and Bolivia. This was done by demoralizing, through a mixture of half-truths and lies repeated with Goebbelsian obsession, intellectuals as well as labour or proletarian movements (in the widest sense), cutting that link between them the presence of which makes for the success of every revolution at its beginning, and the absence for its failure due to ossification. The giant capitalist colonization of imagination has on the Left been recognized by isolated thinkers, who therefore tend to obscurity both in their writing and their success or impact outside a narrow academic group: the list of such lone intellectual giants goes from Walter Benjamin and Alfred Sohn-Rethel to the US rethinkers around Fredric Jameson, and the only non-obscure exception would be poets like Brecht and a few others. (If I have any valid insights, it would be from standing at their crossroads, while sharing the double obscurity.)

However, capitalism (and all of us in the Leviathan's belly) stands today in the presence of Yeats's rough beast advancing toward Bethlehem. Let me bracket his shambling, as in gunnery, by one very general and one very particular shot. General: in Braudel's view, finance capitalism is not simply a stage but a recurrent "Autumn" signal of transition from one world regime of accumulation and domination (e.g. the Genoese, Dutch,

British, and US ones) to another (246); it signals the destruction of the old regime and creation of a "new" one—a Winter which might be better or worse (cf. Arrighi ix-xiv). Particular: the Chicago "ghetto" in 1988 was found to harbour "silent riots of everyday life," no less destructive if usually less than spectacular. Private capital had completely withdrawn, in the years 1950-80 manual jobs fell from 36 to 5 thousand and white collar jobs from 15 to less than 7.5 thousand. There was starkly insufficient welfare support, but lots of alcohol and gun-selling shops—since police was incapable to protect victims from gangs, families had to protect themselves; the school system served mainly for "parking" of children, and infant mortality was higher than in Chile or Turkey. The informal economy was mainly based on mass drug use, a veritable industry with sales in millions of $; drug pushing was also the main job readily accessible to ghetto youths from under 10 on. There was "organizational desertification": no banks but only currency exchanges, no public schools, cinemas, skating rinks, bowling alleys, the last two clinics closed in 1989 (all in Wacquant). In short, we are here amid Weber's "plunder capitalism" that leads to pandemics of violence; and while Chicago might (or might not) have improved in the meantime, the situation is still such in many other slums of capitalism, US or Latin American or otherwhere, where by now live 1,200 million people. Winter is arriving fast and it doesn't look pretty. Particularly if one figures in all the wars from the First Gulf One through Serbia, Second Gulf, and Afghanistan plus Libya—with more certainly to come. By their fruits ye shall know them.

Gentle reader, you might wish to ask me: but what of a way out of our global trap? Of course I'd have many ideas, not invented by me, about components of a way out—beginning, say, with universal guaranteed income sufficient to modestly live on for all adults working 35 hours a week, and a stress on education and health (and don't tell me there's no way to pay for this: just pay trillions to people instead of banks and the military). Thus I honour the question as supremely important:

we need to get into health, activity, and tenderness—Hays's and Seeger's "love of my brothers and my sisters." But this book is primarily not about the way out (though that is its vanishing perspective point) but about the trap of hunger, despair, and violence. For truth shall maybe not make you free, but certainly enable you to become free.

2. Why the Essays in This Book

> It is necessary to depict landscapes by images and remarks because of the nature of the investigation. For it compels us to travel over a wide field of thought crisscross in every direction. The...remarks in the book are, as it were, a number of sketches of landscapes made in the course of these long and involved journeyings.... [A]lmost the same points were being approached from different directions, and new sketches made....Thus this book is really only an album.
>
> Wittgenstein, *Philosophical Investigations*

This book has three essays explicitly on Bert Brecht, and implicitly he has been shaping my understanding for over half a century. Essay 1 (finished in 2000) deals with his concept and image of stance or bearing (*Haltung*) as fundamental for fixing the dynamics of a body—any body or all bodies—poised and enabled to intervene into matters that concern any and all. I use fixing in the sense of photography, where it means stabilizing and rendering visible, thus also sharable, a latent image potentially existing earlier. This *Haltung* is opposed to the concept and image of "world view," which may be momentarily useful but does not wear well because it is not anchored in the ineluctably present labouring and enjoying (or exhausted and painful) body but reduced to a pseudo-scientific eye only, passively observing. To the contrary, as in Marx, people's work and pleasure produce the world, meshing subject and object in a feedback: love is for Brecht a production, indeed, the supremely pleasurable production of an intimately complementary human relationship.

Such a stance is also the central link in a Brechtian chain of terms and images about personality, involving equally everyday "upright posture" (Bloch) and the furthest horizons of death— in our epoch much more urgently a societal rather than a biological decision, for example in wars or the readiness to die for a cause, matters Brecht dealt with in most of his great plays from *Saint Joan of the Slaughterhouses* and the *Lehrstücke* to *Mother Courage and Her Children* and *Life of Galileo*. Further, it enables us to rethink with him the most muddy hollywoodian and TV reliance on emotion planned and deployed as an opposite of reason (see much more in Suvin, "Brecht and Subjectivity"). Contrariwise, their fusion in a *Haltung* enables a body to understand and withstand.

In a long-duration view, Brecht's opus gives us the most persuasive example of how to sublate—redefine and yet preserve—the great Enlightenment discovery of reason, outside which there is no salvation for any or all. Not by "weak thought" or sickly emotion but by the loving union of clarified emotion and precise reason, itself embracing both concepts and topologies, that is configurations in empirical or imaginary spacetime such as metaphors.

The present volume fully participates in such an impossibility of keeping apart subject and object, in the sense that each essay has a defined object but was also felt and held by me to be most pertinent for myself and those who would be open to similar arguments, feelings, and stances. This is obvious in the case of war caused by capitalism (Essay 3) but in more mediated ways all essays have been enforced by its enraged and inflamed state in the last two decades. As for stance, it has led me to reflect on and attempt to perfect my own. Within it, the other most important opus to be constantly revisited, quarried, and updated has for me since my teens been that of Karl Marx.

Essay 2 (1993) reacts against Post-Modernist truly weak

thought tabooing the central Marxian category of "totality." It concedes that Hegel's and the Positivists' (in fact theological) use of it as the presupposition of a static and "natural" ontology out there, as a Stoic necessity providing a stable yardstick for everything (as in Lenin's weakest book, *Materialism and Empiriocriticism*), is no longer tenable. But it then affirms that no useful epistemology—no way of understanding our societal and natural environment—is possible without using a provisional totality for well-defined purposes. This puts paid, as Walter Benjamin realised, to the bourgeois concept of automatic progress: any progress we might achieve will be contingent and threatened. History has proved that to the hilt.

Essay 3 is encapsulated in the two verbs of its title, "Capitalism Means/Needs War." On the one hand, psychologically, war is more than a metaphor for capitalist human relationships, it is their essence: in them, man is wolf to man (with excuses to the maligned wolves, who never kill more than they could eat). On the other hand, economically, capitalism has not only never prospered without warfare, it could not survive more than a few years without the trillions of dollars of "military Keynesianism." I cite a conservative estimate of world spending for military purposes from twenty years ago standing at one trillion dollars per year or 2,500 millions daily; today I guess it might be anywhere up to the double. Humanity will <u>never</u> have the food, education, and medicine it needs until wars are stopped. This means changing our whole way of life and power system, so it may fail. Then we are—remember the Welfare State?—descending into nuclear-cybernetic-nano barbarism.

It will be obvious from the essay's section "Wars of Reterritorialization" how for this author, born and bred in Yugoslavia, this theme became mandatory after the NATO bombing of Serbia in the late nineties. This was, I found, a crass example of the worldwide warfare waged by the capitalist class using the criminal or *Lumpen* class against the working and middle classes. This has by now finally led me to return to Marx's and Lenin's not entirely clear but crucially necessary category of class in Essay 11—better culpably late than never.

As to the Essay 3 Postscriptum of 2002, it uses one of my essays on terrorism ("Access," and see "Exploring") to compare it with war, and concludes that the boundary between them is being erased.

A pleasing union of my masters and preoccupations then resulted in Essay 4 (2001) on Brecht's reworking of *The Communist Manifesto* for our age of world wars. To the last moment of preparing this volume it was unclear whether The Brecht Heirs (an institution which is in the production of The Brecht Industry analogous to capital owners, not least in fettering production) will accord me the copyright permission for the translation of that text. This was finally given against a small payment, but the problem remains.

A theoretical point embodied by that essay is whether poetry (and its sister arts, from narrative prose through painting to music and dance) has a cognitive status. Having learned from them at least half of what I know and cherish, my pragmatic answer is: yes, poetry is cognitive—though in different ways than science and philosophy. I put some arguments to buttress this into Essay 8 (and more in my case study "Cognition"), but this is only incipient greening of—so far as I know—a theoretical desert.

Essay 5 (2003) was sparked by chance and kind friends but gave me a chance to look, with growing dismay, at the discipline of English Studies, in which—though I had other interests too—I faithfully laboured for over one third of a century, teaching much from medieval drama, Shakespeare, and Swift to Woolf. It is a case study of how ideology under capitalism infiltrates and bends an intellectual profession. It tallied with my reflections on my own class, the intellectuals (see "Utopianism" and "On Cognition") and its "treason by clerics" against emancipation and against its own reason for being. With bitter poetic justice, this class of mine has now been downgraded into a push-pen amanuensis and gofer for the brainwashing at the basis of capitalist power. Only a Swiftian stance can hope to render justice to this monstrosity, and I have stolen from this all-time favourite of mine as much as I could lift.

Indignant frustration at my yearly bouts with residence permits led to Essay 6 (2006-07; and cf. its predecessor "Exile"). It is a case not only of direct link between autobiography and intellectual production, but also of what I feel is the latter's psychic beauty: that creativity renders the creator omnipotent, albeit only inside the tiny sub-creation and while it is being appreciated by others. But even limited divine status—fortunately also challengeable within a vast pantheon of creative godlets—is preferable to none. Inside the cognitions and pleasures of my work, police bureaucracy is held at bay. As Adorno remarked, "theory is a kind of stand-in for happiness" (53)—and it shared the ambiguous nature of all such *ersatz*es. Also, the alternative of "civil cohabitation" I argue for is toothless, but it is young and may get some milk teeth at least, if given a chance to grow. Which is why I'm republishing it, inside Leviathan.

Another lucky chance, the review of a misguided periodical issue, led to the brief Essay 7 (2008)—for how could I pass by an issue called "Brecht and Communism"? At the time I had begun work on my major preoccupation in these last years, the anatomy of SFR Yugoslavia, a self-proclaimed socialist State led by a self-proclaimed communist party. Most of the reviewed articles provided a perfect case of what I had to shun if I were, beyond praise or blame, to make sense of either—and Brecht was there to help me along. The essay led to the tangent of how to initially disentangle the term communism (is it a place, a horizon or an orientation?):

> You've heard much untruth about it from enemies, from friends
> Much untruth also.... (Brecht, *Das Manifest*, vv. 14-15)

Essay 8, "On the Horizons of Epistemology and Science" (2008-09) is, together with the one on war, the longest and possesses the widest scope in the volume. It is, so far, the culmination of what I have understood about cognition in class society: the pernicious Unique Truth, the refusal of human history, technoscience as the life-destroying bludgeon of capitalism, plus how to use Hesiod's concept-splitting to understand these and how to begin tracing "whither now?" To my initial two (or with Walter Benjamin three) paragons, Nelson Goodman, Gramsci, Marcuse, and Nietzsche had to be adjoined for guidance.

Essay 9, "Death into Life" (2009), was on the contrary an attempt at a summation in 5,000 words of what I would have to say to a more politically awake audience. It is not a foray onto new terrain but a consolidation of already visited terrains. It ranges widely, it had to be compressed; and I decided that I had to overcome my pusillanimous use of verse separately from prose (I've published three collections of poetry, see the entries in Suvin, "Bibliography B," on *Armirana Arkadija*, *The Long March,* and *Abiko Annual* nos. 24 and 25), or as citations to prove a point—say, Blake in the preceding essay—or, at best, as an object of inquiry (say, Brecht in Essay 4). I interleaved in each of the five essay sections a poem with expository prose, and hope the brief repetition in those sections of what I've mostly written before would gain a new dimension through the condensed poems' interaction with them and with each other.

Essay 10 arose from thinking of what I could bring to a conference of Left-wing European economists in 2009, at the beginning of our Great Depression (but before the manmade tsunami had devastated most of beautiful Greece). I went back to basics: having studied thermodynamics and read much in ecology, I tried to bring this into a critical economics, issuing in some initial policy proposals. The presupposition for them is that the power of capitalist financing would be broken. As Buckminster Fuller told us in the 1960s, we are at Utopia or Oblivion.

Essay 11 is the working hypothesis for my forthcoming study of classes in ex-Yugoslavia. My stance here, as elsewhere, is one of a mildly sceptical reuse of classical Marxism—which for me cannot taboo some insights of Lenin—not as a dogma of Truth but as a flexible guide for possible understanding and action today.

So, at the end, are these "sketches of landscapes" by the road of life in these times a well-planned and homogeneous album? I'm afraid not. I believe they share a single *Haltung*, with a horizon of poetic justice and an intolerance against what degrades people. They might be a collection of some oil paintings interspersed with gouaches and drawings. Perhaps pictures from an exhibition in progress?

Lucca, Italy, April 2012

Works Cited

Presupposed: the opuses of Brecht, Marx, Benjamin, Gramsci, some Nietzsche and much poetry.

This book is, as it were, the third in a trilogy embracing also my two books of 2010 and 2011 cited below; ideally, it should be read together with them, since they look at similar or identical landscapes from various angles and heights.

Adorno, Theodor, and Max Horkheimer. "Towards a New Manifesto?" Transl. R. Livingstone. *NLR* no. 65 (2010): 33-61. [cited as H-A]

Arrighi, Giovanni. *The Long 20th Century: Money, Power, and the Origins of Our Times.* London: Verso, 1994.

Braudel, Fernand. *The Perspective of the World. Civilization and Capitalism*, vol. 3. Transl. S. Reynolds. London: Collins, 1984.

Hobsbawm, Eric. *Revolutionaries.* London: Abacus, 2008 [original 1973].

Suvin, Darko. "Access to an Identification of >Terrorism<" (2001) and "Exploring >Terror/ism<": Numinosity, Killings,

Horizons" (2004), both in his *Darko Suvin: A Life in Letters.* Ed. Ph.E. Wegner. Vashon Island WA 98070: Paradoxa, 2011, 263-305.

——. "Bibliography B," in his *Darko Suvin* [see above], 355-62.

——. "Brecht and Subjectivity" (1989-2006), in his *Darko Suvin* [see above], 133-57.

——. "Cognition, Freedom, *The Dispossessed* as a Classic" (2007) in his *Defined by a Hollow: Essays on Utopia, Science Fiction, and Political Epistemology.* Oxford: P. Lang, 2010, 509-51.

——. "Exile as Mass Outrage and Intellectual Mission," in Maria Teresa Chialant ed., *Viaggio e letteratura.* Venezia: Marsilio, 2006, 69-95.

——. "Utopianism from Orientation to Agency: What Are We Intellectuals under Post-Fordism to Do?" (1997–1998) and "On Cognition as Art and Politics" (1997–1999), in his *Defined* [see above], 217-351.

Wacquant, Loïc J.D. "America as Social Dystopia," in Pierre Bourdieu et al. T*he Weight of the World: Social Suffering in Contemporary Society.* Transl. P.P. Ferguson. Cambridge: Polity P, 1999, 131-39.

1. ON STANCE, AGENCY, AND EMOTIONS IN BRECHT (1989-2000)[1]

—To Jochen Fiebach, friend for fifty years of worrying about theatre and socialism: er bewahrte die Haltung—

0. Preliminary

It is well known that Brecht focused on a thinking capable of intervention into relationships among people (*eingreifendes Denken*) through the condensed and displaced guise of poetry and art. In order to do this he needed a mediation which would be sufficiently incisive without being simply doctrinal ideology.

I have a twofold thesis in this paper: First, <u>the red thread or</u>

1. This essay would have been difficult to write or even conceive without the stimulating surveys by Haffad on love as productivity and by Steinweg on pedagogy and learning in Brecht. Except where otherwise noted, all translations are mine, with thanks to my students Andrew Wood and Caroline Schütze who helped to translate some of the *Me-Ti* stories. I have added punctuation and caps when translating the notes from the Brecht Archive, and made some changes in other translations. My thanks also go to Marianne Conrad, Joachim Fiebach, Dorothea Haffad, Wolf Haug, Walter Hinck, Ishida Hiromi, Franz Norbert Mennemeier, Tilman Reitz, and Cornelia Thiels. Parallel and often overlapping arguments are to be found in a number of my items listed below, especially in "Brecht and Subjectivity."

central insight which unites all the periods and all the genres of his work and life was the concept of *Haltung*. It is a posture-cum-attitude, imperfectly translated as stance or bearing. That Brecht thought of *Haltung* as supremely important may be suggested by two examples, about literature and theatre. In an early *Me-ti* story Brecht claimed "to have renewed the language of literature...by putting only stances into sentences and letting the stances always appear through the sentences" [GKA 18: 78-79]; and in his sketches for "dialectical dramaturgy," the stage should be composed of groupings "in which or toward which the single person assumes particular stances" while the audience groups change their stances and grow into productive co-workers by studying and judging the stage stances [GKA 21: 440-42]. I shall discuss Brecht's overarching views about it, and two principal ways he sought to particularize this general, so to speak syntactic, concept by finding sociohistorically pertinent macro-stances. As of ca. 1928 on, he formulated it as a semantic cluster around the concept of a redefined pedagogy, but after his emigration this concept was dropped as no more pertinent and too narrow, and replaced by meanings clustering around a redefined notion of production, productivity or productive critique.

My second thesis is that this bearing is (as any interest) not to be disjoined from certain kinds of emotion. In fact, I assume that for Brecht any *Haltung* implied an emotion, and viceversa.

A few other key overarching rubrics could perhaps be found. I shall here mention only, in order to get it out of the way, the term of *Wissenschaft* (science). It seems to have been first used by Brecht in 1929 (GKA 21: 270-75), at the confluence of his enthusiasm for flying machines—evident in *The Flight of the Lindberghs*—and for the first Soviet Five-year plan; and it was foregrounded in his most finished and deservedly famous but—as usual for Brecht—open-ended and not final theoretical tractate, the *Short Organum for the Theatre. Wissenschaft* is in German, first of all, much wider than the English term of "science" (see Suvin "'Utopian'"), since it denotes any systematically organized body of knowledge, for example theology or literary studies. Second, Brecht finally recognized its inadequacy for serious theorizing, based on abuse of science by the "Western" and of Marxism by the "Eastern" class societies: "the term [scientific age] by itself, as it is usually used, is too polluted" (GKA 23: 289, ca. 1954). What he permanently retained from this semantic field was his insistence on the necessarily experimental, Baconian character of genuinely modern art. At any rate, the writer of the *Life of Galileo* could scarcely be suspected of an uncritical scientism, just as the lifelong proponent of self-management should not be supposed to have had any illusions about technocracy (or bureaucracy).

1. On *Haltung* or Stance

Gegen Abend fand mich Brecht im Garten bei der Lektüre des *Kapital*. Brecht: "Ich finde das sehr gut, dass Sie jetzt Marx studieren—wo man immer weniger auf ihn stösst und besonders wenig bei unsern Leuten." Ich erwiderte, ich nähme die vielbesprochnen Bücher am liebsten vor, wenn sie aus der Mode seien.
Benjamin, *Gespräche mit Brecht*, 25/7/1938

[Toward evening, Brecht found me in his garden reading *Capital*. Brecht: "I find it very good that you are now studying Marx—when he's met with ever less frequently, and especially among our people." I answered that I preferred to take up the frequently mentioned books when they were not in fashion.
Benjamin, *Talks With Brecht*, diary note of 25/7/1938]

1.1. The *Haltung* of Pedagogy
(Teaching and Learning)

I begin with the story *Tu Wishes to Learn Fighting and Learns Sitting* from Brecht's *Me-ti: The Book of Turns*:

Tu came to Me-ti and said, I wish to take part in the struggle between classes. Teach me. Me-ti said, Sit down. Tu sat down and asked, How should I fight? Me-ti laughed and said, Do you sit well? I don't know, said Tu surprised, how should I sit differently? Me-ti explained that to him. But, said Tu impatiently, I didn't come to learn how to sit. I know, you want to learn how to fight, said Me-ti patiently, but for that you must sit well, for we are just now sitting and we want to learn while sitting. Tu said, If one always strives to take up the most comfortable posture and get the best out of what there is, in brief if one strives after enjoyment (*Genuss*), how can one then fight? Me-ti said, If one does not strive after enjoyment, does not want to get the best out of what there is nor take up the best posture, why then should one fight? (GKA 18: 176-77)

What is here translated as posture (*Lage*, how or where a body lies; also situation, position, location), Brecht usually calls, more actively, *Haltung*, which is in German—as most other key Brechtian terms—a fruitful polysemy or pun centrally involving <u>dynamics</u> and <u>full bodily involvement</u>; while *Genuss* is stronger than enjoyment, much like *jouissance*, and I have argued in the essay on *Life of Galileo* how central it is to Brecht's Epicurean horizon (see Suvin, "Brecht's *Life*"). This may be seen developed in a poem about Weigel preparing for the role of señora Carrar:

Thus my body is relaxed, my limbs are
Light and on their own, all the prescribed bearings
Will provide them pleasure.

[So ist mein Körper gelockert, meine Glieder sind
Leicht und einzeln, alle Haltungen, die vorgeschrieben
    sind
Werden ihnen angenehm sein.]

("Lockerer Körper" [Relaxed Body], ca. 1937, GKA 14: 376)

In our epoch, the pragmatic orientation toward concrete situations of human relationships (*Situationsbezogenheit*) and the need to present them as alterable entails that texts should be experimental, and that they present *Haltungen* that unite the subject's body-orientation in spacetime with that body's insertion into major societal flows of things.

The preoccupation with *Haltung,* present from early on (cf. GKA 19: 285-91), underwent a first crystallization during the great economic and political crisis of 1929 to 1933, when Brecht focussed on a vanguard which should teach others the proper ways of such a union of personal orientation and collective location. Parallels to the Leninist concept of a political vanguard are clear, and may indeed help to explain Brecht's conditional adhering to Lenin's central notion of the Party—alongside with Brecht's lifelong adhesion to Rosa Luxemburg's notion of worker's councils; yet Brecht gave it a characteristically heterodox twist by positing a theatre (and radio) vanguard. This meant, first, allotting theatre an at the time totally new (though historically well-known) function, that of a teaching-cum-learning apparatus or *Pädagogium*, a term denoting "educational institution" but to which Brecht provided a new connotation on the model of *Planetarium* or *Laboratorium*. Obversely, it also meant planning "a chain of experiments which used theatrical means but did not need theatres proper" (GKA 22.1: 167), so that it might perhaps be better to categorize it within the superordinated category of spectacle or public show.

Brecht envisaged a wide spectrum of educational practices in such a radically new institution. However, for reasons both of practical organization and of self-clarification, Brecht began writing fictional performance texts for these "pedagogical experiments" which he called *Lehrstücke*. His term was somewhat misguided in its kinship to *Lehre* (doctrine) or *lehren* (instructing), concepts which were not at all central for Brecht, so that in 1936 he insisted to have it translated into English as "learning plays" (GKA 22.2: 941, Steinweg *Lehrstück* 48).

At the height of such work, expecting a civil war and revolution in Germany, Brecht envisaged two different forms, the Great Pedagogy and the Small (or Initial?) Pedagogy. A note in the Brecht-Archiv (further BBA with file/leaf numbers) reads:

> The Great Pedagogy utterly changes the role of playing. It abrogates the system of player and spectator. It knows only players who are at the same time students.... The mimetic playing becomes a principal part of pedagogy. The Small Pedagogy in the transitional period of the first revolution, on the contrary, merely democratizes theatre: the division still fundamentally exists, but the players should if possible be amateurs (the roles should be such that amateurs have to remain amateurs), the professional actors and the existing theatre apparatus should be used to weaken bourgeois ideological positions in the bourgeois theatre itself, and the spectators should be activised. Plays and way of playing should turn the spectator into a statesman.... <u>The actors must estrange figures and events for the spectator, so that he finds them remarkable.</u> The spectator has to take sides instead of identifying himself [with the figures and events]. (BBA 521/996, ca. 1940, in Steinweg *Lehrstück* 23-24)

As is made clear from a number of passages, the Great Pedagogy presupposes a post-revolutionary state of democratic socialism based on a dialectics between the vanguard and the self-organizing masses, the lineaments of which Brecht saw in the Soviet 1920s on the model of Lenin's program in *The State and Revolution* (cf. GKA 21: 398 and Steinweg *Lehrstück* 207-10). In such a dynamic state of permanent cultural revolution people's acts would no longer be constricted by overriding *Not* (necessity and misery) but they would be educatable through learning new bearings (cf. GKA 18: 34; BBA 112/54, ca. 1929, in Steinweg *Lehrstück* 18). All this should have been developed in an extensive theory of pedagogy which at that point Brecht was planning (cf. GKA 24: 90 and both the Steinweg titles). One is titled "Theory of Pedagogies":

> Bourgeois philosophers make out a huge distinction between those who act and those who reflect. The thinker does not make this distinction.... There is no distinction between true philosophy and true politics. A result of this understanding is the thinker's proposal to educate young people through theatre playing, that is, to make of them simultaneously those who act and reflect, as it is proposed in the guidelines for the pedagogies.... (GKA 21: 398)

A defining and fundamental characteristic of the learning process Brecht envisaged was his enmity to a closed "world view" or systematized doctrine. For one thing, knowing is necessarily dynamic: "in the teaching, the learning must be preserved. The Lehrstücke are not simply parables that provide an aphoristic moral with emblems, they also investigate." (BBA 827/13-15, ca. 1930, in Steinweg *Lehrstück* 23) As Benjamin formulated it, the traditional, Schillerian statement that the stage is an ethical institution is justified only if a theatre does not only communicate cognitions but also <u>produces</u> them (18); Benjamin went on to perspicaciously characterize Brecht's whole theatre by connecting investigation with the gestual attitudes.[2]

Even more important, however, Brecht diametrically counterposed two kinds of learning. One, using theatrical means, engages the whole body without splitting the sensorium from the brain and dovetails emotion and reason precisely under the concept of bearing or behaviour (*Verhalten,* cf. for example

---

2. Benjamin was the first and remains the best commentator on Brecht's *Haltungen*; another full study would be needed to do justice to his rich discussion of Brecht's plays and poems (cf. also Steinweg *Brechts* 403 and 491).

GKA 21: 421-22); this makes it possible to fruitfully use contradictions. The other kind is a learning through systematized notional constructs, which tend to false harmony and univocity, for Brecht necessarily present in any doctrine. Therefore, "the teaching should not spread a specific cognition but carry out a specific bearing (*Haltung*) of people.... When taking up a proper bearing, truth, that is the right cognition of circumstances, will manifest itself." (BBA 827/07, ca. 1930, in Steinweg *Brechts* 101) Brecht is astonishingly modern in such considerations, pitting the juggler-philosopher as educator against the priest, and again best exemplified through some *Me-ti* stories. One of them, "Vorsicht bei der Verwahrung von Erfahrungen" ("Prudent Custody of Experiences") distinguishes between experiences and judgements, and calls for great caution not to take the latter for the former: "A proper technique is necessary to keep the experiences fresh so that they can remain a permanent source of new judgements.—Me-ti called that kind of experiences best which resembled snowballs. They can serve as good weapons but they do not keep too long. For example they cannot be held ready in the pocket for long." (GKA 18: 90-91) Another, crucial Me-ti story warns forthrightly, "*Make No Image of the World*":

> Me-ti said: The judgements which are won by dint of experiences usually do not correlate with each other as the events which led to the experiences. The unification of the judgements does not give an exact image of the events lying beneath them. When too many judgements are tied to one another, getting back to the events is often very difficult. It is the entire world which generates one image, but the image does not include the entire world. It is better to associate judgements with experiences than with other judgements—if the judgements should serve the purpose of governing things. Me-ti was against constructing overly comprehensive images of the world. (GKA 18: 60)

Across a quarter century, very little had changed when the director Brecht in the 1950s carefully grounded the believability of each stage event on analogous events possible in everyday life, that is, "vertically" athwart and against any pre-established harmony of the syntagmatic notional and textual, "horizontal" concatenation (cf. Bunge 332 and passim).

Of course, Brecht's goal was to influence people and society as a whole. Furthermore, the determining context of all of his "pedagogical" exertions was the clear realization that the education he wanted was only feasible if favoured by the general drift of society: "Thus the lack of bread in the shack educates to stealing, or the Bible educates to hungering. He who has to have a potato must bow down, because the ground demands it or the boss. Such is the education to bowing down." (GKA 22.1: 55) Brecht's pedagogy is one for stormy but favourable winds. A provisional summing up, provided in a short note called "On the Theory of the *Lehrstück*" (GKA 22.1: 351-52), did not at all aim at a transmission of judgements, even of general or parabolical ones, but at a critical appropriation of a way of thinking, of a method, incarnated in the players' bearing (cf. Steinweg *Lehrstück* 102). The goal of such learnings is to learn the method of learning. For Brecht, "The concept of the right way is less good than that of the right walking" (GKA 22.1: 569).

Brecht's project could be articulated by discussing his concept of experiment and his even more sophisticated concept of a scientific or epistemological model. More briefly, it may be illustrated by his stance toward jazz. Though that stance was complex, since he found jazz mostly used in brutal and stupid ways, Brecht wanted his kind of playing to follow the technical method of jazz, "namely the montage way which makes the musician into a technical specialist. Here possibilities were shown of arriving at a new union of personal freedom and ensemble discipline (improvising with a fixed goal)...." (GKA 24: 99-100, cf. GKA 21: 188) Another analogy was that to team sports: "These players should play so that...all attempt to work out the few basic ideas, like a football team" (BBA 521/95, ca.

1930, in Steinweg *Brechts* 105). Brecht hated one-way transmission so much that he was, at the same time as he planned a
theory of pedagogies, also planning a radio theory whose main
plank was the demand for a two-way teaching communication
between the radio performers and the listeners (GW 18: 117
ff., esp. 127-34). Another *Me-ti* story goes so far as to say, "If
anybody affirms that 2x2 = 4 because 8 minus 5 equals 7, I shall
immediately say that twice two is not four.... I cannot stand it
when truth is believed or spoken like a lie, without proof or
out of calculation." (GKA 18: 110-11) The clear polemical point
goes here against official Marxism in Stalin's time; it is paral-
leled somewhat more tactfully in the *Messingkauf* speech on
the useful "judgments, forecasts, and pointers" of Marxism's
engaged thinking as opposed to the harmonious "world views"
in many "sentences/propositions [*Sätze*] by the Marxists" (GKA
22.2: 717).

In practice, this meant that Brecht wanted the players of his
"plays for learning" to radically distinguish those of his guidelines that contained views about <u>performing</u> from those about
<u>meaning</u> and application. The former were to be tested through
mimesis (and Brecht frequently expatiated, both theoretically
and practically, on such mimetic criticism), the latter were
personally untestable and thus at best temporary scaffolding
("working hypotheses," GKA 21: 415) and at worst disembodied
doctrine:

> The study of the guidelines about meaning is not neces-
> sary for the study of the guidelines about performing,
> and thus neither for the performing, while the study
> of those guidelines about meaning without studying
> the other ones and without playing is even danger-
> ous. Therefore the guidelines for playing should be
> read first, and only after the student has performed the
> document [that is, the play text], the study of meaning
> and application should follow.... The guidelines are

full of mistakes as far as our times and its virtues are concerned, they are unusable for other times.
(BBA 112/57 and 66, ca. 1930, in Steinweg *Lehrstück* 21)

A final but omnipresent aspect, which too can here only be suggested, is Brecht's dialectical stress not simply on critique but on outright negativity, such as would be usually considered "bad" or indeed dangerous and horrifying. Any "positive" action is meaningful—rather than automatic and unfree—only as a choice out of a spread of stillborn possibilities: for example, "To consent means also: <u>not</u> to consent"; or, faced with a teaching, one can adore it or despise it (BBA 529/14 and BBA 112/69, both ca. 1930, in Steinweg *Lehrstück* 24 and 19). But more than logic is at stake here. At stake is, first, the dialectical sublation of the <u>asocial element</u>. From the figure of Baal on, Brecht was obsessed by sensual and other values inherent in anti-social behaviour. In the already cited "Theory of Pedagogies" he allots it a central role in the development of the post-revolutionary state or community: "The State can best correct human asocial instincts, since they arise out of fear and ignorance, by extorting them from each in an as far as possible perfect form, almost impossible to attain for the individual. <u>This is the basis of the idea of using theatrical playing in pedagogies.</u>" (GKA 21: 398, underlined by DS) And further, in the *Lehrstück* "an educational effect may be expected from an (as magnificent as possible) reproduction of asocial acts and bearings" (GKA 22.1: 351). While it is possible that Brecht was here building on the Soviet experiences in educating the huge numbers of *besprizornye*, the post-Civil-War nomadic orphaned children sometimes treated by playing out a kind of psychodrama, and while he was—more remotely—perhaps also trying to socialize Freud's return of the repressed (cf. Steinweg *Lehrstück* 138 and 142), the central impulse at work here is not clear though obviously of supreme importance for Brecht's thought and work.

What is finally at stake in Brecht's "pedagogy" is the full socialization of the community. Using his frequent image of a roaring river, what should happen is not only a channelling of the deviant energies but also a redrawing of the rationalistic norms for channels or riverbeds. To anticipate my next section on productivity: "Not all human productivity is included in the always limited present production.... Very sharp ears for the productive element are needed. It is a masterpiece to keep it from destruction, that is, to keep it from destroying and to keep it from being destroyed." (GKA 22.1: 132) In fact, Brecht finally concluded that there was no such thing as asocial people or instincts in themselves, only asocial roles or functions, such as that of the private possessors of the means of production (AJ, GKA 26: 331).

1.2. The *Haltung* of Producing (Productivity, Creativity)

The Nazi victory deprived Brecht of any chances for teaching with help of an organized societal network. Furthermore, it interacted with Stalinism to take off the historical agenda Lenin's and Luxemburg's ideas about, and early Soviet experiments with, self-management and a gradual elimination of State apparatus. In the new situation Brecht abandoned the project of *Pädagogium* but not the underlying impulse at organized learning of a method that centers on bearing. The method and bearing to be learned, it turned out, was one of a productive critique, or of a critical productivity.

My thesis in this section is that in the Marxist tradition, beginning with Marx himself, there are two largely incompatible but intimately associated meanings of "production": the economistic one, taken from Adam Smith and other bourgeois political economists, and the anti-alienating or creative meaning which is part of Marx's central utopian critique, taken from a revolutionary fusion of Enlightenment and Romanticism; and furthermore, that Brecht largely and very originally moved from the first to the second meaning. These two meanings may be associated with Marx's central opposition between exchange-value and use-value, in which the inherent limit of capitalism is precisely restriction of production of use-values by exchange-value and, as its obverse, the growth of productive forces at the expense of the "main force of production, the human being itself" (Marx, *Grundrisse*, discussed further in Suvin "Living Labour," 437-52; cf. Harvey 2, 105, and passim). In these circumstances, as already the young Hegel had noted, "The value of labour decreases in the same proportion as the productivity of labour increases" (239). Marx's examples for production in the first sense are all quantifiable productions founded on capital and produced for profit. In this case, "our production is not a production of man for man as man, that is it is not a social production. As person, none among us has a relationship of pleasure to the other's product." (Marx 459) Most interestingly, his examples for qualitative production in the second sense, not reducible to profit, are actors producing a play, piano players producing not only music but also "our musical ear," and the madman producing delusions (ibidem 109). Artistic production is indeed (together with scientific production) taken as a paradigm for such non-alienated production of use-values.

Brecht has his share of "vulgar economist" references to production (and of course this economism is not so vulgar when applied to situations of poverty and low productivity). His defence of Stalin was, for all strong reservations, based on the great surge of production in the USSR (cf. GKA 18: 108, 139, and passim), just as his objections to capitalism were based on its being "no more able to further the production of life's necessities in the form of free competition" but of having to resort to "production of instruments of destruction" (GKA 18: 146-47)—of, in effect, making for death rather than life. However, some usages from the 1930s already show an ambiguity or passage between this meaning and production in the wider sense of productivity meaning any creativity. This turning seems marked by compromise terms such as "productive behaviour" (GKA 18: 152, and cf. the *Me-ti* story *On the Productivity of Individuals*,

GKA 18: 138).

While the term "pedagogy" is abandoned by Brecht by the mid-1930s, references to creative production become especially frequent from 1940 on, as testified by Brecht's journal. Non-Aristotelian theatre, always tied to an "evaluative *Haltung*" (GKA 21: 440-42), is now defined as "simply [one with] a spectator who produces the world," and as using for the basis of its emotions, alongside curiosity and helpfulness, "human productivity, the noblest of them all" (AJ, GKA 26: 439 and 441-42). "Learning" is now equivalent to "mental producing" (GKA 22.1: 63). The key passage, which explicitly identifies production as non-economistic productivity, seems to be a notation from March 7, 1941:

> The great error which has prevented me from making the little Lehrstück of *The Evil, Asocial Baal* was my definition of socialism as a <u>great order</u>. It is, on the contrary, much more practical to define it as a <u>great production</u>. Production is, of course, to be taken in the widest sense, and the struggle goes for the full unfettering of everybody's productivity. The products may be bread, lamps, hats, pieces of music, chess moves, irrigation, complexion, character, plays, etc. (AJ, GKA 26: 468)

The concept of an all-sided deployment of productivity is amplified in a note of 1949. In a characteristic move, this begins with a counterproposal to (or, ambiguously, amplification of—at any rate in a supersession of) Lenin's famous dictum that communists deduce their morality from their struggle, which was shared by Brecht as late as 1931 in *The Measures Taken;* and it ends by punning on the theatrical sense of *sich produzieren*, "showing off" and/or "producing itself":

> If one wishes to deduce all morality from productivity and one sees the highest thing in a huge exfoliation of

everybody's productivity, one must take care to lift the interdict from mere existence, indeed from the resistance against being used. I love: I make the beloved productive; I repair a car: I make the drivers drive; I sing: I ennoble the hearing of the hearer, etc. etc. But then society has to have the ability to use everything, it must possess such a "capital" of what has already been produced, such a plenty of offers, that the individual's production becomes as if a superfluous, so to speak unexpected thing. If productivity is the highest thing, then strikes must still be honoured. (In the esthetic domain it is already so. The asocial element also pleases; it is taken as sufficient that it "produces itself.") (AJ, GKA 27: 305)

Obversely, to produce oneself is also to show off, as in the conclusion of the *Short Organum*: "The spectator should produce himself in this theatre in the easiest way: for the easiest mode of existence is in art" (GKA 23: 97).

Around 1954, planning a series of songs for a play on the Chinese God of Happiness, Brecht noted: "The highest happiness is called productivity" (BBA 204/71, in Tatlow 546). When first thinking of this cycle of songs, he had also noted it should be an entirely materialist work, "praising 'the good life' (in both senses). Eating, drinking, dwelling, sleeping, loving, working, thinking, the great pleasures." (AJ, GKA 27: 159). Though he probably didn't know the works of young Marx, the parallel to Marx's "Seeing, hearing, smelling, tasting, feeling, thinking, opining, perceiving, willing, being active, loving" (MEW *Ergänzungsband I*.: 539), is striking.

A whole Brechtian theory of personality could be reconstructed around the axis of productivity; for example, "indignation, this socially highly productive affect" (AJ, GKA 27: 140). I shall therefore insert a discussion of some main points about Brecht's notion of agency and character before I get to emotions as such.

As can be seen in the above diary note, in a rare series of exceptions to the interdict he had put on himself in the mid-1920s against writing about erotics (which he never observed in poems), Brecht identified love as a paradigm of productivity: "Love is the art of producing something with the capacities of another person. To this purpose one needs regard and affection from the other person." (GKA 18: 40—see on this theme Haffad). Here are some further *Me-ti* and *Keuner* stories with this horizon (the first story was probably stimulated by the anecdote about Picasso's portrait of Gertrude Stein):

When Mr K. Loved Somebody

"What do you do," Mr K. was asked, "when you love somebody?" "I make a design of that person," said Mr K., "and I take care that it turns out similar." "What? The design?" "No," said Mr K., "the person." (GKA 18: 24)

Kin-jeh on Love

I speak not of carnal joys, although there would be much to say about them, nor of being in love, of which there is less to say. With these two phenomena the world would get along, but love must be examined separately, as it is a production. It changes the lover and the beloved, whether in good or bad ways. Already from the outside, lovers appear as producers, and of a high order at that. They show passion and unstoppability, they are soft without being weak, they are always looking for friendly deeds which they may do (in the end accomplished not only for the beloved). They build their love and bestow upon it something historical, as if they reckoned upon the writing of a history. For them the difference between no mistake and only one mistake, a difference which the world can safely ignore, is immense. If their love makes of them something out of the ordinary, they have only themselves to thank; if they fail, they may excuse themselves almost as little with the faults of the beloved as the leader of the people with the faults of the people. The obligations which they take on are obligations against themselves; the severity in relation to the violations of obligation which they muster up is unparalleled. It is the nature of love, as of other huge productions, that the lovers take many things earnestly which others would treat lightly, the smallest touches, the most unnoticeable half-tones. The best succeed in bringing their love into full harmony with other productions; then their friendliness becomes universal, their inventiveness is of use to many, and they support all that is productive. (GKA 18: 175-76)

Love, critical productivity, and the making of images memorably intertwine in these texts (cf. also the "Lai-tu" stories, GW 12: 583-85, and the texts *Lovers Make Images of One Another* and *On the Drawing Up of Effigies*, GKA 18: 61 and 20: 168-70). Their dynamic and personalized images, verified by integral bodily contacts, are the symmetrical obverse of those systematically all-encompassing "images of the world" forbidden by Brecht's pedagogy as unproductive.

This approach may also throw a new light on Brecht's well-known predilection for female, and especially for maternal figures. The maternal ones (*die Mütterlichen*)—as Grushe is called at the end of *The Caucasian Chalk Circle*—love the children productively: not simply, nor even primarily, as their biological bearers but as their social enablers and nurturers. This is largely why Shen Te loves Sun, in *The Good Person of Setzuan*: she sees in him the potential aviator furthering human communication. A truly productive love is not privatizing: the lovers who "are always looking for friendly deeds which they may do" in the end accomplish them "not only for the beloved."

Love and motherhood are equally revolutionary within an unjust society, just as they converge in the call for a utopian future of friendliness when people will be helpers to people. Grushe takes up little Michael because she had just avowed her love to Simon; Shen Te's necessity (and misery) in resorting to her alter ego Shui Ta to defend her unborn child is the strongest intrinsic critique and condemnation of capitalism à la Setzuan, and so is Mother Courage's necessity to deny her dead son in the long war of Germany (there is little or no fathering in Brecht's work). Erotics in a wider, diffuse and sublimated sense, are strong and omnipresent in Brecht's plays, but in the sexual sense rather rare. The male relationships in his early plays cannot in my opinion be interpreted as sexual, and thus neither as homo-sexual. However, after an initial tinkering with the whore as businesswoman, his plays somewhat shamefacedly slighted erotics. If female figures are still clearly privileged in them, it is because they stand for the ultimate alienation of the subject under capitalism, "precisely because [women] can be physically reduced to a commodity," as well as for "what [Brecht] saw as 'productive' or 'unproductive' responses to socio-political situations" (Nussbaum 229 and 231)—for example Grushe or Kattrin vs. Natella or Courage. Negative critique and positive production thus embrace in the *Haltung* of love as "a micro-model" of the great productivity (cf. Haffad 212-13 and 246).

Another emblem of nurturing, parallel and subsidiary to love, is <u>cultivation</u> of a garden or of a fruit-tree, one of Brecht's favourite ancient *topoi*, present in many of his poems and notes. It is perhaps best explicated by contraries, in the poem on The Plum Tree (*Der Pflaumenbaum*, GKA 12: 21) rendered justly famous by Benjamin's commentary (GS II/2: 566-67). The plum tree, railed round in a city courtyard, can't grow for lack of sun: "The plum tree never bears a plum/ So it's not easy to believe./ It is a plum tree all the same/ One tells it by the leaf." (adapted from translation by J. Willett and R. Manheim).

Mothering, irrigated cultivation, and good car-driving are bundled together in the farewell words of *The Caucasian Chalk*

Circle, since they all bear fruit:

> And you
> Who have heard the story of the chalk circle, take note
>   of
> The wisdom of our fathers, that what there is should
> belong
> To those who do well by them, and thus:
> Children to the Motherly, that they thrive,
> Cars to good drivers, that they be driven well,
> And the valley to the waterers, that it bear fruit.
>   [adapted from Manheim-Willett]

Again, coincidences with some of the best in contemporary feminist thought could, probably to the dismay of both sides, easily be found here (cf. Nussbaum 241-42 and passim). In this play, his supreme achievement, "Brecht created the mother-educator of the future in which all traditions are revised or replaced by new, more productive...relationships between people" (Nussbaum 238-39). It is a frontal clash between, on the one hand, the self-management of productive cultivation and of engaged art together with social motherhood and—discreetly—love against, on the other hand, the society of class injustice and civil as well as ethnic warfare. The constellation of the producing cooperatives and the Singer of the framework, plus Grusha and Azdak inside it, versus the upper class is one of productivity against possessivity (cf. Suvin *Brecht*, ch. 6).

At some points, thus in the *Short Organum,* Brecht inclined to call the basic societal bearing of this productivity simply criticism (*Kritik).* Such a critical *Haltung* (GKA 22.1: 226) or productive critique is "the grandest characteristic of a human being, it has created most of the goods of happiness, best improved life" (GKA 22.1: 569). Therefore, "if only it is left unhindered, [productivity] may prove the greatest pleasure of them all":

21.

If we want now to give ourselves to this great passion for producing, what ought our representations of
people living together to look like? What is that productive bearing in face of nature and of society which
we...would like to take up pleasurably in our theatre?

22.

The bearing is a critical one. Faced with a river, it consists in regulating the river; faced with a fruit tree, in
grafting upon the fruit tree; faced with locomotion, in
constructing vehicles and airplanes; faced with society, in overturning society....

(GKA 23: 73, translation J. Willett)

Such a bearing entailed a lifelong mistrust of ethics, which
Brecht saw as a set of idealist notions that had little in common
with the necessities in and of life. Nonetheless, just as he had
in the *Messingkauf* and *Short Organum* finally adapted rather
than abandoned theater and esthetics, he finally also found a
way to refunction rather than refuse the categorical imperative
in favour of a "productive mode" of imagination, creating what
is not present to sense (Kant 164). Here is a testimonial of the
revocation:

Me-ti and Ethics

Me-ti said: I haven't found many "You must" sentences which I would desire to pronounce. I mean now
sentences of a general nature, sentences addressed to
the generality. But one such sentence is: "You must
produce." (GKA 18: 179)

Two consequences following on this stance should be briefly invoked. First, the lovers' friendliness and the producers' good humour are conducive to a "joyous criticism" (GW 16: 637) which is not too far from Nietzsche's joyous knowledge and quite near to Bakhtin's gay plebeian truth. An autonomous creative force of socialized humanity, it is its own measure. At best, a kind of qualitative felicific calculus may be applied to it, as in: "The proposition: <u>A man's goal is to have pleasure</u> is bad for the reason that it boxes the ear of the good proposition: <u>Humankind's goal is to have pleasure</u>." (GKA 23: 361) Second, the presupposition for all such constructive production is the destruction of destructivity. Brecht's analysis of his best transposition of our age's contradictions, *The Caucasian Chalk Circle*, shines as a lighthouse to our present:

> The more Grushe furthers the child's life, the more she endangers her own; <u>her productivity works for her own destruction</u> (underlined DS). This is so under the conditions of war, of the existing jurisprudence, of her isolation and poverty. (GKA 24: 346)

1.3. *Haltung*: Language and Class History

How did Brecht arrive at this central tool of his, *Haltung*? As usual, by productively refunctioning the German language as the concrete consciousness of both the upper and the plebeian classes. Also as usual, he went back to and built on the meanings stemming from before the caesura of the bourgeois or Romantic split of people into an "inner" and an "outer" image and life. He took from it the full bodily involvement and changed it by a melding with his peculiar variant of dynamics from below.

I shall proceed in this subsection by an abbreviated overview of the material from the great historical dictionary of German semantics by the Grimm Brothers (see a fuller account in Suvin "*Haltung*"). It shows that *Haltung* becomes a frequent term only in and after the Romantic period. *Haltung* is a sign of two fundamental changes: first, of growing demographic density in the budding capitalist economy and city life; second, of aristocratic need to insist on "proper" behaviour in all social classes and of subaltern German bourgeois fear of failing to do so. The main meaning of *Haltung* may be identified as "orientation toward a precise way of somebody's behaving," which always involves the body and a bearing toward other people. Only beginning with ca. 1848 *Haltung* is also applied to "inner" mental activity (cf. the Heyne ed. 1877 edition of the Grimms' *Dictionary*, and even more so in the Duden dictionary of 1993).

In particular, within the meaning of *Haltung* as precise bodily bearing in a hierarchical interpersonal relation, the Grimms show it as positively evaluated in the meaning of strong, determined, worthy behaviour (*festes, energisches, würdiges Verhalten*), for example "eine Frau von Haltung"; it also borrows connotations from physical and moral solidity: "Gesimse, die wenig Haltung haben," "eine Neigung die ohne Haltung...ist" (both from Kant).

What is most important here: the dominant semantics was <u>a discourse originating in the ruling class</u>, whose own stance is from above downward and requires from subordinates the stance from below upwards—in both cases formalized as a stiff vertical: "[er] blieb Bedienter in Wort, Gebärde, Haltung" (Immermann, *Münchhausen*); Brecht too uses "servile bearing" *(lakaienhafte Haltung)* for subaltern intellectuals and for clerics (GKA 21: 428). This is often found when *Haltung* is taken absolutely (and thus without adjective), as strong, determined, dignified—or obversely servile—self-discipline; it is then cognate to two significant lexemes: *Fassung* and *Beherrschtheit*, taking hold or controlling as a vector uniting social pressure and personal acquiescence (which is echoed in Max Weber's and Brecht's *Einverständnis*s, consenting). Most suggestive for these clearly moral and political evaluations is *eine militärisch stramme Haltung*, "a military upright bearing" (a metonymy for rigid behaviour). It inserted the body personal into the body politic, just as did widely used stock phrases such as "die

Haltung verlieren, oder sich Haltung zu geben", "etwas mit Haltung aufnehmen."[3] Brecht knew this all-pervasive original meaning very well before refunctioning it, and used it first in a Strindbergian movie scenario of his from 1921 (GKA 19: 106) and also at the end of 1926, in the sense of "taking hold of oneself" in poem 7 from the *"Lesebuch für Städtebewohner"*: "Sie brauchen jetzt keine Haltung mehr zu bewahren/ Es ist niemand mehr da, der Ihnen zusieht" (GKA 11: 1963).

From Aristotle's *heksis* and Cicero's *habitus* on, *Haltung* always "stands" or mediates between potentiality and action (as well as between nature and nurture, necessity and choice, thus malleability and teachability). This diachronic tradition is in Brecht synchronically renewed by means of materials and insights from the early writings of Marx (alone or with Engels) with their orientation on *praxis*. The classical formulations are in the *Theses on Feuerbach*: "Praxis is a sensual human

---

3. The "military connotations" and "conservative tradition" of *Haltung* are discussed in Nägele 141-57. Very usefully, he connects its use in Brecht both with *Halt!* (Stop!) and *Verhalten* (behaviour), as well as with the usage in Benjamin who stressed more the stop or caesura, and concludes that *Haltung* represents "an intricate economy of movement and rigidity." Earlier important investigations are to be found in Steinweg, especially 134-39. I should mention three interesting though subsidiary clusters of meaning, possibly of special interest to a playwright and the author of *St. Joan of the Stockyards*. First, an old one pertaining to the "holding" of festivities: "Haltung eines Spils mit grosser Versammlung des Volks, celebratio ludorum" (vgl. "Verhalten" in "das V., gestus, motus corporis..."—Kasp. Stieler, *Der teutschen sprache stammbaum...*, Nürnberg 1691: 746, cited in the Grimms 25: 514). Brecht's important though somewhat opaque concept of *Gestus* could to my mind only be clarified within this semantic field: Nägele adopts, after Benjamin and Steinweg, the idea that *Gestus* is "the smallest element of a *Haltung*" (152). Second, a newer semantic cluster indicating the momentary "stand" of affairs and of prices on the market, including the stock-market: "Spiritus in steigender, festen, flauer, weichender, sinkender Haltung" (*Weserzeitung* 1853); in *Meyer's Konversations-Lexikon of 1908* (671), this is the only entry s.v. *Haltung*: "it means the course of affairs," for example "matte, feste, abwartende Haltung." Third, a tradition within mime which used "attitude" as its basic theoretical term, intricately connected with arrested emotion, see Wylie, esp. 48-52.

activity" uniting subject and object (#1) and mediating between the "changing of conditions and people changing themselves" (#3); the human subject "is the ensemble of social relationships" and not "an abstract—isolated—human individual" (#6); last not least for the participation of the observer in the observed, "the standpoint" of the "practico-critical" materialism is "social humanity" (#1 & 10) (MEW 3: 5-7). And in the first section of *The German Ideology*: "Consciousness can only be conscious being, and the being of people is their real life process" (26). To the contrary, in the later Engels "praxis" is rarely used or substituted by references to applied science and technology (for example in his *Dialectics of Nature*, MEW 20: 393). Furthermore, in Engels's influential formulation, people are supposed "to draw their moral views in the final instance" from the economic relationships in which they live (*Anti-Dühring*, MEW 20: 87).

The Marxian orientation on practice is quite compatible with possibly secondary but not unimportant confluences of Brecht with US pragmatism and behaviorism, primarily Watson (and US movies); with translations of Chinese philosophy, primarily of Mo Ti, Lao Tse, and Confucius, and the impact of Chinese and Japanese dramaturgy[4]; and with early bourgeois philosophy, primarily of Descartes and Bacon. All the above were assiduously studied by Brecht from the end of the 1920s on, with much reliance on Korsch and on translations of Lenin (Brecht praised the *Haltungen* of Ford, Einstein, and Lenin and planned to write "Die Haltungen Lenins," GKA 21: 383 and 26: 319). One could perhaps illustrate Brecht's position as being

---

4. Brecht cherished the Chinese cultural sphere precisely because of its rich culture of clear stances (he planned to write a play on Confucius). For example in Japanese *kamae* means physical-cum-psychological "assuming an attitude" or "attitude assumed" both in formal arts such as judo, flower arranging or tea ceremony and in everyday life, and it is defined as "action in [the] reduced form [of]...a single moment." The parallel between "Tu Wishes To Learn Fighting..." and the famous swordsman Musashi's instruction to a novice—itself in all probability heavily indebted to Chinese models—is so close that it amounts to an overlap (see Lee 55 and 57).

synchronically in the middle of a square on whose angles were the German semantic tradition, Marx, Lenin, and pragmatism and diachronically an updating of Eaast Asian collectivism.

1.4. A Conclusion

If one is now to inquire into the reason and meaning of Brecht's redefining the semantics of *Haltung* and allotting to this "bearing" a central role in his work and approach to the world, my thesis would be the following: <u>*Haltung* is Brecht's semantic micro-unit of *praxis* for the active subject</u>. In conscious opposition to several important social usages, *Haltung* has simultaneously three functions: 1/ a refusal of the bourgeois and individualistic concepts of an internalized and atomic character (*Charakterkopf, Seelenkäse*); 2/ a revaluation of the Rightwing and militaristic-cum-servile stress on *Strammhalten*, that is, statics and hierarchy; 3/ an alternative to the faceless "economics as last instance of all behaviour" in orthodox "Historical Materialism" from Engels through Kautsky to Stalin. As such a witty alternative, *Haltung* mediates between two uses of "intervening thinking": in practical relationships of people to each other and in systematic cognition about people (*Menschenkunde*).

The anti-individualistic function of *Haltung* is of a piece with the dismantling of the "individual" or the monolithic Self as center of universe. This is a central theme of Brecht's, foregrounded in his work from *Man is Man* and *Mahagonny* to *The Good Person of Setzuan*: "the destruction, explosion, atomisation of the individual psyche is a fact." What remains is, however, not at all a Nothing—"lack of nucleus does not mean lack of substance, we have thus a new structure in front of us, which has to be determined in new ways" (GKA 26: 476)—but subjects capable of action or agency as Marxian "ensembles of social relationships." All of Brecht's figures are confronted with situations of choice, all are bipolar agents (saying yes and no), much akin to the "typified masks" (*Charaktermasken*) from Marx's *18th Brumaire* with flexibly allegorical behaviours and orientations. Possibly the two most important types are the true intellectual or the "Thinker": Keuner, Me-ti, Azdak, and the ambiguously perverted variant of Johanna Dark and Galileo; and the motherly one: Wlassowa, Kattrin, Courage (fully perverted case), Shen Te, Grusche.

Thus, Brecht was constantly preoccupied with *Haltung* as a practical and cognitive tool that ensures the naming—and bestowal of meaning—of a subject's body-orientation. As could be seen also from the little *Me-Ti* story cited at the beginning, the foregrounded materiality of the movements and postures is not only a <u>sign</u> for the orientation of the thinking but also its almost magical <u>induction and guarantee</u>. In other words: the sensual Being-Thus (*So-Sein*) in a given changeable situation is the guarantee that the acting subject in an always already concrete existence will avoid, by means of her enjoyment and critical evaluating, being sacrificed to fetishized abstractions— for example, "the future," "the struggle"—but will instead assume a fertile, sensual, and therefore unshakable orientation toward them. The best presentation of this stance may be found in Brecht's probably most optimistic text, the *Caucasian Chalk Circle*, where a brief Saturnalian interregnum suspending class power allows Azdak to help himself—for example to drink and sex—and to help as well the concrete seeds of the future, Grusche and the Noble Child (cf. Suvin *To Brecht*, chap. 6). Brecht's fascination with helpers—the "motherly" women, but also Azdak or the sage teacher figures—who take practical measures to meld the difficult today with a productive tomorrow, gives a face to and embodies this preoccupation.

For these reasons, *Haltung* proved similar to some other attempts on the Left to fuse theory and everyday practice. Most similar to Brecht are Benjamin's use of the same term, first independent of and then in dialogue with Brecht, Gramsci's notion of "philosophy of practice," and Bloch's notions of "upright posture" *(aufrechter Gang)* combined with orientation toward a horizon. Lukács's use of standpoint *(Standpunkt)* in *Geschichte und Klassenbewusstsein* is characteristically more abstract but has even so allowed highly interesting reinterpretations by materialist feminists (cf. Jaggar *Feminist* and Hartsock) and "theologians of liberation" as "the privileged standpoint of the women" respectively "of the poor" (cf. on both Jameson). There are also parallels to Bakhtin, Sartre, and Merleau-Ponty, as well to Bourdieu's "habitus."

2. Approaching Brecht and Agency

2.0. Introduction

Here would be the place for a theory about <u>agency</u> (and dramaturgic agents) in Brecht. This would test what light the "stance hypothesis" could throw on some crucial <u>practices</u> in Brecht's opus, understandable also as <u>epistemological concepts</u>, such as personality. I cannot develop it at all adequately in this essay, but I shall put forward one main thesis and a few sub-theses as corollaries.

Thesis: <u>Brecht's understanding of agency strongly privileges personality (Subject) as opposed to character (the Cartesian Self)</u>. From this follow some corollaries, such as:
    <u>1/ The downgrading of heroism and upgrading of comedy.</u>
    <u>2/ While character is disembodied (a laicization of soul), personality is indivisible from body.</u>
    <u>3/ While character is a dogmatic or ideological apriori, a mononuclear interiority, and only rational (or better, only conceptually established), personality is a bipolar spread of possibilities permeated by an ensemble of relationships and reposing on a union of reason and emotion, senses and sensorium.</u>

My stark opposition character-personality may be an imperfect instrument, as all Manichean or "digital" dichotomies. As my final table in 3.3 may also indicate, Brechtian productivity is a strange mixture of ostracism and cannibalism, that is denegation as cutting off and supersession by subsumption. However, for all its limitations, I believe this approach is here mandatory precisely in order to clearly refuse fruitless (dogmatic, undialectical) dichotomies between emotion and reason, character and type, distance and nearness, etc., that the individualist Self brings and that Brecht's whole work rebels against.

2.1. Defining Terms

I am here simplifying, streamlining, and sometimes contaminating Jean-Pierre Vernant's and Paul Ricoeur's approaches to individuation (Colloque de Royaumont "Sur l'individu," 1985). They distinguish three notions, which can in French be elegantly called "l'individu *stricto sensu*," "le sujet," and "le soi" (or "le moi"). The first is a not further divisible physical token of any logical type, and especially of a biological species; I have failed to find for it a better term than the French <u>individual</u>, though perhaps we could call it <u>a particular</u>. At any rate, this sense must be sharply distinguished from the ideologized bourgeois sense of individual as Self (the third notion here—which is in fact reached by a deliberate confusion of this first notion with this one). It designates any Something (this cat, piece of bread or province) by three principal means: definite description, proper name or indicator (pronoun, adverb, etc.). The second is a human—and I would argue often an animal—"individual" communicating in her own name, expressing himself "in the first person" with traits that differentiate her from others of the same logical type-token and biological species-variety-race (etc.)— most importantly, from an ethnic, class or gender group. To the individuation of the first term this adds identification, and I shall call it the <u>Subject</u>. For a Subject, the pronoun "I" is no longer a shifter, an itinerant marker applicable to any speaker, but it is anchored in a fixed stance or bearing; this makes dialogue possible, where—however—the anchoring is reversible, "I" can be understood as "thou" and viceversa (cf. Ricoeur 62). Finally, the Self (*ipse, Selbst)* is constituted by the practices and stances "which confer upon the subject a dimension of interiority..., which constitute him from within as...a singular individual whose authentic nature resides wholly in the secret of his inner life, at the heart of an intimacy to which nobody, outside of herself, can accede..." (Vernant 24; cf. Suvin, "Polity").

To ground this a bit in terms of agential theory and literary genres: the biography and the epic would correspond to a particular human—usually a famous, type: the warrior, the statesman, the Amazon. The autobiography or the pre-bourgeois lyric correspond to the Subject, which can perhaps be deciphered as a type seen from within (for example, the poet, the lover, the hermit). Vernant remarks that in Hellenic lyrics the first-person subject gives his own sensibility the status of "a model, a literary *topos*...[so that] what is felt individually as interior emotion...acquires a kind of objective reality" (30-31). Only the genres of confession, beginning with Augustine of Hippo, the intimate memoir, and the profoundly changed post-Renaissance lyric and prose epic (that is, the novel) would correspond to the Self, the interiorized character seen simultaneously from inside and outside, as public and private, therefore stereometrically or "in the round." No doubt, all kinds of grey zones, precursors, and anachronisms must be conceded to this scheme if it is to work. Nonetheless, it seems to be at least getting at a very significant, perhaps central set of distinctions. In this optic the best Modernist practice, most clearly in Brecht, is playing off against individualism and its agential interiority the medieval, Antiquity or Asian featuring of Subjects as types rather than a Self as character (more in Suvin "How Can," "Subject," and "Brecht and Subjectivity").

2.2. The Downgrading of Heroism and Upgrading of Comedy

The Cartesian character is a Thing-in-itself, a Kantian *noumenal* interiority understandable only through its phenomenal outer manifestations. Its supreme attempt to become a Thing-for-us, indeed a Thing-and-Image-for-the-Community, is hero-ism. It is well known that Brecht hated heroism deeply. The community must be extremely bad, he argued repeatedly in his plays, if it asks for the Subject's sacrifice unto death. Obversely, the ethical consolation that this is *post mortem* idealistically compensated by tragic glory (or assumption into Paradise) looked to him as wedded to the concept of individualist charac-ter and therefore as hopelessly unrealistic. Notoriously, Brecht preferred the materialist comedy, which he upgraded from the depths of repressed and often alienated short semiotic forms as a great subversive form. As the fulminations of Sloterdijk against metaphysical subjectivity (the "Self") have it,

> "[in] the confrontation between the mega-thinker Plato and the gutter mime Diogenes....[t]he clown as philosopher shows the philosopher that there is an al-ternative to the spiritually heroic ascent into the life of ideas.... [A]t the time of the breakdown of metaphys-ics, the voices of [such] wisdom are becoming audible again. These are the voices of the oldest dissidence, they belong to women, children, ecstatics, rogues, plain people...." (209-10)

Brecht put it pithily as the title and upshot of his seminal 1930 Herr Keuner story: "Weise am Weisen ist die Haltung" (*Haltung* Is the Wisdom of the Wise, GKA 18: 13); this coinci-dence too testifies to Brecht's pertinence for our times. And as Benjamin found out on the material of the "plays for learning," the Brechtian protagonist is not a traditional hero, the athlete of fixed certainties, but a quick and changeable, that is wise, learner—including teachers who can still learn (776). As the learning teacher in *The Naysayer* remarks of the Boy's refusal to die unless upon an extremely good and defensible cause: "What the boy says is reasonable, even if it is not heroic" (cf. Suvin, "Use-Value"). Conversely, when such cause exists, when it is the salvation of the Mother and the *res publica* as in *The Yeasayer,* or of the children of Halle as in *Mother Courage and Her Children*, then the Boy's or Kattrin's death are, their heroism is (exceptionally!) necessary. But even then, it testifies to the contrary rule that ought to prevail on a habitable planet.

2.3. Body—>Death—>Politics

Sub-thesis: <u>Character is disembodied (a laicization of soul), personality is indivisible from body:</u>

Dialectically, the affirmation (or with Spinoza, the determination) can best be gauged from the negation, as convex from concave. Does the elimination of Self, of individualist character—as in the re-mountable *(ummontierbar)* Galy Gay—also necessarily mean the elimination of Subject or personality? This may be a central theme in Brecht's plays, foregrounded from *Baal* and *Man Is Man* through *Mahagonny* and all the *Lehrstücke* to the large post-Hitler plays. Descartes would say it does: he taught that "this 'me,' that is to say, the soul by which I am what I am, is entirely distinct from the body"; "I am a thinking thing," proclaim the *Meditations*, whereas "I <u>possess</u> a body with which I am very intimately conjoined" (1:101 and 190). But in a Brechtian (or Marxian) optic, if Self disappears, the Subject's <u>body</u> does not. It remains the Subject's anchorage and validation for saying "here" or "now," for inscribing the Subject's time and space into the socially recognized time and space. This holds not only for location and dating but also for the name (cf. Ricoeur 64-65) and what Brecht often—especially in the *Lehrstücke*—calls, in the Chinese tradition, "the face." The body, phenomenologically pinpointing and validating the "inscription" of its here, now, and name/face into the central collective categories of space, time, and agency, grows in a devaluation of Self not less but much more important. How does it relate to other bodies, how does it perceive the natural and social universe? We can call the perception question (even etymologically) esthetics, and the relationship question politics. Clearly, there is no wall between them, since (for example) sexual relations belong to both; as explained earlier, they subtend and suffuse much of Brecht's work, though he did not choose to focus on sexual relationships in his later plays. On the other hand, however, both the esthetics of rightly perceiving the world of bodies and their stances, and the politics of collective bodies and their interplay with, including shaping of, singular bodies (cf. Suvin, "Subject" and "Polity"), became for Brecht necessarily foregrounded discourses and domains.

Furthermore, most of Brecht's plays, with a few important exceptions, end with an actual or a living death, and the *Lehrstücke* usually with a killing. The immensely significant *Baden Lehrstück on Consenting*, for example, turns on the question of who is able to die: and Brecht noted that from the answer "Nobody" there follows the necessity of turning everything upside down, of a radical all-sided revolution (BBA 827/25, ca. 1930, in Steinweg *Lehrstück* 24). That people should become able to die properly—presumably with a wise consent to a proper community which will go on—seems therefore one of the main anthropological reasons for personal and political radicalism. Once more the surprising modernity of Brecht's horizons, here comparable to Bakhtin's account of the people's immortal body and its breakup under the bourgeoisie in his *Rabelais* book, becomes apparent.

I do not have spacetime here to discuss at appropriate length even the third corollary of my general thesis about Brecht's agents: Character is a dogmatic or ideologically aprioristic, mononuclear interiority, only rational (as opposed to senses and emotion); while personality is a bipolar spread of possibilities permeated by an ensemble of relationships, and reposing on a union of reason and emotion, senses and sensorium.

3. A Conclusion: Emotions Intertwining with *Haltung* as Basis for Acting

<u>3.1.</u> Here would be the place for an extended argument just why and how emotions are not split from cognition, and how Brecht may help us to understand emotion. I have written about this at length in a separate essay (Suvin, „Emotion"). Here I shall repeat from it merely Brecht's foundational diary note of November 15, 1940, where he defined his theatre "in emotional categories...for a change" from the usual "bad definitions as especially intellectualistic":

> This is possible without any problems, since in the epic theatre the emotional line and the intellectual line remain identical in the actor and in the spectator. It would be necessary [for such a defining] to build on the basis of curiosity and helpfulness a set of emotions which balances the set based on terror and pity. Of course, there are other bases for emotions too. There is above all human productivity, the noblest of them all. (GKA 26: 441)

I have tried to indicate how a whole Brechtian theory of personality, including emotionality, could be reconstructed around such a stance. It is variously associated not only with curiosity and productivity but also with happiness, friendliness, love, and "indignation, this socially highly productive affect" (GKA 27: 140). A constant tenor of Brecht's may be found in his defense of a certain type of flexible but critical reason, refusal of uncritical submersion in both stupidity and corrupt emotions, and attempt at <u>contradictory reconciliations of emotion and reason in a proper *Haltung*.</u>

While it is important to show some serious—though not central—blind, and sometimes black, spots in Brecht's treatment of the female gender in life or in effigy, it is at least equally important to show that he had an understanding of subjecthood or personality that refused the patriarchal or militaristic downgrading as well as the Hollywoodian or philistine misuse of emotion. This understanding crystallized out of Brecht's own cognitive emotions and insights as the image and concept of *Haltung*.[5]

Haltung is akin to *Halten*, "to stand" in the sense of *Was ist haltbar?*, what may withstand or stand up (to pressure etc.). Brecht is much exercised with flexibility and a Daoist softness winning over rigidity; this is perhaps most memorably encapsulated in his poem *Legend on the Coming About of the "Tao-te-king" Book*. But understanding leads to withstanding: the insistence on durability is also of supreme importance to Brecht, one of whose favourite slogans was "Steel stood," taken from an ad for a skyscraper that withstood the 1923 Tôkyô earthquake (GKA 22.2: 801). Thus, emotion is an integral part of any action; in any consideration of agency, such as Brecht's meshing or intervening thinking, emotion cannot be split from cognition, from thought in the widest sense.

How and why do, then, emotion and bearing fit together? I shall here attempt to sketch only two matters. First, what general stance toward the cognitive value of a refusal of the emotion-reason split may we read out of Brecht (and some feminist theoreticians)? Second, what are some innovations directly readable in Brecht as regards a possible feedback between emotion and stance (*Haltung*) as a gestural critique of ideology?

3.2. The powerfully hegemonic division of reason vs. emotion, where reason is seen as: masculine, analytic, proper to the mind, cold, objective and universal, public, etc., while emotion would

---

5. I find with pleasure that this conclusion has been earlier arrived at by Dümling (626), whose excellent book is most useful for discussing Brecht's bearings—not only as concerns music.

be: feminine, synthetic, proper to the body, warm, subjective and particular, private, and so on is, obviously, both intellectually and politically scandalous:

> it is necessary to rethink the relation between knowledge and emotion and construct conceptual models that demonstrate the mutually constitutive rather than oppositional relation between reason and emotion. Far from precluding the possibility of reliable knowledge, emotion as well as value must be shown as necessary to such knowledge. (Jaggar, "Love" 156-57)

This does not confer any magical efficacy on emotions as compared to concepts. Like concepts, emotions have an epistemic potential. But both may be erroneous; both need subsequent validation, though possibly in incommensurable ways (for example, asymmetrically, by each other). "Although our emotions are epistemologically indispensable, they are not epistemologically indisputable. Like all our faculties, they may be misleading, and their data, like all data, are always subject to reinterpretation and revision." (163)

In order to begin such a rethinking, I propose two converging directions. First, to ground the relation of emotion to reason in Raymond Williams's "structure of feeling," a crucial site of social knowledge and conflict, which he defines as:

> not feeling against thought, but thought as felt and feeling as thought: practical consciousness of a present kind,...as a set, with specific internal relations, at once interlocking and in tension.... [S]tructures of feeling can be defined as social experiences in solution.... [Yet this solution] is a structured formation...at the very edge of semantic availability....(132-34)

Second, even more radically, I propose querying the terms of debate (as I did at length in Suvin, "On Cognitive"). Rather than speak about emotion vs. reason, it might be useful to say that <u>the class of "not conceptually expressibles" is not cognitively empty</u>: for example, that a quartet, a sculptural frieze, a theater or video performance, a metaphoric system or indeed a personal emotional configuration may be no less cognitive than a conceptual system (though, no doubt, in different ways). Obviously there may and will be cognitively empty or banal symphonies, paintings, metaphors, and emotions galore, just as there are concepts and conceptual systems galore to which almost all of us would deny a cognitive status: Disney movies or 20th-Century Great Man charismatics are cognitively neither better nor worse than—say—sociobiology or "Creation theory," since all zeros tend to be equal. Obversely, both the conceptual and the non-conceptual ways of understanding, when they are actualized epistemic potentials and not institutionalized mimicries, may <u>allow people to deal with alternatives</u>, that is with not merely or fully present objects, aspects, and relationships. The entities which were not present to people's perception and reflection now become available for evaluative inspection, choice, and subsequent intervention by means of a cognitive organon: conceptual, emotional or whichever.

What can, in this hypothesis, count as understanding, cognition or knowledge? Anything, I would maintain, that satisfies two conditions or, better, two aspects of one condition: that it can help us in coping with our personal and collective existence; and that it can be validated by feedback with its application, modifying existence and being modified by it. I see no permanent or "anthropological" reason to allot (or withdraw) a special privilege to any human activity or faculty here, for example to words, numbers, geometrical figures, arranged sounds, concepts, metaphors, movements or what have you; though it might almost go without saying that particular social groups in particular historical chronotopes will always have specially privileged activities and sign-systems.

<u>3.3.</u> As to feedback between emotion and a gestural critique of

ideology, I shall summarize my views in the following table. Since theatre as an activity (performing) is for Brecht simultaneously an experimental laboratory for and a condensation of everyday life, the table holds for behaviour-patterns in both theatre and life:

BOURGEOIS CHARACTER—BRECHTIAN SUBJECT	
Gesturer, hidden under the character's emotion, induces the same emotion in him/herself	Gesture may be emotional, gesturer is not. Stage role may induce same or different emotion in spectator.
Gesture always depends on emotion	Gesture sometimes causes emotion
Conflation, fusion of elements/media on stage to infect spectator	Separation of elements/media on stage, addition in spectator
Emotion continuous and contagious, submerges passive spectator identifying with central character/s/	Emotion fluctuating, depends on active traffic spectator/ characters
No psychic distance to undisputed central value	Fluctuations of distance to disputable values
Empathy only	Sympathy/antipathy
Necessarily ideological	Critique of ideology possible

Works Cited

1. Texts by Brecht

Brecht, Bertolt. *Gesammelte Werke in 20 Bänden.* Werkausgabe Edition Suhrkamp. Frankfurt a.M.: Suhrkamp, 1967. [GW—retained where better organized than GKA].

Brecht, Bertolt. *Werke.* Grosse Kommentierte Berliner und Frankfurter Ausgabe. Suhrkamp & Aufbau V., 1988-2000 [GKA; within it, the *Working Diary* (*Arbeitsjournal*) is preceded by AJ].

Steinweg, Reiner. *Das Lehrstück.* Stuttgart: Metzler, 1972, 6-67.

—, ed. *Brechts Modell der Lehrstücke.* Frankfurt: Suhrkamp, 1976, 31-221.

2. Secondary Literature

Bakhtin, M.M. *Rabelais and His World.* Transl. H. Iswolsky. Cambridge MA: MIT P, 1968.

Benjamin, Walter. *Gesammelte Schriften.* Frankfurt: Suhrkamp, 1980-87 [GS].

—. *Versuche über Brecht.* Frankfurt: Suhrkamp, 1966 (now in GS II/2. Frankfurt: Suhrkamp, 1980).

Bunge, Hans Joachim. "Brecht probiert." *Sinn und Form* Zweites Sonderheft Bertolt Brecht (1957): 322-36.

[Descartes, René.] *The Philosophical Works of Descartes*, 2 Vols. Eds. E. Haldane and G.R.T. Ross. Cambridge: Cambridge UP, 1911.

Duden—Bildwörterbuch der deutschen Sprache s.v. "Haltung." Mannheim: Dudenv., 1993, 3: 1453.

Dümling, Albrecht. *Brecht und die Musik.* München: bei Kindler, 1985.

Gorelik, Mordecai. *New Theatres for Old.* New York: Dutton, 1962 (orig. 1940).

Grimm, Johann, and Wilhelm Grimm. *Deutsches Wörterbuch.* Bearb. v. M. Heyne [1877]. München: DTV, 1991, Bd. 10 and 25.

Haffad, Dorothea. *Amour et société dans l'oeuvre de Brecht.* Alger: Office des Publ. Universitaires, 1983.

Hartsock, Nancy C.M. *Money, Sex, and Power.* New York: Longman, 1983.

Harvey, David. *The Limits to Capital.* London & New York: Verso, 1999.

Hegel, Georg W.F. *Jenenser Realphilosophie*, Vol. 1. Ed. J. Hoffmeister. Leipzig: Meiner, 1932.

Jaggar, Alison M. *Feminist Politics and Human Nature.* Totowa NJ: Rowman & Allanheld, 1985.

—. "Love and Knowledge," in eadem and Susan Bordo eds. *Gender/Body/Knowledge.* New Brunswick: Rutgers UP, 1989, 145-71.

Jameson, Fredric R. "*History and Class Consciousness* as an Unfinished Product." *Rethinking Marxism* 1.1 (1988): 49-72.

Kant, Immanuel. *Critique of Pure Reason*, 2nd edn. New York: St. Martin's, 1968.

Lee, O-Young. *Smaller Is Better.* Tokyo: Kodansha Int'l, 1984.

Lukács, Georg. *Geschichte und Klassenbewusstsein.* Berlin & Neuwied: Luchterhand, 1968.

Marx, Karl. *Werke. Ergänzungsband I.* Berlin DDR: Institut für Marxismus-Leninismus, 1956-58.

Merleau-Ponty, Maurice. *Phenomenology of Perception.* Tr. C. Smith. London: Routledge & Kegan Paul, 1962.

—. *The Structure of Behavior.* Tr. A. Fisher. Boston: Beacon P, 1963.

Meyers Grosses Konversations-Lexikon. Leipzig: Bibliographisches Institut, 1908, Bd. 8.

Nägele, Rainer. *Theater, Theory, Speculation.* Baltimore: Johns Hopkins UP, 1991.

Nussbaum, Laureen. "The Evolution of the Feminine Principle in Brecht's Work." *German Studies R* 8.2 (1985):

217-44.

Ricoeur, Paul. "Individu et identité personelle," in *Sur l'individu*. Paris: Seuil, 1987, 54-72.

Sloterdijk, Peter. *Eurotaoismus.* Frankfurt a.M.: Suhrkamp, 1989.

Steinweg, Reiner. *Das Lehrstück.* Stuttgart: Metzler, 1972.

—ed. *Brechts Modell der Lehrstücke.* Frankfurt: Suhrkamp, 1976.

Suvin, Darko. "Brecht and Subjectivity," in *Darko Suvin: A Life in Letters.* Ed. Ph.E. Wegner. Vashon Island WA: Paradoxa, 2011, 133-57.

—. "Brecht's *Life of Galileo*," in *Darko Suvin* (see above), 107-57.

—. "Emotion, Brecht, Empathy vs. Sympathy." *The Brecht Yearbook* 33 (2008): 53–67, also at www.arts2.tau.ac.il/mofa/article.php?id=175

—. "Haltung," entry in *Historisch-kritisches Wörterbuch des Marxismus*, Vol. 5. Hamburg: Argument, 2002, col. 1134-42.

—. "How Can People Be (Re)Presented in Fiction?" in *Darko Suvin* (see above), 53-71.

—. "Living Labour and the Labour of Living: A Little Tractate for Looking Forward in the 21st Century," in his *Defined by a Hollow: Essays on Utopia, Science Fiction, and Political Epistemology.* London: P. Lang, 2010, 419-71.

—. "On Cognitive Emotions and Topological Imagination." *Versus* no. 68-69 (1994): 165-201.

—. "Polity or Disaster: From Individualist Self Toward Personal Valences and Collective Subjects." *Discours social/ Social Discourse* 6.1-2 (1994): 181-210.

—. "The Subject as a Limit-Zone of Collective Bodies." *Discours social/ Social Discourse* 2.1-2 (1989): 187-99.

—. *To Brecht and Beyond.* Brighton: Harvester P, 1984.

—. "The Use-Value of Dying: Magical vs. Cognitive Utopian Desire in the >Learning Plays< of Pseudo-Zenchiku, Waley, and Brecht," in his *Lessons of Japan.* Montreal: CIADEST, 1996, 177-216.

—. "'Utopian' and 'Scientific': Two Attributes For Socialism From Engels," in his *Defined by a Hollow* (see above), 49-66.

Tatlow, Antony. *The Mask of Evil.* Bern: Lang, 1977.

Vernant, Jean-Pierre. "L'individu dans la cité," in *Sur l'individu.* Paris: Seuil, 1987, 20-37.

Willett, John. *The Theatre of Bertolt Brecht.* New York: New Directions, 1968.

Williams, Raymond. *Marxism and Literature.* New York: Oxford UP, 1981.

Wylie, Mary Kathryn. "An Analysis of the Concept of >Attitude< as a Basis for Mime." Diss. CUNY 1984. Ann Arbor: Univ. Microfilms, [1984?].

2. TWO CHEERS FOR ESSENTIALISM AND TOTALITY: ON MARX'S OSCILLATION AND ITS LIMITS (AS WELL AS ON THE TABOOS OF POST-MODERNISM) (1993)[6]

—For Fredric Jameson—

The heretic spoke to the Buddha: "Yesterday, what kind of law did you preach?" The Buddha replied: "Yesterday I preached the Definite Law." "What kind of law will you preach today?" "Today I shall preach the Indefinite Law." The heretic asked: "Why

---

6. My reflections are much indebted to Balibar's stimulating *La philosophie de Marx,* as well as to Haug, Jameson, and Witt. Some aspects sketched in this essay are developed further in Suvin, "Living Labour" and "On the Horizon" (essay 8 in this book).

All non-attributed translations are mine.

The territory I am attempting to sketch in for my own purposes, and much too rapidly, is of course a well-traversed one. In particular the debate about Marx's supposed scientism has raged from the nineteenth century to the present day, since it is centrally a political debate about the claims to predictive authority by movements claiming to follow Marx. I have assumed that documenting the echoes of and/or dissents from many earlier writers would unduly clutter up this essay.

do you preach the Indefinite Law today?" The Buddha responded: "Yesterday's Definite Law is today's Indefinite Law."

Variant on a Zen dialog or mondô of Dôgen,
Shôbôgenzô, Section 73 (13th C)

—We've lost touch with reality. Don't worry, it'll find us.

—Down with phallogocratic physics: free fall for all!

—Whoever today sticks his head into sand, will grind his teeth tomorrow.

Graffiti in Germany (late 20th C)

...we understand theorizing as an open horizon, moving within the magnetic field of some basic concepts, but constantly being applied afresh to what is genuinely original and novel in new forms of cultural practice, and recognizing the capacity of subjects to reposition themselves differently.

Stuart Hall, "On Postmodernism" (late 20th C)

0. Introduction

Why revisit and revise Marx, or our opinion of Marx, today? Because he remains a quite indispensable beacon; yet his forecasts (or what were taken for such) seem to have been, and in part certainly have been, massively confuted by historical practice, by what he called in the 1847 *The Poverty of Philosophy* "history's wrong side" (noting that it usually advances by that side). But as Balibar remarks, this will apply to 1848 and 1871 in Marx's lifetime, and then 1914, 1933, 1968, and 1989. No doubt, this is an one-sided list, to which can be opposed 1917 and 1945, for example, but it is equally doubtless that it is today the dominant list. For all his significant oscillations, Marx on the whole believed he could subsume this bad and most painful side of history under a rhetorics of double negation, where (for example) poverty means not only poverty but also revolt, so that in the proper Hegelian fashion it is materially necessary that the latencies of history have to pass through the Purgatory of defeats but will then prove so powerful as to issue in the positive resolution. Perhaps we are too panicky after the number and quality of defeats, but it seems to me this "Marxist" confidence is for our generation or historical moment irretrievably a Paradise Lost: rather, Rosa Luxemburg's alternative of "socialism or barbarism" and its dialectics of determinacy/indeterminacy remain as our realistic horizon. But then it becomes quite indispensable to envisage what is lost and what is not necessarily lost with this fool's paradise—at least for me, and for people like me.

I shall enter here only into a few points pertinent to a discussion arising out of the triumphalist and determinist aspect visible, for example, in the *Communist Manifesto*. My thesis is that what is lost today is a scientistic, that is deterministic, belief in progress, directly descended from theological triumphalism, and what is not lost are two major methodological pointers: the demystificatory vision and the open-ended concreteness of analysis and of recategorization (the setting up of new signifying categories). These latter allow a new take on, indeed refusal of, the undialectical and irrational onslaughts on any essence and totality which today predominate in the ideology of "cultural studies." More substantial arguments about labour-power, production/self-creativity, and an intelligibility of history posited against the horizon of social struggles and of a (however distant) revolutionary practice, I can only mention as desiderata at the end.

I believe that Marx's overriding category is the critique. I shall propose a brief sketch of this master's oscillation toward but also away from scientism and triumphalism, accommodated within such horizons.

1. What Is Well Lost:
Scientism, Automatic "Progress"

In a strictly Marxian optic, the division of labour results within antagonistically split societies in a division into exploiting and exploited social groups—by race, class, gender, etc.—and exfoliates as a series of historical, productive and societal, formations. Modern natural sciences (and all other ones) arose within that division: they are not only as it were accidentally within history, subordinating it to some cognitive or technological imperative; they are not a pure transcendence of the regrettably impure history; they are a stuff interacting most intimately with all other stuffs of history. In fact sciences arose together with the rise of capital and the bourgeoisie—as visible in the methodology of Bacon, Descartes, and Galileo—in fierce opposition to the clerico-feudal Aristotelianism, "qualitative physics," and similar theological deductions. It is therefore counter-indicated (to use a term from medical science) or historically dubious to adopt the paradigm of bourgeois science for an anti-capitalist mode of systematic cognition. That is, the dynamics of science are arrested by presenting them (as Marx's critique of Mill puts it) "as encased in eternal natural laws independent of history, at which opportunity <u>bourgeois</u> relations are then quietly smuggled in as the inviolable natural laws on which society in the abstract is founded" (*Grundrisse* 87). Therefore the term "science" strongly invites confusion with the bent institutionalized practice thereof in the service of capitalism, which made it possible for Wallerstein to stress, on the negative side, that "we have come to call rationality or universalism or 'science' ...[those cultural] pressures that seek to discipline and channel the world's cadres or 'middle' strata" (107). It would be much safer to find for positive use a disambiguating term like "articulated and systematic understanding," or indeed, as Jameson most perspicaciously suggests, non-alienated production (*Ideologies* 2: 141; cf. Suvin, "Living Labour"). The logic of Marx's analysis and what followed it in both bourgeois and supposedly socialist history strongly suggests that—with all due caution against a return into irrationalism—a new cognitive epistemology is on the order of the day (cf. Suvin "On the Horizons," essay 8 in this book, and Wallerstein's suggestions 115-19, 181-83, and passim).

In particular, the quintessentially capitalist and liberal ideology of progress is a highly suspect vehicle for such a mode of cognition. Balibar rightly notes that the catchword of progress fuses two factors: the notion of irreversible temporal flow (time as a river rather than, say, an ocean or an electric current or...), which presupposes an overall linearity regardless of local eddies, and the notion of technical, moral or other improvement (87—I would actually foreground the economic one). But one would have to add to this a third notion (which Balibar approaches in the same section), that of a monocausal determinism in the guise of "if atomic A then, necessarily, complex B," in which there is a necessary relation between a given beginning and the "end" of history (even if that end is in Marx conceived as the beginning of another, radically better history, that of classless society). History is then seen as having a predetermined goal in the laicized form of strict and, in spite of Engels's plea for multi-causality, "ultimately determining" (Engels 692, cf. Balibar 91) immanent necessities. Only such a trinity, it seems to me, melds to make a pseudo-Darwinian upward arrow of evolution.

This brand of evolutionism was the "scientific ideology" par excellence of Marx's time and probably its unavoidable furthest imaginative horizon (cf. Canguilhem, also Suvin "Cognitive"). It was in part shared by Marx, when for example he speaks of a kind of Newtonian "natural laws" that "make one's way by iron necessity" *(diese [Naturg]esetze, diese mit eherner Notwendigkeit ...sich durchsetzenden Tendenzen)* in the Preface to *Das Kapital* (12). But even here the immediately apposed concept weakens the laws into "tendencies"; and to Marx's great honour, in the body of *Das Kapital* he ceases to use the term "progress" without critical irony (Balibar 98). To the contrary, "progress" was later on fully embraced by Engels and orthodox Marxism of most stripes: with a minor difference in favour of its egalitarian extension, it rejoined the liberal idea of progress as "essence and law of society" (Larousse, and cf. Nisbet and Sorel). Both Gramsci and Benjamin have, under the twin impact of Fascism and Stalinism, convincingly noted how history itself dispelled such illusions and indeed delusions about history. Their diagnosis of the 1920s-30s could today be repeated in spades. Using Marx's own method of demystificatory analysis based on *praxis*, we can today see behind this over-reified image the ungainly bones of a theological pre-established plan for mankind (directly inherited from Christianity through Hegel) sticking out.

2. What Remains: Approach

But if not progress, then what is it that makes history intelligible? What can be used to organize events into a story that makes sense? Making sense is to my mind "anthropologically" inescapable: what various PoMo (supposedly "post-"Modernist) Lyotards are saying in their epic story to end all epics—bound to the same apocalyptic delusion which made US President Wilson believe he was entering a world war to end all wars—is that nonsense makes sense to them; this primarily means that both the World-Bank and the Marxian intelligibility or historicity do not make sense to them. Demonizing totality and essence means making ontology out of delight in panic disorientation.

Yet if history is a process rather than a final product, what are the forces or the collective agents in it, and what is their logic? It seems clear today that Marx's unconcluded opus does not give what we can today accept as an operative answer. But then, this difficulty is also, dialectically, an advantage, from which we may crystallize two major achievements and methodological lessons that set the stage for articulating any acceptable answer.

2.1. What Remains #1: Critical Demystification

First, I see no reason to retract the laudation of the Marxian demystification and its inner logic, about which I have written elsewhere.[7] What this amounts to is quite akin to a procedure that Brecht will later develop as a stance of estrangement (*Verfremdungseffekt*). That is, once a configuration of phenomena has been described in a "normal" way—as they immediately appear to the contemporary socialized eye, subsumed under the dominant alienated, bourgeois or positivistic, norms—Marx sets out to demystify or demythologize them; his analytic yield is to reveal a different configuration hidden behind or under, and even more precisely encoded within, the phenomena. In other words, the norms of the initial description are to begin with, pragmatically, not considered irrelevant since they represent the "commonsensical" hegemony from which one has to begin one's analysis in order to have a chance of making it both relevant and understandable; yet they are finally, axiologically, considered not as simply erroneous but as an alienation which is in itself significant and has to be accounted for (as it were by subtraction) in order to get at the really operative categories that permit an interventionist understanding. This Marxian proceeding refuses the bourgeois subject-object split: in a central example, the commodity objectively generates a fetishized world which is then rightly perceived by subjects as reified and opaque; but the fetish draws its power from incessant alienation of surplus labour in the specific capitalist form of a market(able) equality and "freedom," and this alienation is also both collectively objective and distributively or serially

---

7. See Suvin-Angenot. Instead of discussing here Derrida's very interesting, though insufficient, *Specters of Marx* his conclusion about Baudelaire's pamphlet will be approvingly cited: "The critique or polemic of 'The Pagan School' would have the virtue of demystification. The word is no longer fashionable but it does seem to impose itself in this case, does it not? It is a matter of unfolding the mystagogical hypocrisy of a secret, putting on trial a fabricated mystery...." (112)

subjective.

The PoMo vogue, which possesses and is possessed by strong elective affinities with intellectual prohibitionism akin to psychic terrorism, would prohibit the positive turn of this demystification. Expressions such as "subjective and objective alienation" and others suggesting an operative assumption of reality as something to be understood and intervened into are in this vogue tabooed as "essentialist." The shrewdest *tu quoque* ("you too") formulation I am aware of is Althusser's observation that "the total ['expressive'] presence of essence in existence which reduces all opacity to zero ...makes us suspect the presence behind it of the tenebrous religious phantasm of epiphanic transparency" (1: 41; for direct critiques of *Capital*, cf. among many others Cutler et al.; see also 2.3 below).[8] And there is no doubt that Marx repeatedly envisages a fixed inner structure (for example composed by economic relations) in a way which we would today wish to rephrase. Yet, obversely, washing one's hands of the world we live in and that lives in us is epistemologically, ethically, and—not least—politically futile. But the question is important and necessitates a little detour into the problem of essentialism, and later on of totality.

2.2. On "Essentialism"

---

8. Thinking back to my first acquaintance with Althusser's and his *Lire "le Capital,"* I remember my centrally negative reaction to its scientism, as in the famous epistemological break between the young humanistic and mature "scientific" Marx (later repudiated both by a self-critical Althusser and by Balibar). The pernicious insistence on scientificity has sterilised many Althusserians; it is in him coupled with an exclusive horizon of conceptuality as epistemic criterion, when the best analyses in *Lire*...indicate that totality and other matters should also be discussed as topological discursive necessities (cf. for example 2: 329). But the foundational gesture of rereading *Das Kapital*—as well as some loosenings of determinist orthodoxy, such as the rejection of the subject-object split and identification of structures with shifting dominance in their strong readings—were useful. One of the consequences of reading it closely is that I am citing it in my own translation.

Essence is one half of the doublet or pair "essence vs. appearance (or existence)," which stands as perhaps the longest unresolved quarrel in philosophy (cf. for example Marcuse). From a materialist point of view it sounds tempting to privilege appearance which, being here-and-now, seems immediately accessible to sensual perception. This can be done either in the nihilist (for example Buddhist) version of a bad appearance—we can never get beyond appearances, so reality can't be known at all; or in the phenomenological and indeed positivist version of a good appearance—appearance is reality, there is nothing else to know (people like Baudrillard hybridize this "hyper-reality" into a kind of nihilist phenomenology—cf. Hall 136). However, questions such as just what are the limits of any spatiotemporal present and just how sovereign may any perception be, lead into veritable minefields: semiotics has been grappling with them since ancient divination and Chinese or Greek medicine. But even outside these central epistemic conundrums, there are excellent reasons why taking appearance at face-value is suspect. First, it does not allow for human foresight and intervention outside of the present instant (so: no long-range agency). Second, even in the present instant it remains unclear which of the many facets of appearance—and how and why—to intervene into for a probable result (so: no strategic choices). Third, in a commodified and therefore fetishized world, where money and commodities are "the alienated essence of people's work and existence" (Marx, translation modified from Tucker ed. 48), direct experience is even more radically polluted (so: common sense is not to be trusted). Thence the no doubt partly justified downgrading of appearance as a naive or indeed degraded, merely "subjective," experience of or take on or view about reality, as opposed to "reality itself."

But obversely, all approaches to essence, especially when it is postulated to exist independent of appearances, are notoriously complex, difficult, and very often disappointing in their results (say in Kant's noumena as opposed to the phenomena). The narrow (Cartesian or Positivist) rationalists and—in an apparent paradox—the mystics, beginning with Plato, believe that the really real can be known directly without passing through appearance, either by logic or by direct mystical communion. While all of these stances may have useful or even admirable elements, none of them seems able to allow for lastingly intelligent agency. They all lead to rigid Aristotelian or monotheistic norms of what is "natural," therefore eternal and valuable, in a social order (see Jameson *Seeds* 33-34). Moreover, the liberal or bourgeois version of strict essentialism bans concrete political questions from its abstract universality of what is "naturally human," treating them as accidents (cf. the good critique of Gould). Thus, one has to exclaim "a plague on both your houses!" about the strict essentialists and the strict existentialists. As Marx noted, "if the appearance and the essence of things directly coincided ...all science would be superfluous" (*MEW* 25: 825): we need both terms of this distinction, and its feedback dialectics, for any systematic cognition or understanding. This leaves us with the necessity to either find a place for essence in our knowledge or to invent some hitherto undreamt of new terms. The second alternative is not only uneconomic and strongly subject to privatization of language but also favours the pernicious extinction of historical memory, and is to be rejected.[9]

Thus, the real or demystified question becomes: Whence the dislike of essentialism anyway? What functions does it fulfil? Let me start, for example, from Jameson's most interesting and

---

9. While some central stances of Durkheim appear today too limited, we can still profit from his observations that:

The categories of human thought are never fixed in any one definite form; they are made, unmade, and remade incessantly; they change with places and times. (21)

[The categories are not] very simple notions which the first comer can very easily arrange from his own personal observations, [but] priceless instruments of thought which human groups have laboriously forged through the centuries.... A complete section of the history of humanity is resumed therein. (27)

suggestive analogy between such anti-foundationalism and economic circulation in Post-Fordist capitalism with its "drive to liquidate inventories" (*Seeds* 41)—and I would include here the human "inventories" of full employment. If terms such as "exploitation" or "full employment" are demonized as essentialist, all opposition to savage capitalism is disarmed. So the tabooing of essentialism by the promoters of the "post-modern condition" turns out "to be the very paradigm of every sort of [buckling under and] compromise with the existing status quo" (Guattari 40), a godsend to World-Bank ideology. Diachronically, it is a liberal habit stemming from the breakdown of fixed feudal "estates" and similar slots in the "historically unique democratization of oppression" (Chéla Sandoval, in Gardiner ed. 97), that is, in the diffuse, more hypocritical, and much more "internalized" bourgeois oppression of our age. The intellectuals' anti-essentialism agenda today may well stem from a repugnance against being lumped together or identified with <u>any</u> kind of articulated collective, except the privatized and narcissistic identification with market competition and consumerism. PoMo, as Stuart Hall has well put it, "<u>is</u> about how the [intelligentsia] dreams itself to be 'American'" (132). Its anti-essentialist slogan has by now petrified "into a kind of norm in its own right...wide open to the objection that it has itself become something of a dogmatic foundation..." (Jameson, *Seeds* 34-35).[10] The quite indispensable hermeneutics of suspi-

10. In a work to my acid surprise often invoked on the Left, Laclau and Mouffe's *Hegemony and Socialist Strategy*, the authors have totally equated Marxian theory with economic determinism. Their shell-shocked hyper-essentialism in the guise of radical anti-essentialism concludes that Marx's key concepts of labour-power as commodity, of class, and of exploitation have to be totally rejected. While it may be in places useful to look at some insights from their critiques of orthodox Marxism (both social-democratic and Leninist), though even those have since been superseded by better critiques, I totally reject their framework, tone, and conclusions. Even this note would not be necessary except for their claim to speak as radical democrats and indeed socialists. Yet their banner of anti-essentialism logically leads them to anti-socialism (cf. a similar conclusion by Stabile

cion and demystification are either incomplete or counterproductive unless accompanied by the readiness for and attempts at reconstruction of meaning.

A proper usage of essence, a term which I think signals a real unresolved problem within understanding, would then seem to be a "soft" one, open to historical practice and therefore limited both in time and in scope; in it, essence is neither to be dogmatically rejected because it provides a movable focus permitting choice and agency, nor dogmatically accepted as static, natural, and eternal. As Jameson has argued, such abstractions are a unique resource and way to escape the viscous confusion of immediacy, "a more global characterization of the secret affinities between those apparently autonomous and unrelated domains, and of the rhythms and hidden sequences of things we normally remember only in isolation and one by one." He acknowledges the danger of confusing such a concept with the thing itself, that is, of surreptitiously perverting materialism into idealism. But he rightly concludes that "the escape from the nightmare of history, the conquest by human beings of control over the otherwise seemingly blind and 'natural' laws of socio-economic fatality, remains the irreplaceable will of the Marxist heritage..." ("Marxism" 35-37). My proposal for the proper usage of essentialism is to decisively reject the monotheist topology (taken over by bourgeois understanding in Cartesian, Lutheran or other guises) of identifying human or any other essence with a spheric interiority of the kernel-in-a-shell type (cf. Althusser 1: 44, 2: 174-75, and passim). As Sève repeatedly phrases it, human essence is "socially de-centered." Our *bon usage* should therefore use essence simply as a supremely important "rational abstraction" which not only underlines the common traits of a subject and thus avoids repetition but furthermore allows us to define and intervene (first discursively and then pragmatically) into any subject at all. Not being the Truth—a spherically

284-85, which identifies their position as that of privileged intellectuals bidding to become a new center for political struggle, and the painstaking critique by Haug, *Pluraler* 41-47).

internal, or polar or diametrical, opposite of empirical appearance—this essence is only there as an indispensable mediation toward a richer concretization (see 2.3 below). In human affairs—history—essences are created by actions of people, they are changeable or dynamic (cf. Gould 440-41).

In this area, Marx is precisely the high point of a "Copernican revolution" in the whole European philosophical tradition, to the effect of seeing essence as <u>relational</u> rather than substantive (Sève 331, also 194, 510-11, and passim). This relationality has a synchronic and a diachronic aspect. First, the essence of (for example) money, labour-power, production, class, exploitation or any other major concept is a nexus and a node of multiple, <u>pluricausal</u> interactions. One of the major necessities of a reasonable epistemology today is to discuss the conundrum of causality and get rid of the reified cause-effect dead-end (and especially of using only the efficient cause, and most especially the single cause vs. complex effect) without throwing the baby of causality out with such a dirty bath: "Any historical event comes about," noted Brecht, "[...as a result of] contradictory tendencies, which were decided by struggle, this is much less than 'sufficient causes'" (20: 156), and further on he speaks of a "bundle of motives" (GW 20: 157).[11] In other words, I would argue that all complex concepts such as those above are—Marx stresses it time and again—not merely general or abstract, "horizontally" referring to each other as fixed pseudo-things in a closed and unfalsifiable doctrinal system, but also "vertical" feedbacks from and to dynamic material practices (see more in Suvin "Cognitive," and the preceding essay here, section 1.1). When Marx refuses Feuerbach's fixedly "naturalized" or reified human species-essence and totality, a fixed idea of the whole German Idealism from Schelling to Schiller, he does so because it is an "internal and mute generality, which connects

---

11. That Brecht is to be taken quite seriously as a critic not only of theatre or even of culture but also of our epoch and *épistémé* has been a well-kept secret among the specialists, but should become apparent as soon as Haug's *Philosophieren* is made accessible in English.

individuals in a merely <u>natural</u> way" *(Theses on Feuerbach* 6, translation modified from Tucker ed. 109).

Second, as against such old-style philosophizing, history is not accidental and extrinsic to but constitutive of bodies and concepts:

> This sum of productive forces, [a historically created relation of individuals to nature and to one another,] capital funds and social forms of intercourse, which every individual and generation finds in existence as something given, is the real basis of what the philosophers have conceived as "substance" and "essence of man"...(*The German Ideology*, Tucker ed. 128-29).

In a vivid *exemplum* for our lives:

> The "essence" of the fish is its "existence," water—to go no further than this one proposition. The "essence" of the freshwater fish is the water of a river. But the latter ceases to be the "essence" of the fish and is no longer a suitable medium of existence as soon as the river is...polluted by dyes and other waste products and navigated by steamboats...(ibid. 132)

In sum, for Marx each essential concept is "a <u>generative process</u>, [a] self-constructing dynamic" (Sève 332, cf. Berman 93), which participates in the no doubt imaginatively constructed yet also reality-constricted feedback with material bodies and processes. A good example would today be the difference between the simultaneously abstract and reified atom from the Greeks to Rutherford, as opposed to the infinitely subdivisible and recombinable dialectics of atom in 20th-Century physical sciences—whose "essential" existence nobody has nonetheless put into doubt, simply because operative physics functionally, strategically or epistemologically must have this concept. Thus, a Marxian essence is organized into formal topologies (see also Sève 328-33, and Suvin "Cognitive"): "human essence," concludes Thesis 6, "is an ensemble of social relationships." As such relationships change with ever-increasing speed under capitalism, essences or "natures" change too, prominently including human nature. That is a ground bass of *Das Kapital*.

It is noteworthy that two among the central lines of epistemic insight in our century, namely the best formulations by Antonio Gramsci and Bertolt Brecht as well as by some critics arising out of feminism, develop such a flexible "soft" essentialism. Among many of Gramsci's and Brecht's propositions of this kind (both also have "hard" essentialist statements), which foreground the role interest plays in such determinations (see also Marcuse 76), one for each might here suffice:

> every "truth"...has had practical origins and has represented a "provisional" value (historicity of every conception of the world and of life), ...without in so doing shaking the convictions that are necessary for action. (Gramsci 406)
>
> ...truth has become a commodity to such an extent, ...that the question "what is true" cannot be solved without answering the question "whom does this truth avail." Truth has become an entirely functional matter, something that does not exist (above all, not without people) but must be created in each case, certainly a means of production but a produced means! (GW 20: 87)

Finally, those feminist theoreticians whom I take to be useful beyond the internal debates of that movement, picking their way through the antinomy between valorizing a women's standpoint and seeking equality, agree with Gayatri Ch. Spivak that we need a "strategic essentialism" used in a vigilant way in place of "the totally counter-productive gesture of repudiating it.... Whereas the great custodians of the anti-universal...are actually run by a great narrative even as they are busy protecting their theoretical purity by repudiating essentialism." (12) Such a "weak" essentialism might be "based on the creative force of labor" (Weeks 299), as "a performative discourse seeking to constitute a political effect and a political community" (Judith Butler quoted by Patricia Stamp in Gardiner ed. 88; many other examples could be found, beginning with bell hooks and Spivak).

2.3. What Remains #2: Critical Dialectics

A second strong (and presently very useful) aspect in Marx's opus, and a central implication of his methodology, is that in fact there can be no final answers in a quickly changing history (after the Industrial Revolution/s). His central stance and concept of critique (for example the critique of commodity fetishism) constitutes a firm refusal of all static fixity, of any eternally natural categories and undialectical determinism (cf. Haug *Pluraler,* Balibar, Berman 20 and passim, Amariglio-Callari 56 and passim): there is no dialectical determinism; there are only more or less strong tendencies that can succeed or be counteracted in a multicausal world. This stance may be, for example, educed from the definition of dialectics in Marx's Afterword to the second edition of *Das Kapital* in 1873, which is:

> a scandal and abomination to bourgeoisdom and its doctrinaire spokesmen because it includes into the positive understanding of the existing state of things at the same time also the understanding of the negation of that state, of its necessary decline; because it regards every form that came about as in fluid movement, thus also in its transient aspect; because it lets nothing impose upon it, and is in its essence critical and revolutionary. (28; translation modified from McLellan ed. 420-21)

Dialectics can only be found by interacting with a temporal horizon of a potentially different and a potentially better (less oppressive) set of human relationships. Obversely, "all categories that describe the given [historically mutable] form of existence...become 'ironic': they contain their own negation" (Marcuse 86). The stance of critique, which is necessarily always dialogical and ironical, is never absent in Marx, and it predominates wherever the level of concrete analyses—which was for Marx always the most important one—is his strategic choice: in the *18th Brumaire* rather than in the *Communist Manifesto*, in *Das Kapital* (perhaps most clearly) rather than in the *Preface to A Contribution to the Critique of Political Economy* of 1859. Rather than in the programmatic and thus inevitably schematic—though still immensely stimulating—summaries, Marx attained in such feedbacks, where the inductive verticality from actual messy historical processes intertwines with thought-experiments, the maximal richness of all his concepts, as well as their maximal plasticity, visible in the modifications they underwent whenever new analytic exigencies arose. Marx himself defined this inductive-deductive methodology as going from an empirically superficial and/or banal conception first to "ever thinner abstractions," but then from such simplest conceptual determinations spirally back to a reconceptualized and enriched concreteness: "The concrete is concrete," he concluded, "because it is the concentration of many determinations, hence unity of the diverse" (*Grundrisse* 100-01, the last phrase coming as a direct quote from Hegel's *Encyclopädie der philosophischen Wissenschaften* and going towards Althusser's "overdetermination").

It is one of Balibar's (and before him, W.F. Haug's) great merits that he has drawn attention to the methodological consequences arising from Marx's letters to Mikhailovsky and Zassulich in 1877-81 on whether Russia could jump from the medieval peasant commune directly to socialism, namely that "one has to descend from pure theory to Russian reality in order to discuss that"; that his historical discussion of capitalism in

Western Europe is not "a general historico-philosophical theory of development...regardless of historical circumstances" but that it would have to be independently argued for a different geopolitical spacetime; and that the answer is finally a matter of possible political contingencies rather than predetermination— so that "the Russian commune can be saved by a Russian revolution" (*MEW* 19: 108 and 926, English excerpts in McLellan ed. 571-80; cf. Haug *Pluraler* 44-46 and Balibar 105-07). The very linearity of historical time, indispensable for making it the space of progress, is here decisively doubted in favour of a Riemannian or Einsteinian "qualitative" dialectics of time (cf. Balibar 112) which depends on its constituent matter; this will be developed further by Ernst Bloch's reflections on the asynchronicity of global history, by Althusser's approach to historical time, and by Wallerstein's topology of the global centre vs. periphery.

Thus, in order to discuss Marx's concepts in less than several hundred pages, the finite schemata have inevitably to be used— but not without correction by his most highly developed philosophical practice as in *Das Kapital* (cf. on this Balibar 91-94). These are at times accompanied by sarcastic disclaimers such as the one in the letter to Mikhailovsky against applying the *passe-partout* masterkey of "a general historico-philosophical theory, the supreme virtue of which is to be supra-historical." That is why the early Marx's generous attempt to substitute the proletariat as "universal class" for the Chosen People of World History would not work even if the incidence of workers' resistance were happily much higher than it is, even if revolutions made in the name of and together with the working classes were still on the horizon: the whole constellation, notion or image is still within a monotheistic or hard essentialism.

2.4. On Totality

From this vantage point, it would be useful to attempt a differentiation within (and if you wish demystification of) the outcry against <u>totality</u> similar to that attempted above for anti-essentialism. It is of course possible to illegitimately reduce totality to what Althusser identifies as the Leibniz-Hegel (in fact, as he says in Vol. 1, the monotheistic) "expressive" model, which presupposes that the whole that is being discussed "possess such a unity that each element of the whole, be that a material or economic determination, a political institution, or a religious, artistic or philosophical form, is always only the presence of the [essential] concept to itself in a given historical moment" (2: 40), so that at each such monadic moment it is possible to employ the equation "element" = "the inner essence of the whole" (cf. also Witt 748-49). What has thence come to be called "expressive totality"—though this somewhat unfortunate ellipse should properly be "totality with an expressive causality" (2: 173)—is, as argued in 2.2, clearly to be rejected as a static, "bad" essentialism. However mediated and overdetermined the vivifying warmth of this Sun Deity may be, in Althusser it is a "code word for Stalin" (Jameson, *Political* 37), even if it is in the texts under discussion mainly applied to Lukács's *History and Class Consciousness*.[12] Before Althusser this was perhaps even more convincingly articulated by such undoubted totality-seekers as Bakhtin/Vološinov, Brecht, and Benjamin (for example in "The Author as Producer"). All of them protested against the Platonic impoverishment of experience, the reduction of new understanding to a re-cognition (*anamnesis*) of eternal Ideas, and the concomitant assumption of the text's author into the systematic heavens of prophetic transmission.[13]

---

12. This work on the whole may merit it, though I have argued (in Suvin, "Lukács") that Lukács is not a dead dog, and I agree with Jameson that even *History and Class Consciousness* still carries many lessons for today.

13. But nonetheless, there also undoubtedly exist "expressive" totalities, for example all Euro-American works of art between the Middle Ages and Modernism. The Leibniz-Hegel mistake was to illegitimately extrapolate such "soulful" construct (cf. Suvin" Soul") from art to State, a procedure then foregrounded by Burckhardt for the Renaissance.

No doubt, interesting variants of predetermining reality can be found: it may become an <u>illustration</u> of what existed (or in fact, was believed to exist) earlier, or an <u>indication</u> of simple "underlying causes," or an onset or <u>seed</u> which is seen backward from its teleological perspective-point as a "baby figure of the giant mass /Of things to come" (Shakespeare, *Troilus and Cressida* II.i—see Witt 755-56). But all of these allegories suppress agency and actors between its rigid poles, that is, they suppress the possibility of a Blochian Novum, of something new and not previously known resulting from the existing; all of them occult the author's situation; and all of them fully subordinate and incorporate induction from possibly new practice to hegemonically deductive modes of thought handed down from the past.

Again, there is no doubt that Marx had such a Hegelian or messianic heritage of combative "hard" essentialism and totality which he grew increasingly critical of but never quite outgrew (though even Hegel never quite articulated his "thick" arguments according to his programmatic essentialism but let all his decipherments of appearances function exclusively within history). However, the Althusserian or monotheistic totality is not the only, nor even the most important, model of totality available. In Marx, much more frequently and significantly, we are within *Capital* confronted by <u>two different ways of cognizing</u> reality. A crucially ambiguous case is one of outer appearance vs. inner laws of movement. I have discussed in Section 1 the unfortunate paleotechnic vocabulary of rigid laws, issuing forth with metallic ("iron," or in the original German in fact "brazen") necessity, on the example of his Preface to *Capital* (and cf. on this post-Cartesian and scientist dualism also, for example, *Das Kapital III, MEW* 25: 324, discussed in Witt 750-51). Much more interesting is the relation between veiling or mystifying and unveiling or manifesting, omnipresent in Marx from *The Communist Manifesto* through *Capital*. Though it contains a Platonic element of a solid truth stolidly waiting to be found out, it usually does not rely on "laws" but on critical work constituting both these poles in an unceasing weaving back and forth between them (see for an extended discussion Angenot and Suvin). We could call these two models rock-solid vs. ocean-fluid: on the one hand, an uncritical linkage of notions (*Vorstellungen*) which follow a "common sense" that is usually more conceptual than sensual, and on the other hand a critical reasoning that reconstructs the given in its becoming, having become, and functioning—as well as according to subversive norms of desire and value—into an articulated, fluid, and dialectically contradictory "concrete": "Beneath the apparently solid surface, they [the 1848 revolutions] betrayed oceans of liquid matter, only needing expansion to rend into fragments continents of hard rock" ("Speech at the Anniversary of the *People's Paper*," Tucker ed. 427; see on this remarkable passage Berman 90 and passim). This dynamics is in fact the exemplary Marxian whole or totality (cf. Althusser 2: 43ff. and Haug *Pluraler* 49 and passim). Marx's oscillation between the two models may be phrased also as his not having "adequately and articulately conceptualized (*pensé*) the ...theoretical implications of his theoretically revolutionary proceeding" (Althusser 2: 75).

In that latter, fluid vein, totality is a twin of "system"— and in particular, as already Durkheim pointed out (629-35), a synonym of the social system or society or, as Raymond Williams repeatedly insisted on, of "the whole social order." It is thus "an indispensable [family] name" for any generalized understanding today (Jameson, *Late Marxism* 28 and 29); and I would maintain that we need to strive for both extensive totality (understanding the capitalist world-system which beats Western trade unions by shifting to Taiwan or Georgia) and intensive totality (a standpoint able to see the shifting paradigms under the extension). After all, a total, and negative, world-system exists beyond any reasonable doubt—let us take only the examples of the sale and use of arms and chemicals; so, to refuse thinking it as such is an act of imaginative and political abdication. It is just this that happened in the PoMo vulgate, which took to heart

Lyotard's slogan "the answer is this: war on totality" (16). This is also why the PoMo horizons are singularly unhelpful and *passé* today: my answer is, *qui totalitate ferit, totalitate perit*—he who offends through denial of totality shall perish by that denial. Further, the present movement by many ex-Leftists of "back to Kant" (from whom we can no doubt learn much, including how to shun his dead ends) forgets the "quasi-religious motive behind [his] desire for an ultimate, unified reality" and all the antinomies of reconciling phenomena and noumena that he found must necessarily follow when one wishes to apply relativized stances to "hard" totality. Hegel's providential philosophy of history was then an attempt to resolve such antinomies, and I doubt one escapes it by returning to its root cause (Hawkes 71, and cf. 78-80).

To the contrary, Jameson's insistence on a dynamic and open-ended value-horizon of possible totalization that yet criticaly refuses spatiotemporally closed totalities—"the absent totality that makes a mockery of us" ("Actually" 172, and cf. *Late Marxism* 26-31, 131-32, and 251)—is a necessary presupposition for criticism and for positive counter-proposals, indeed for any politics of social transformation. Such a totality is not expressive of any divine essence or ultimate end, but on the contrary, as I argued earlier, resolutely divorced from any imaginary spheric centrality analogous to Christian soul or Ptolemeian Earth. However, it is only thinking about one finite matter— best as an ensemble of shifting relationships—that enables us to grasp it at all. If my argument about essence is found persuasive, the analogous conclusion about totality seems to necessarily follow: whatever has a (however dynamic) essence also has some (however provisional) defining limits and thus constitutes a whole.

In other words—just as for essence—we can and have to use an epistemological or hermeneutic but not an ontological totality: this trope is quite indispensable in understanding anything and everything, even though not present in any "deep" or "interior" way within an Engelsian "(dialectics of) Nature." As Brecht lucidly remarked, in a note called "Totality" from the 1930s: "In fact, we can only construct, make, put together a totality, and this should be done quite openly, but following a plan and for a given purpose" (GW 20: 131). Symmetrically obverse, I understand open-endedness in Jameson's and Marx's sense not as liberal pluralism or simply mush, but as a Brechtian productive doubt entailing an articulated stance and clear value-horizon. The resulting inescapable totality is always provisional; it is an epistemic category which should not, in Williams's terms, "as so often in idealist thought..., almost unnoticed, become [a] substantive description..." (80). Yet it, simultaneously, remains operative for this constellation as well as necessarily wedded to change, consubstantially with a dynamically changeable stance or bearing in order to render justice to the coming about of different situations and to the agent's self-reflection and self-correction (see the preceding essay).

3. A First Conclusion

In sum, we have to read Marx's opus as a rich and uneven force-field. His rupture with traditional philosophy had not resulted in a monolithic system. Nonetheless, it certainly included an aspect and stance of deterministic scientism, founded in his hopeful enthusiasm of the 1840s and echoed as late as the 1867 Preface to *Das Kapital*. This proved an inspiration but also finally a snare to the socialist movements in the century after his death: it answered their legitimate need for clear and simple slogans, but it also easily slid into a pernicious impoverishment and doctrinaire encapsulation toward which the monotheistic "Marxists" had tended since the late Engels and which was consummated in Stalinism. Yet in Marx this stance went always hand in hand with, and by the time of *Das Kapital* became on the whole superseded by, his "thick" effort of a demystificatory critique of ruling illusions and capitalist fetishism, advancing finally toward a dynamic and unceasingly renewing, open-ended illumination. The result is a plurality of stances unified by Marx's constant horizon of revolutionary practice as the agency needed to rid people of devastating capitalist exploitation of human labour. However, this oscillating and in many respects even contradictory plurality-in-unity, arising out of his reflection on changing phases of capitalist power during his lifetime and in particular out of the defeats of the revolutionary hopes both in 1848 and in 1871, "in no way signifies a weakness of Marx's" (Balibar 6).

At the end, I would like to return the reader, with what I hope is some additional illumination, to what I began with. I hold that if we cannot accept the deterministic Marx, we cannot do either without such a final horizon, to be read out of and no doubt also partly read into Marx. I accept Guattari's characterization of our historical moment:

> A certain idea of progress and of modernity has gone bankrupt, and in its fall it has dragged along all confidence in the notion of emancipation through social action. At the same time social relations have entered an ice age: hierarchy and segregation have solidified, poverty and unemployment tend now to be accepted as inevitable evils...(40).

Nonetheless, especially in our time, the heritage which the *Manifesto of the Communist Party* was willing to accept from the revolutionary bourgeoisie, remains the quite indispensable beacon—though today taken as hope and horizon to be devoutly striven for rather than as prophecy:

> All fixed, rusted-in circumstances, with their train of ancient and venerable notions and opinions, are swept away, all new-formed ones become antiquated before they can ossify. All that is solid melts into air, all that is holy is profaned, and people are at last compelled to face with sober senses their position in life and their

relations to each other. (translation modified from Tucker ed. 338)

Facing soberly our position in life, we cannot cease talking (for example) of labour-power and production, and how they provide the stuff of human reproduction: of history, of its hegemonic occultations, and some of its central—finally no doubt revolutionary—tensions; they are, after all, verified daily even in the somewhat epicyclic regions of our work in academia. All such essences and totalities are, I repeat, not ontological realities but epistemic tools: as Nagarjuna put it about analogous problems in Buddhism, "the feeble-minded are destroyed by the misunderstood doctrine as by a snake ineptly seized by the tail rather than by the neck" (in Loy 59, and cf. Inada). Thus, we cannot do without operative synonyms for essence and totality—providing we never fail to supply their limits of validity for each particular case under discussion.

Works Cited

Althusser, Louis, et al. *Lire le Capital*, 2 Vols. Paris: Maspero, 1965; [*Reading Capital.* Tr. B. Brewster. London: NLB, 1975, but here cited from original].

Amariglio, Jack, and Antonio Callari. "Marxian Value Theory and the Problem of the Subject." *Rethinking Marxism* 2.3 (1989): 31-60.

Balibar, Etienne. *La philosophie de Marx.* Paris: La Découverte, 1993.

Berman, Marshall. *All That Is Solid Melts Into Air.* New York: Simon & Schuster, 1982.

Brecht, Bertolt. *Gesammelte Werke,* 20+ Vols. Frankfurt: Suhrkamp, 1973 [GW].

Canguilhem, Georges. "Qu'est-ce qu'une idéologie scientifique," in *Idéologie et rationalité dans l'histoire des sciences de vie.* Paris: Libr. Vrin, 1977.

Cutler, Antony, et al. *Marx's "Capital" and Capitalism Today*, Vol. 1. London: Routledge & Kegan Paul, 1977.

Derrida, Jacques. *Spectres de Marx.* Paris: Galilée, 1993.

Durkheim, Émile. *Les Formes élémentaires de la vie religieuse.* Paris: PUF, 1968.

Engels, Friedrich. Letter to J. Bloch, Sept. 21, 1890, in Marx-Engels, *Selected Works in One Volume.* London: Lawrence & Wishart, 1968, 692-93.

Gardiner, Judith Kegan, ed. *Provoking Agents.* Urbana: U of Illinois P, 1995.

Gould, Carol C. "The Woman Question," in M.B. Mahowald, *Philosophy of Woman.* Indianapolis: Hackett, 1983, 415-45.

Gramsci, A. *Selections from the Prison Notebooks.* Ed. and transl. Q. Hoare and G. Nowell-Smith. New York: International Publ., 1975.

Guattari, Félix. "The Postmodern Dead End." *Flash Art* [Milan] 128 (May-June 1986): 40-41.

Hall, Stuart. "On Postmodernism and Articulation," in David Morley and Kuan-Hsing Chen, eds., *Stuart Hall: Critical Dialogues in Cultural Studies.* London & New York: Routledge, 131-50, 1996.

Haug, Wolfgang Fritz. *Pluraler Marxismus*, Vol. 1. W. Berlin: Argument, 1985.

—-. *Philosophieren mit Brecht und Gramsci.* Berlin: Argument, 1996.

Hawkes, David. *Ideology.* London & New York: Routledge, 1996.

Inada, Kenneth K. *Nâgârjuna.* Tokyo: Hokuseido P, 1970.

Jameson, Fredric. "Actually Existing Marxism." *Polygraph* no. 6/7 (1993): 170-95.

—-. *The Ideologies of Theory*, 2 Vols. Minneapolis: U of Minnesota P, 1988.

—-. *Late Marxism.* London & New York: Verso, 1992, 33-49.

—-. "Marxism and Postmodernism," in his *The Cultural Turn.* London: Verso, 1998,

—-. *The Political Unconscious.* Ithaca: Cornell UP, 1981.

—-. *The Seeds of Time*. New York: Columbia UP, 1994.

Laclau, Ernesto, and Chantal Mouffe. *Hegemony and Socialist Strategy*. Transl. W. Moore and P. Cammack. London: Verso, 1985.

Larousse, Pierre. "Progrès," in his *Grand dictionnaire universel du XIXe siècle*. Nîmes: Lacour, 19: 224-26, 1990-92. [rpt. of original 1866-76 edn.].

Loy, David. "Preparing for Something that Never Happens." *International Studies in Philosophy* 26.4: 53-66, 1993.

Lyotard, Jean-François. *The Postmodern Explained: Correspondence 1982-85*. Eds. J. Pefanis and M. Thomas, transl. D. Barry et al. Minneapolis: U of Minnesota P, 1994.

Marcuse, Herbert. "The Concept of Essence," in his *Negations*. Transl. J.J. Shapiro. Boston: Beacon P, 1969.

Marx, Karl. *Grundrisse*. New York: Vintage, 1973.

—-. *Das Kapital, Erster Band. MEW,* Bd. 23. Berlin: Dietz V., 1993.

—-. *Das Kapital, Dritter Band. MEW,* Bd. 25. Berlin: Dietz V., 1962.

—-. *Selected Writings*. Ed. David McLellan. Oxford: Oxford UP, 1978.

[—-, and Friedrich Engels.] *The Marx-Engels Reader*. Ed. Robert C. Tucker. New York: Norton, 1972.

—-. *Werke [MEW]*. Berlin: Dietz, 1962.

Nisbet, Robert A. *History of the Idea of Progress*. New Brunswick & London: Transaction Publ., 1994.

Sève, Lucien. *Marxisme et théorie de la personnalité*. Paris: Ed. sociales, 1972.

Sorel, Georges. *Les Illusions du progrès*. Paris: Rivière, 1927.

Spivak, Gayatri Chakravorty. "Criticism, Feminism, and the Institution," in S. Harasym ed., *The Post-Colonial Critic*. New York: Routledge, 1990.

Stabile, Carol A. "Feminism Without Guarantees," in Antonio Callari et al., eds., *Marxism in the Postmodern Age*. New York: Guilford P, 1995, 283-91.

Suvin, Darko. "On Cognitive Emotions and Topological

Imagination." *Versus* no. 68-69 (1994): 165-201.

——. "Living Labour and the Labour of Living: A Little Tractate for Looking Forward in the 21st Century," in his *Defined by a Hollow*. London: P. Lang, 2010, 419-71.

——. "Lukács: Horizons and Implications of the 'Typical Character'." *Social Text* no. 16 (1987): 97-123.

——. "The Soul and the Sense: Meditations on Roland Barthes on Japan," in his *Lessons of Japan*. Montreal: CIADEST, 1996, 27-61.

——, and Marc Angenot. "L'aggirarsi degli spettri. Metafore e demifisticazioni, ovvero l'implicito del manifesto (Elogio, limiti e uso di Marx)," in M. Galletti ed., *Le soglie del fantastico*. Roma: Lithos, 1997, 129-66.

Wallerstein, Immanuel. *Geopolitics and Geoculture*. Cambridge: Cambridge UP, 1992.

Weeks, Kathi. "Feminist Standpoint Theories and the Return of Labor," in Callari et al., eds. [see in Stabile], 292-300.

Williams, Raymond. 1977. *Marxism and Literature.* Oxford: Oxford UP .

Witt, Thilo. 1994. "Ausdruck," in *Historisch-Kritisches Wörterbuch des Marxismus.* Ed. W.F. Haug. Hamburg: Argument, 1: 748-56.

3. CAPITALISM MEANS/ NEEDS WAR (1999-2001)[14]

—To the memory of Luigi Cortesi,
a late but dear friend—

...Anyone can understand that war and conquest without and the encroachment of despotism within mutually support each other; that money and people are habitually taken at will from a people of slaves to bring others beneath the same yoke; and that conversely war furnishes a pretext for exactions of money and...for keeping large armies constantly afoot.... In a word, anyone can see that aggressive rulers wage war at least as much on their subjects as on their enemies, and that the conquering nation is left no better off than the conquered.

J.-J. Rousseau, "Abstract and Judgment
of Saint-Pierre's Project for Perpetual Peace," 1756

When, when, Peace, will you, Peace?...

---

14. This essay was first presented as an abbreviated French lecture in Paris 1999 and amplified in Montreal in 2000; a few factual points were added up to March 2002 for periodical publication. However, no attempt has been made to rewrite it in view of the huge militarization imposed on the world by the USA after Sept. 2001. This matter is briefly addressed in a P.S. at the end.

That piecemeal peace is poor peace. What pure peace
  allows
Alarms of wars, the daunting wars, the death of it?
G. M. Hopkins, "Peace," 1879

War is distinguishable from murder and massacre only
when restrictions are established on the reach of battle.
Michael Walzer, 1977

mékhris téo katákeisthe...
...en eirénei dè dokeîte
êsthai, atàr pólemos gaîan hápasan ékhei
(How long will you go on being inert?
...In peaceful sloth
You are lying down, while war keeps command of the
whole land.)
Kallinos, after 700 B.C.E.

Counter-revolution by the center against the periphery
Blood on stone   blood & stones
Thou shalt not get out from under world banks
                        fish mouth silently
This is Moses & the prophets.
Roland Wyser, "The Ashes of Tito," 1999

0. Introductory: War?

Amid systematic obfuscation, I wish to recall Dorothy
Dinnerstein's great confession of faith:

> ...we must try to understand what is threatening to kill
> us off as fully and clearly as we can.... And...to fight
> what seems about to destroy everything earthly that
> you love—to fight it...intelligently, armed with your

central resource, which is passionate curiosity—is for me the human way to live until you die. (viii)

I shall be unable here to go, as she did, into the murky psychic depths of what drives the lust to power, profit, and killing. These are initial soundings, to limn what is afoot.

The overriding question for today is: What may be workable, embodied answers to the present stunted rationality of wars, of the exchange-value rule of bureaucracy and army? How are we to delineate the new collective body, the new sensorium humanity needs for survival? For if we don't at least guess at the alternatives, approximate them, try to forecast them, pave the way for them, help—however feebly—to make the alternatives possible or maybe bring them about, capitalism may well destroy all that humanity has achieved in the last 1000 years or longer. A radical change in reasoning is needed for us to use Marx's great insight that no theory or method can be understood without the practice of social groups to which it corresponds.

We have to find our answers in action. As Vico argued, whatever we cannot intervene into, we cannot understand. But for action we need a clear horizon and possible vectors toward it. The horizon for our opposition seems clear: only use-values can stand up to capitalist unequal exchange. Ancient designations for the life-furthering use-values were compassion, indignation, and love: they are today gathered up into communism and poetry. We need also to realize that there is no poetry without communism, and no communism without poetry. All poets know this is their encompassing horizon, often in fantastic metamorphoses; few communists apart from Marx, Morris, Brecht, Césaire or Neruda have allowed their suspicion to flower. When sundered, what we get are caricatures which compromise the potential horizon of either.

My initial question on how to at least begin understanding the spreading blight of warfare in all of its forms, literal and metaphoric, may today be only answered fragmentarily, since it is one aspect of a consubstantial unholy trinity: mass murders, mass prostitution, mass drugging. For it is the case that by mass prostitution one could mean not only that of the sexual services (in majority female) but also, as Balzac did, the prostitution of the mind (of intellectuals, in majority male) making death-bringing commodities seem sexy. It is also the case that drugging is the inflecting of the mind to momentary euphoria bringing death, so that one could definitely include in it the identical effects wrought without pharmaceutical substances, such as most PR and the prevailing Disneyfication of consumer virtues. And finally, by mass murder could be meant all the victims of starvation and poverty-induced illnesses, as well as of the drugs. I have tried to indicate their inextricable links in a previous essay, "On Cognition"; here I concentrate on war only.

To begin with, I shall cull from my readings on war a provisional, operative definition: war is a coherent sequence of conflicts, involving physical combats between large organized groups of people, that include the armed forces of at least one state, which aim to exercise political and economic control over a given territory. One or more fights or skirmishes, even between groups of people, do not qualify. The aim of war was originally the forcible expropriation in favour of a given social class (sometimes tribal or ethnic group[15]) of booty, land— or other productive forces—and/or labour power from the vanquished: "A simple definition of a warrior might be a person who survives by taking what others have or have produced" (Love and Shanklin 283). However, in developed class societies war has also always been *ultima ratio regum,* a means to evade inner revolutionary tension by outer conquest, while in a

15. Whether there is war in pre-State (tribal) societies is a disputed question, depending on one's definition of war, which in turn depends largely on the researcher's ideology. Those who hold that war is biologically innate to *Homo sapiens* must find war in all human groups, but the evidence is against them—I tend to agree with Bourne that war and State are coterminous (16-17). The rest is a matter of finding out how far a particular tribe or similar group is on the road to State (class) society. See the conflicting opinions of Mead (whose definition of war seems too large) and Lesser, in Fried et al. eds. 215-17 and 94-95.

multi-State system other indirect and intermediary (but crucial) aims may be added, such as securing advantages for coming tensions and conflicts—for example dominion over sea lanes or oil resources—and the destruction of commodities and people.

It ought to be noted that the demarcation line to mafioso gang clashes, indicated by my "that include..." clause, grows increasingly thin as unchecked private wealth balloons and the moral legitimacy of many States converges toward zero: practically all wage undeclared wars using civilian killings; all States are today "rogue States" to different degrees, most clearly in the undeclared US wars on Vietnam and Serbia bombing them back into the Stone Age; terror killings cannot be differentiated morally but only by scale (cf. Virilio and Lotringer 25-27, Lens). The ratio of military to civilian casualties in wars has in the course of twentieth Century "progressed" from 8:1 to 1:8 (eight civilians killed for each combatant), while the fighting units diversified from regular armies into paramilitary groups, police forces, mercenaries, local warlords and "pure" criminal gangs (Kaldor, *New* 8). It is by now received Western media wisdom to treat the ex-Yugoslavia civil wars or the Russo-Chechen war as conflicts between exploitative gangs in power, but the same could be said for both Gulf Oil Wars and for the NATO-Serbia War.

This means that Clausewitz's restriction of war to the politics of State-like entities reflects only the historical rise of capitalist nation-States which arrogated to themselves the monopoly of organized violence through their armed forces in exchange for "civil" pacification through police (cf. Weber and Giddens). The monopoly was always threatened by gang and revolutionary violence, and there are indications this "State dominance period" may have been limited to 1600-1990. The "privatization of violence" (Kaldor, *New* 92), an unintended but logical result of the corporate enforcing of economic privatization at the expense of State authority, also means that the line between the "policing operations" of the army and a technoscientifically beefed-up police (and then private militias and illegal gangs) grows almost indistinguishable. Nonetheless most major armed conflicts—defined ad hoc as "battle-related deaths of at least 1000 people" (SIPRI 1998: 17)—are still conducted by State or aspiring proto-State entities.

1. War and Classes

In the twentieth century probably more people have been murdered in mass killings than in all of world history up to 1900. Around one hundred million people have been slaughtered by bomb and bayonet, and probably billions by imposed starvation and maladies of poverty—the class war of the few ever more rich against the many ever more poor. Tuberculosis, the malady testifying to misery, is back in force, and even the plague has returned in India. The excuse that, proportionately to the number of people alive, the century is no worse than any other may or may not be statistically correct, but it is irrelevant. If we have the knowhow to ensure the survival of more people beyond their twelfth month, then we surely must use it to ensure their survival to their (our) natural end. Each person is a body in hope and pain, in theological terms in direct one-to-one relation to divinity. No proportions apply.

The first materialist rule in societal affairs is to ask of major events and trends in whose interest do they happen, *cui bono*? I believe there is an iron rule according to which those societal classes in whose interest these events did happen have in fact brought them about—in however direct or indirect, monocausal or overdetermined ways. In the Malthusian world of keeping poverty safe for the rulers, war has presented many advantages for them and for the State they rule, but at a minimum it has always had at least three systematic and consubstantial objectives. The first one is huge new profits, buttressing an always endangered economy; the second one, mass destruction of commodities, to match the mass production that cannot be disposed of in a pauperized world and to enforce development of new technologies able to kill more people and dispense with more people as workers. A few more words might be useful to discuss the third objective, keeping population—and especially the poor, humiliated, and marginalized, the threatening masses—down.

Summarizing immemorial ruling-class practice, Adam Smith had coolly observed that "The demand for men, like that for any other commodity, necessarily regulates the production of men" (80); and Marx supplied the decisive understanding why this demand leads within the capitalist mode of production to waves of (for capitalists) surplus population through periodical waves of higher salaries, which population is then in the next—our present—wave redundant (cf. *Kapital. MEW* 25: chap. 13 and 14, esp. 228-33, and *Theorien* 2: 569-72). War is a prime technology of population control, and—if we have forgotten the lessons of the World Wars—the last twenty years teach us that its role in modern class struggles should be accorded much more attention. For obviously, the present Post-Fordist social system does not *need* even approximately as many producers as Welfare State Fordism did. To the contrary: since the rise of living standards caused by Leninism and the Keynesian response to it has led to overproduction of people, they have to be overdestroyed (cf. the splendid book by George). Consumers are still needed, but the poorer ones—non-"Whites," most women, the very old and very young—don't count for much: "Nearly two-thirds of the world's population is basically written off as far as foreign investment is concerned" (Tabb 22)! One average North American citizen consumes thirteen times more energy than one Chinese and 1,300 times more than a Bangladeshi: in direct proportion, the US media count carefully their own body-bags but not the dead of its bombing and starving out.[16]

---

16. Cf. C.H. Gray 136-37. By contrast, the US army in Vietnam was obsessed with the "kill ratio" proportion between enemy and own killed (see Gibson 111-20, Caputo 160) but did not take into account the criterion of "cost tolerance" (the same one that bankrupted the USSR) by which the USA could not, as Ho Chi Minh predicted, tolerate even a 10:1 ratio of

All statistics we have are inadequate because the indirect effects of wars will kill people in Vietnam or Iraq (and in the USA) for generations to come. But even inadequate, the statistics are revealing: in Vietnam, ca. 60,000 US soldiers vs. over 3,000.000 Vietnamese killed; in the first Iraq War, a few dozen NATO soldiers vs. 1,200,000 to 1,500.000 Iraqi dead of bombing or the subsequent embargo. In the vein of Swift's *Modest Proposal*, I can propose that for the rulers of our globe, the corporate-military complex, major demographic bloodletting among the poor is most welcome (more than a touch of racism may be found here). At the very least, there is no reason to spend serious money on preventing wars (Angola, Rwanda, Bosnia, and further to come), epidemics, terminal drugging or endemic famines. About (organized!) starvation alone, cautious international sources speak of some forty million people dying from its immediate consequences each year, while "about 500 million are chronically malnourished," that is, on the way to dying soon, and a further 800+ million in "absolute poverty," that is, bordering on famine and dying a bit more slowly (Drèze-Sen 35, *Human...1996* 20, idem *1998*). War, with its attendant politico-ecological catastrophes, such as hundreds of thousands of refugees as well as delayed killings by toxic ingredients of the explosives used and by not yet exploded mines and bombs, much accelerates such "population control" (see Thompson, and cf. the satirically sharpened but serious arguments in *Report* 72-75).

The cannon fodder or mortified meat in wars, prostitution, and drugging, the mass casualties, are as a rule people who are marginal to "White" patriarchal capitalism: the poor, the "colored," women. "Lower" class, race as well as gender, are expendable, though spoken of with nauseatingly sentimental hypocrisy: and especially when these categories overlap in, say, Black volunteers for the US armed forces or prostitutes displaced into big cities (cf. A. Davis). "Colored, sexed, and

---

Vietnamese vs. US killed (in Rosen 168).

laboring persons" are denied epistemological visibility and thus political agency (Haraway 32, and cf. 26-30), they have traditionally not been Cartesian and Lockean "individuals" (who were, before the onset of counterrevolutionary hypocrisy in the 19th Century, forthrightly defined as those who have possessions). The blended out—the unemployed, the "criminal," and the female people—bear the full weight of the enforcement of super-profits, the degradation, and the legal persecution that were formerly focussed on the dangerously organized male White industrial workers and on intellectuals, who now advance to privileged bearers of social-democratic reformism (cf. Marcuse 134 and passim, Haug 190 and passim). However, it should be stressed that Post-Fordism and the US New World Order has also especially targeted the middle classes and "middle" nations that threatened to rise, such as Russia, Yugoslavia and Iraq. Indeed, it seems that the social basis of at least the al-Qaeda cadres are the middle classes of Egypt and Saudi Arabia (cf. Minolfi 19). Beyond outright killing in wars and enforced misery, all such colonial and semi-colonial vanquished swell the ranks of the super-exploited today in all our cities under mafioso debt slavery as they did in times of chattel slavery.[17] Both the social-democratic and the communist movements catastrophically undervalued the significance of this change in exploitation modalities toward a kind of sub-proletariat (though the Bolsheviks were, at their revolutionary beginning, the first to indicate it).

2. War as a Dominant in Necrophilic Capitalism

As I was elsewhere arguing that war, drugs and brainwashing were the present dispensation's Three Riders of the Apocalypse, I found out that war is the lead rider—the determining spring of

---

17. The NGO Anti-Slavery International estimates there are more than 27 million slaves in the world today (in Merlo), roughly twice the number of chattel slaves captured in Africa 1450-1900, which is estimated at between 11 and 17 million enslaved people (Suret-Canale 24-30).

life under capitalism. Before I get to some empirical data, it has to be stressed that deep forces are at work here. The heartbeat of capitalism is antagonistic competition regardless of human lives: for one small example, there were more dead and maimed per year in US car crashes than US casualties at the height of the Vietnam War. Any sane society, unwilling to sanction killing for the sake of profits to a few, would have prohibited highway traffic of the kind known in the USA; instead the US model has conquered the world. Considering both the emotional main-spring and the brute result in humans killed, the capitalist way of people cohabiting is Hobbes's "time of war, where every man is enemy of every man"; extrapolating from the English Civil War after 1640, he realized this was centrally a permanent civil war. Two centuries later, the best European codification noted that war is properly likened "to business competition," and even more to "State policy, which...may be looked upon as a kind of business competition on a great scale" (Clausewitz 1: 121). While "competition...does not establish [the laws of bourgeois economy]," it is its "essential locomotive force": "competition is generally the mode in which capital secures the victory of its mode of production" (Marx, *Grundrisse* 552 and 730). War is therefore more than a metaphor for bourgeois human relation-ships, it is perhaps their allegorical essence. This was always understood in the workers' and socialist movement: Jean Jaurès phrased it as "le capitalisme porte la guerre comme la nuée porte l'orage" (capitalism brings war as the cloud brings the tempest). Much before Lenin, who did something about it, the socialists' slogan was "war upon war" (cf. Angenot, *Antimilitarisme*).

Nonetheless, even when we limit ourselves only to warfare in the narrower sense defined above, that is, involving one or more entire States, continuous warfare has *never* ceased under capitalism. In that respect, at least, capitalist States did not centrally differ from preceding social formations in which the main government departments were, as Marx observed, "that of Finance, or plunder of one's own people; that of War, or plunder of other peoples" (Marx, "Die britische" 129; cf. Avineri 239).

There are strong claims that the economic basis for the triumph of capitalism was colonial warfare-plunder from the fifteenth to the eighteenth and nineteenth centuries (Headrick, Parker), prepared by Venice in the eastern Mediterranean as well as by the "internal colonies" of England's "Celtic fringe" and France's Languedoc. At the same time it provided the major impetus for mass production for a standardized "population," pioneered by the famous arsenals of Venice. Armies strongly influenced the process of industrialization with its "reserve armies" of workers, and as Marx noted, they were important for division of labour within one branch and had since Antiquity the first developed wage system (Marx-Engels 529-30). War financing—which constituted throughout the eighteenth century three-quarters of state budgets in Europe—resulted in the setting up of modern bureaucracy and central national banks (Anderson 31-33, Kaldor *New* 18).

A temporary lull in European wars ensued after 1871, when the metropolitan powers had divided the world and the British navy was policing this division; this was accompanied by mass colonial and semi-colonial murderings of more than sixty million peasants and tribals (Watts 125, and cf. M. Davis). But the warfare returned home from brutal domination of Asian, African, and Latin American labour to roost in the "North" at the latest from 1911—date of the first carving up of a precapitalist European empire, the Ottoman one, and the first major world revolution, the Mexican one—in a permanent chain of war carnages, which show no signs of abating. The Oslo Peace Research Institute (PRIO) counted sixty-six wars in the year 1992 and a German peace research consortium thirty-four in 1999. Definitions of war differ, but around 160 wars seem to have raged between 1945 and 1993, of which about three quarters were civil wars, and in them more people were killed than in World War II; the frantic search of the US corporate-military class for enemies that might justify further hundreds of billions out of the pockets of taxpayers shows the USA-USSR competition was only a welcome excuse for "a permanent war economy" (phrase by Wilson, chairman of General Electric in 1944—in Lens 14). Summing up, we are already within the most terrible (almost) Hundred Years' War in human history. Is this an accident? No. Just as capitalism came about in plunder wars, there is no evidence it could climb out of economic depressions without huge military spending, a "war mega-dividend" (best examples: the 1930s and the 1990s—cf. Amin 48). I shall return to this in Section 3.

The strictly political fall-out of militarization, which is not the focus of this article, is the spread of military rule that subordinates all other aspects of civil society to its barbarity not only during wars but in times of official "peace" (cf. Pannekoek 183-85). Before colonial liberation movements, dictatorships enforced by bayonet and gun muzzle were the rule in all imperial possessions; in the twentieth century they are more common in nominally independent States than at any time since the rise of the bourgeoisie, marking well its degeneration. This is technically facilitated by the enormous elaboration of armaments, accessible only to large economic systems, and it is underpinned by the spread of both organizational complexity (cf. Andreski 69-72, 87-88 and passim) and of the brainwashing industries such as cinema and TV. It should never be forgotten that the armies' sabers, bullets, and bombardments—first by the feudal landowners' armies and then by those of the centralized State— were always the upper class's final answer to any uprisings for justice from below. All these factors were behind Foucault's question: "[I]sn't power simply a form of warlike domination...a sort of generalized war which assumes at particular moments the forms of peace and State?" (123) I am uneasy at politico-economically unanchored generalizations such as "power." But they may be useful if historicized into actual mediations, focussed not on the question why the ruling classes need and wage war, but rather on how come that they're as a rule able to find plenty of lower class cannon-fodder. Bourgeois power under capitalism is thus in feedback with and exercised through strong institutionalizations and ideologies disciplining huge masses: beside outright military dictatorships whenever necessary, I can only refer here to technoscience and identity politics (chauvinisms and ethnic exclusivisms). One could call these the two faces of bribing the middle and lower classes: by finance and by ideology.

Technoscience: "[B]y and large, technoscience is part of a war machine and should be studied as such," concluded Latour, looking at data which in 1986 showed that ca. 80% of the US federal budget for research and development was devoted to "defense" (171 and 172); half of all US scientists and engineers work today for military priorities (C.H. Gray 231, cf. Tirman ed.). At the very least, "value-free" technoscience is the central means for—and thus intimately shaped by use for—war, literal and metaphorical: mass production in capitalism needs mass destruction for the cycle to go on (cf. C.H. Gray; also Toffler 42, 64ff., Virilio 11-12, Virilio & Lotringer 20). As soon as "classical" primitive accumulation of capital—pushing down the cost of labour, dispossessing the peasants—is no longer possible, capitalism is threatened by "global crises and led, inexorably, to the kinds of primitive accumulation and devaluation [that is, physical destruction of both capital and labour] jointly wrought through...wars" (Harvey 443). Furthermore, the effect of wars is not spread evenly over the globalized globe; on the contrary, the destruction is unevenly distributed to benefit the victors, as a rule the strongest capitalist countries. But this unnatural state of affairs generates so much misery that drugs and brainwashing have to be resorted to, in the finally vain endeavour to find a breathing space, to shut out Death. Fidel Castro in his speech at the "Summit of the South" (G-77, Havana, April 2000) summarized the only partially available, undervalued data from *Human...1998* as: "800 billion dollars are spent yearly for arms and armies...; at least 400 billion for drugs [not including alcohol and tobacco], and a further 100 billion for commercial propaganda which obfuscates reason just like drugs."

Identity politics: Among the most efficient brainwashings that have developed since the collapse of credibility of socialism and rampant immiseration is mega-group exclusivism, usually named after its psychological motivation "identity politics." Any means of helping downtrodden and impoverished groups, such as most women or racially oppressed people, to fight for justice are welcome, and identity-based awareness may become such a means for a while. But its perversion into resentful exclusivisms "triggers violence [and] diminishes solidarity with the victims of that violence" (George 93; cf. Angenot, *Idéologies*). The perversion may be pinpointed as coming about when justice is demanded only for one's own group, regardless of whether this might lead to injustice or even crass humiliation and exploitation, up to genocide, of those defined as enemy Others. It is unavoidable that the hundreds of millions of unemployed people rejected to the margins of society, with third-rate or no social services in Post-Fordism, should fall prey to "isolation, shame, depression and violence" ("Éditorial" 19). But it is not fatally unavoidable that this should lead to hatred of other, usually equally downtrodden "identities," ethnic cleansings, and civil war; however, this worst case is a clear possibility. It is practically always keyed to a sudden rise of misery and disorientation. A PRIO study of 98 wars in 1990-96 concludes that "a particularly strong correlation exists between high external debt and the incidence of civil war"—especially "crucial" are the IMF conditions imposed on the country!—and between "falling export income from primary commodities [and] the *outbreak* of the civil war" (cited verbatim in George 95, PRIO's emphasis; cf. Smith). The three civil wars in ex-Yugoslavia—in Croatia, Bosnia and Kosovo—are a prime example that "the economy, stupid!" is an absolutely necessary, though not sufficient, cause for such wars (cf. at least Woodward). The increasingly direct entry of major European nations and then the USA into such wars fits well into their swap of internal welfare (for all people) for external warfare (profiting only capitalists and to a minor degree employees of armament industries), as the capitalist ruling classes seek by all possible means to stabilize military expenditures and profits at the Cold War level.

3. Weapons Commodities as Extra-Profit and System Pillar

In the "metropolitan" sites of mature capitalism (the countries of the Trilateral: North America, Western Europe, Japan and a few other places), the appropriation of surplus value is carried on "democratically" through economic instruments, that is, primarily by means of brainwashing, with the police visible but the army only called out in emergencies. In very rarefied liberal societal theory, abstracting from the existence of States and of all other factors of uneven development, as well as from the internal inexorable limits to capital (cf. Harvey), this might be taken to mean that war could be dispensed with. As usually presented by bourgeois common sense, military coercion was the rule for pre-capitalist societies but seems to be a thing apart from capitalist economic production. And it has in fact today, from the global point of view, shifted either into (so to speak) non-metropolitan local politics inside one State or between two States, or into threatening but not fully ripened intercontinental rivalries: the US does not today need war to dominate in North America, nor does Germany need it in Europe. However, armament production is, as Kaldor noted ("Warfare" 262), not only an object of consumption—finally but not always immediately needing wars—but also an object of production bringing profits. I'd add that its enormous size and central position—the world war industry was calculated as 10% of the world GNP in the 1960s; it is surely more than that today, and disproportionately more in major powers such as the USA—bring also system stability.

True, the money value of the huge international armament trade—oscillating between twenty and over thirty billion US$ yearly in the last thirty years according to the SIPRI yearbooks—dropped abruptly after the collapse of the USSR because the burgeoning conflicts did not as a rule need superbombers and heavy tanks but infantry gear and helicopters, which could also increasingly be local products or bought cheap either at the huge stockpiles in the black market belt between Cambodia and Russia or direct from the major pestiferous trader of retail arms, the hundreds of legal US producers. And armament outlays have not only been again steadily climbing from the mid-'90s on, with a noticeable spurt in the USA as of 1998, so that its military budget was at the end of the 90s again 95% of the Cold War one: armament production has remained at the heart of this epoch's financial capitalism. Furthermore, in the '90s the trend toward global business alliances has reached the arms commodity, which is also increasingly incorporating advanced non-military technoscience, such as electronics (Keller x). I can best indicate it by a summary from McMurtry:

The capital-intensive market systematically favours armaments commodities for production because of:

(1) their uniquely high value-added price...(for example $26 billion for the first five years of the US "Star Wars" programme...);
(2) their specially rapid rate of obsolescence and turnover...;
(3) the monopoly or semi-monopoly position of armaments manufacturers which flows from: (a) the designation of military production...as state secrets; (b) the high capital costs of armaments technology and manufacture; and (c) the privileged linkages of established military producers with government defense and procurement agencies;
(4) the large-scale and secure capital financing of military research, production, and cost additions...ensured by...public taxation, [and]...available to no other system of commodity production. (*Cancer* 170)

No moralistic wailings about the madness of this almost unimaginably enormous institution, correct as they may be, will matter a whit unless we zero in relentlessly on this fact: from the inception of the modern State and market, wars have always been "the greatest and the most profitable of investments" (Lefebvre,

Production 275). By the time of the First Gulf War, a conservative estimate of spending for military purposes was nearly a trillion (one million millions) US$ annually (the Tofflers 14), or between two and two and one-half billion dollars daily. Of this, the armament-commodity production accounted for ca. 200 billion US$ annually, or for about one fifth (SIPRI 1999: 9), of which half was located in the USA. Its imperial outlay dwarfs its British predecessor: the US spends on armaments as much as the next twelve strongest States combined, whereas the Royal Navy only wanted to be greater than the next two combined. For one huge example: of the eighteen US nuclear submarines, "each one carrying the equivalent in injuring power to 4,000 Hiroshima bombs [...or enough] to destroy the peoples of an entire continent,...eight have been made...since the opening of the Berlin Wall" (Scarry 28). The USA also accounts for more than half of the world armament exports (Keller 12). A huge part of these trillions goes to the superprofits of "Northern" corporations, and a smaller but appreciable part for the maintenance of practically all the ruling mafias and classes of the world. Last but not least, "[t]he new wars could be viewed as a form of military waste-disposal—a way of using up unwanted surplus arms generated by the Cold War, the biggest military build-up in history" (Kaldor, *New* 96). Disposal of surplus commodities that simultaneously disposes of surplus people: what a neat trick!

In particular, as is well known to all specialists though obscured by media blather, the military-industrial establishments of corporate capitalism, led by the US one, which produce "life-killing commodities" as the most profitable part of global trade (cf. McMurtry, *Understanding*), are the strongest factor of organized international violence. However, only a few critics have begun to show that these establishments are simultaneously (marvellous synergy!) possibly the strongest factor enforcing a world cultural revolution for the total colonization of human life-worlds and eco-systems by commodity economy. This was pointed out by Rosa Luxemburg even before the huge acceleration organized through World Wars (see her chapters 27-30) and other globalizations. She concluded that capital cannot accumulate without the productive forces and the consumption markets of more primitive societies (her examples are India, Algeria, and China), whose economies it eventually turns inside out: "Violence [*Gewalt*] is the only solution open to capital: the accumulation of capital employs violence as a permanent weapon, not only at its genesis, but further on down to the present day" (371). This was invariably accompanied by militarism, and by the eradication of rural industries in favour of a sharp rural-urban divide usually called industrialization (her example here is the dispossession of farmers in post-Civil-War USA).

Of course, Marx had already made of "State power, the organized and concentrated violence (*Gewalt*) of society" a lynchpin of his theory of primitive accumulation, which was however still strongly endogenous to his example of England (but also of Scotland and Ireland). Yet the "genesis of the industrial capitalist" proceeed for him too largely from colonial conquest: "The treasures captured outside Europe by straightforward looting, enslavement, and murder (*Raubmord*) flowed back to the mother-country and were turned into capital there" (*Kapital. MEW* 23: 779, 777, and 781). Luxemburg could extrapolate that to a thesis that "Accumulation is...primarily a relationship between capital and a non-capitalist environment" (417), which is in the imperialist phase characterized by: "foreign loans, railroad constructions, revolutions, and wars" (419 & ff.). Militarism is "the executor of [such an] accumulation of capital" (439) under State compulsion. Along with the "normal" metropolitan commodity market, the accumulation of capital needs "colonial policy, an international loan system...and war. Violence, fraud, oppression, looting are openly displayed [here].... In reality, political power is nothing but the vehicle for the economic process. The conditions for the reproduction of capital provide the organic link between these two aspects of the accumulation of capital." (452) Replace direct colonization with nominally independent native elites, and you have the present system.

Thus, what does it matter that the production of armament commodities contributes little to improving any economy's productivity, since the output is used neither for the growth of means of production nor for consumption? What does it matter that, if the US economy sanely spent as much to make the buildings in that country airtight as was spent by the US military in one year of the mid-80s (before the Gulf Oil war) on the forces meant to ensure the West Asian oilfields, no imports of oil from that region would be necessary (the Lovinses 27)? What does it matter that the recurring pork-barrelling and misinformation about the cost of new weapons systems lead in 90% of cases to doubling—or multiplying up to seven times—the original cost estimate (Weisberg 81),which is surely not a rational or economic way of organizing production? And finally, what does it matter that the cost of one war casualty has risen from 29,000 DMark in WW1 to 34,500 in WW2 and to 338,000 in the Korean War (Heinig 25)? For, from a profit point of view, all of these aspects in the development, trade, and use of armament commodities are supremely rational. The tens of millions of dead in World Wars brought about tens of trillions of profitable investments in the huge new opportunities of reconstructing the destroyed homes and industries—a million dollars or more per dead body. And today, from the point of view of the US military-technoscientific bloc—and of analogous, though not quite so central, blocs in a few other major powers (Germany, France, the UK...)—armament maintains the national military-industrial base; for the ruling establishments, dominated by big corporations, its use abroad is equally rational. So are all of the death-bringing improvements from chemistry, atomic physics or electronics; so is selling not only the commodities but increasingly also their means of production, the underlying technologies of mega-destruction, to anybody with ready cash. "A century devoted to the rationality of technique was also a century so irrational as to open in every mind the real possibility of global destruction" (Norman Mailer, *Of a Fire on the Moon*).

What is irrational is the final cause of all these increasingly destructive flows: the profit principle itself. No capitalism without increasingly destructive weapons and wars: and today wars destroy the world. "It is estimated that the single greatest source of environmental destruction in the US is the military-industrial complex, and that one-quarter of the public monies which are expended on weapons commodities across the world would eradicate poverty, homelessness, and illiteracy, as well as pay for the cleanup of all our major environmental pollution at the same time" (McMurtry, *Cancer* 174). This is most apparent in nuclear weaponry and the civilian uses that developed out of it, including not only Chernobyl and Three Mile Island but the regular US government dumping of nuclear waste into the oceans (cf. Weisberg 83). However, ABC—atomic, bacteriological and chemical—weaponry is now being joined by further super-technoscience with incalculable effects. Just one example of a new generation of US weaponry is HAARP (High-Frequency Active Aural Research Program) for "weather warfare."[18] It uses most powerful radiowave beams that heat and then sweep away areas of ionosphere, allowing huge amounts of energy to bounce back to Earth in order (as a US air force scenario put it) to "own the weather" either by pinpointed local modifications of weather patterns (say in a "rogue nation") or by global weather disruption. This would not only disrupt communications but it could be combined with a spacelab to deliver amounts of energy comparable to a nuclear bomb anywhere on Earth, via laser and particle beams. Beside climate manipulation, the returning waves could also affect human brains, and earthquake effects are being envisaged. The dirty megaweapons of today—such as the US uranium-encased bombs and shells in Irak as well as in ex-Yugoslavia and the Adriatic Sea, cf. Chossudovsky "Low"—and even more of tomorrow threaten the survival of a "sustain-

_____

18. All information in the rest of this paragraph is taken from Chossudovsky "It's," who gives nine further printed and Web sources; the US Air Force quote is from its Air University AF 2025 Final Report, www.au.af.mil/au/2025/.

able" vertebrate biosphere (cockroaches may survive). Clearly, there can be no sane ecology or even survival without going against the profit principle and unlimited growth: beginning with wars, armament industries and technoscientific military research.

A crucial factor in the unprecedented post-1940 rise of production was the "permanent military reflation" through World War II, the Korean War, and the Cold War up to today (Went 76). The military cluster of industries, with a locked-in permanent market and assured high profits, seems to be the key sector of the US economy, propping up the national and then the world economic structure. The decisive question may well be whether capitalism could economically and indeed psychically survive without warfare and mega-armaments. Baran and Sweezy made a strong argument that it could not have done so in the 1930s-40s, and the evidence of the first small reduction in new procurements after the fall of the USSR, which resulted in a deep depression in a dozen or more major US states, speaks as strongly in favour of this black argument today. As Benjamin had intuited, capitalism is a permanent "martial law": the bourgeois welfare State (welfare first for the upper class, and then, reacting to the threat of Leninism, for the middle and parts of the working classes) is also a warfare State. Threats "against the 'national interest' are usually created or accelerated to meet the changing needs of the war system" (*Report* 30). In that respect, even the fully degenerate "State socialism" of the USSR was better: it did not need war, it was bankrupted by the armaments race forced on it. True, US armament-commodity procurements jumpstarted startling new technologies—aerospace, semiconductors, medical technology, etc.—out of the trillions given by taxpayers (US$1.5 trillion 1950-75), at the time that 40% worldwide of both research and its financing were devoted to military R&D. But by the same token the high-tech commodities for killing took 40% of world research and material resources *away* from more economical, certainly less destructive, purposes (Tirman ed. 11-16, 46, 148, 216-21 & passim, Brenner 56n).

Finally, the deflection of so much financial and brain-power, so much human labour, into profitable commodities for killing makes a sham of democratic control and decision-making. As Wallerstein has repeatedly argued, ideological and economic liberalism is incompatible with democracy. The war economy palpably marks the divorce between capitalism and civic responsibility for other people and for the planet. But the stakes are even higher: if "the enduring, primary symbiosis between capitalism and war" (Kolko 474) means that wars are indeed necessary for the survival of this social formation, then the capitalist social formation is truly, as McMurtry says, a cancer in the body politic, and the only way we and this planet can survive is to get rid of it once and for all. Pannekoek remarked in his remarkable chapter on war already in 1947:

> When we say that war is inseparable from capitalism, that war can only disappear with capitalism itself, this does not mean that war against war is of no use.... It means that the fight against war is inseparable from fight against capitalism.[19]

4. Wars of Reterritorialization

<u>4.1.</u> As mentioned at the beginning, the totalization of war in the twentieth century leads to "whole populations com[ing] to be more and more regarded as legitimate objects of annihilation" (J.G. Gray 132). This can only be done if wars are waged

---

19. Pannekoek 193; similar arguments may be found in Magdoff and Amin. A revealing if tragicomic instance is the suppression of the 1962 Humphrey subcommittee report on disarmament for fear it might "back up the Marxian theory that war production was the reason for the success of capitalism" (Lewin xiii). *Report from Iron Mountain...*, the book Lewin introduced (and wrote?) is, beneath its guise of a satirical hoax, a most prescient text which ought to be speedily reprinted. To the contrary, Melman has in several books (cf. *Permanent*) argued that this "nonproductive" economic orientation not only leads to industrial degradation but could be offset by saner forms of capitalism, an argument which today seems irrelevant.

in the spirit of quasi-theological hatred, "the enemy" being an incarnation of total evil. An early culmination of such an *odium theologicum* was the insane US and NATO doctrine of nuclear warfare. However, this "emotion-drenched...abstract hatred," compounded of repugnance and fear (ibid. 132-34), has in our post-Cold-War and Post-Fordist age given rise to a dual military world. This is concatenated with the dual economic world, where 90% of world investment and trade are already contained within the "North," meaning North America, western Europe, Oceania, Japan, and the Asian "Little Tigers."

The *genus* war had up to the twentieth century (not counting fights between tribal groups) a few recognized species: a/ war between States or quasi-State entities; b/ civil war within a State; c/ partisan warfare in an occupied State. All of them were defined, among other matters, by a circumscribed territory of warfare, be this Caesar's Gallia, a frontline, or the quarter-worlds of the two World War II "theatres of war" (European and Pacific). This territorial limitation begins to waver and fade with the advent, first, of military air power, and second, of instant global communication, primarily on TV, which brings a "war for hearts and minds" to the nations and the people involved. Leaving "war on terrorism" for a separate discussion, now we have to face two new species: the exogenous war exported by the North, usually the USA, into the "global slums" of the poorer South, and pursued by high-altitude bombing plus internal subversion (which I cannot examine here); and the supposedly—but in reality only partly—endogenous species of "armed turmoil" in the South.

There have been some early warnings about a shift of warfare modes away from the war pitting one State-government-army against another—anyway a recent invention datable to 1648, to what Arrighi would call Europe's "unique fusion of State & capitalism" (1)—notably in van Creveld's astringent and stimulating book programmatically called *The Transformation of War* (other cognate considerations, for example by Gantzel, Gibbs, Chris Hables Gray, Schreiber, and Woodward shall not be explicitly discussed here). Though he says very little about the crucial nexus of economics with wars, he noted that in the age of telecommunications and modern means of transport, controlled by ca. twenty-five states, such Clausewitzian war is becoming outdated. Thus for van Creveld "battles will be replaced by skirmishes, bombing, and massacres" (207). Such a sporadic small scale war leads to regular forces easily degenerating into police or mere armed gangs, while on a global scale it develops a "security business."

The most detailed hypothesis about this latter species, the one manifested primarily or "purely" in African or Yugoslav civil wars, is Kaldor's *New and Old Wars* (further as K with page number; cf. also her "Warfare and Capitalism") which I shall proceed to critically interpret for my purposes. Her approach is rather phenomenological, so that it to my mind suffers from one major failing and one perhaps minor one. The major gap in the diagnosis is a minimization of the external pressures, support, and indeed enablement making for both the outbreak and the continuation of these wars. This is the more regrettable as it is well known in the literature on separatism that "international factors are clearly decisive. Whereas the emergence of separatist movements is determined largely by internal factors, their success is contingent on obtaining a level of external support that is in fact seldom available." (Zolberg et al. 243) In particular for the conflict in Bosnia-Herzegovina, on which much of Kaldor's investigation is concentrated, it is well known that German ruling interests (alongside US Rightwing groups and probably the Vatican) favoured and financed the Croat side, that the much weaker Russian ones backed the Serb side, while the Clinton administration after 1992 supported the Bosnian "Muslim" side, favouring its arming by Iran and Saudi Arabia and the arrival of thousands of Islamist Mujahideen fighters (cf., from among a huge welter of titles, Conert 5-13, Gibbs, Halberstam, Hofbauer, International, Wiebes, and Woodward). There is probably little or no purely endogenous "armed turmoil."

Kaldor's other limitation is signalled by her empiricistic

and inelegant name of "new war/s," a term limiting our understanding. I propose they should be provisionally called "reterritorializing wars," that is: wars conducted to control a limited territory and its goods by an elite claiming to act in the name of an ethnic group (however invented).

Nonetheless, while Kaldor's prescriptions therefore remain insufficient, her description is indispensable.

4.2. The ostensible goal of the new wars is not universal ideologies, such as the no longer fashionable socialist or "national liberation" ones, but "identity politics": ethnic or tribal exclusivism "for the purpose of claiming State power" (K 76) in a new State or for making a new group dominant in an old State. The identities are usually "invented traditions" no older than the nineteenth- or twentieth-century arrival of market economies into those colonial territories and the need of the incipient local bourgeoisie to control its own market. They are culturally constructed communities claiming a "blood" basis which is threatened by impure admixtures. Their fiercely mini-collectivist ideologies have a sweeping disregard for personal rights, often directly inherited from their Fascist or Stalinist roots and re-actualized by their oligopolistic corporate backers. Behind the chauvinisms, however, other interests hide. First, "a politics fostered from above" (K 78) by an ethnic elite that covets State power and enrichment, and enlists for that purpose a small part of its poorer co-ethnics promising them immediate plunder of neighbours, careers and glory. Second, interests of multinational companies over valuable resources (oil, ores) in the disputed territory. Third (overlapping with second), interests of major military powers over its strategic position in relation to other territories.

The necessary precondition for any such "identity" crystallization is a major economic crisis in a world where structural impoverishment of the South is imposed by the global capitalist order: the ratio of real income per head between the richest and the poorest countries was 3:1 in 1800, 10:1 in 1900, and is 60:1 in

2000 (cf. Dummett). This crisis may be partly due to and exac-erbated by internal difficulties or errors by the original State's ruling classes but it is always ignited by corporate interests: Shell in Ogoniland-Nigeria, but usually the World Bank and IMF (cf. for Yugoslavia Chossudovsky 243-63, International, and Woodward). It results in staggeringly massive unemploy-ment and immiseration plus a grab for privatized possessions starting at the power top and spreading downwards. Legal norms are necessarily forsaken in such straits, and livelihood comes to depend on Kaldor's "parallel economy"—"networks of corrup-tion, black marketeers, arms and drug traffickers, etc." (K 83), often linked to previous financial support by the CIA through the diaspora and to international illegal circuits of drug smug-gling (for example the "Kosovar Liberation Army") and arms smuggling. Such a total existential crisis sometimes re-actual-izes but often reinvents factional, "ethnic" or pseudo-religious, conflicts. It fosters ruthless warlord or gang hegemony making for spiralling "violence markets" (cf. Elwert), inculcating fear and hatred of the Other, and leading to redistribution of riches without new production—a primitive accumulation for the new separatist ruling class, usually in a vassal function to foreign powers (the US or NATO, France and Belgium in Africa, some Islamic-expansion States).

Kaldor's account of what happens once the war starts is magisterial. It is "heavily dependent on local predation and external support. Battles are rare, most violence is directed against civilians, and cooperation between warring factions is common" (K 90). The warring units "finance themselves through plunder and the black market or through external assistance". The latter can be remittances from the diaspora, illegal trade in arms, drugs or valuable commodities such as oil or diamonds, and—crucially—financing from outside the war territory: either covertly by a major power and/or a neighbour or through "taxation" of humanitarian and other international assistance. "All of these sources can only be sustained through continued violence so that a war logic is built into the functioning of the economy" (K 9 and 102). I don't know whether the following excerpt would apply to all such wars, but (regardless of some shaky terminology) it is dead on for the Yugoslav civil wars:

> Because the various warring parties share the aim of sowing "fear and hatred," they operate in a way that is mutually reinforcing, helping each other to create a climate of insecurity and suspicion.... Often, among the first civilians to be targeted are those who...try to maintain inclusive social relations and some sense of public morality. Thus...[the new wars] can be understood as wars between exclusivism and cosmopolitanism. (K 9)

The main lever of control is neither front-line occupation of more territory nor the battle for the people's hearts and minds as in revolutionary guerrilla warfare; rather, it is "population displacement." This new warfare adapts US counterinsurgency techniques from Mozambique, Nicaragua, and Afghanistan: "poisoning the sea" in which Mao's guerrilla swims like a fish. This considerably raises the level of inhumanity:

> Instead of creating a favourable environment for the guerrilla, the new warfare aims to create an unfavourable environment for all those people it cannot control. Control...depends on continuing fear and insecurity and on the perpetuation of hatred of the other. Hence the importance of extreme and conspicuous atrocity and of involving as many people as possible in these crimes so as to establish a shared complicity...and to deepen divisions. (K 98-99)

Kaldor discusses at length the techniques of population displacement: by systematic murders of people categorized as the guilty Other; by ethnic cleansing in the narrower sense, that is, forcible population expulsion (see on this concept and its history Rosière); and by rendering an area uninhabitable through land mines, shelling civilians, or enforced famines, powerfully aided "by instilling unbearable memories of what was once home, by desecrating whatever has social meaning," for example by destruction of religious and other historical monuments (say the famous medieval bridge in Mostar) or by systematic rape and sexual abuse (K 99-100).

Such reterritorializing wars are thus characterized by the breakdown of the "distinctions between the political and the economic, the public and the private, the military and the civil" (K 106): they are exemplary Post-Modernist cultural constructions, and should possibly be called neo-Fascist.

4.3. Lest the richer and apparently pacified West grow too smug about its presumed civility, I take Kaldor's warning about budding analogous conflicts in those climes, which only await an economic crisis to erupt, as very significant:

> The characteristics of the new wars I have described are to be found in North America and Western Europe as well. The right-wing militia groups in the US are not so very different from the paramilitary groups in Eastern Europe or Africa...[nor] is the salience of identity politics.... The violence in the inner cities of Western Europe and North America can, in some senses, be described as new wars. (K 11)

In fact, "The new war economy could be represented as a continuum, starting with the combination of criminality and racism to be found in the inner cities of Europe and North America and reaching its most acute manifestation in the [war violence] areas" (K 110).

The inner logic of these new wars is that they are the inescapable anti-successor to the vanished Welfare State (a brutal do-it-yourself welfare for small comprador elites) and the inescapable obverse of capitalist economico-political globalization of plunder. As to the former, the first major German post-1945 venture into military affairs in ex-Yugoslavia coincided with the major dismantling of internal social welfare (Rousseau knew it all!). As to the latter, in the new dispensation, after god and socialism are dead, everything is permitted. Takeovers, dispossession, marginalization, reserve armies: What is good for General Motors is good for the Rwanda warlord.

Finally, it should be noted that these wars unfold within the overwhelming context of capitalist deterritorialization of production and consumption (not of control, still firmly in metropolitan hands). They are a reaction to it by the local ruling classes, employing the most retrograde rhetoric of once perhaps progressive bourgeois nationalism, together with outside financial support for heavy armaments, to enlist a sometimes small fraction of a territory's lower classes to slaughter or in other ways "cleanse" other groups (in the main also lower classes). Although in Bosnia all three warring groups managed together to enlist only ca. six percent of the population to follow them, this was enough to chain the whole thus constructed ethnic group ineluctably to "their" ethnic upper classes' interest and destiny.[20] In class terms, this is <u>a war of the ruling class plus the criminal or *Lumpen* class against the middle and the working classes</u>.

---

20. A semantico-ideological note: It might be of great ideological and semiotic interest to compare this practice to the unqualified praise of "deterritorialized flows" in the *magnum opus* of probably the best theoreticians of Post-Modernism, Deleuze and Guattari, in *A Thousand Plateaus*. For all my admiration of some of their insights, this would, in my opinion, testify to the aporias of irresponsible anarchism. My use is returned to earth from such theoretical stratospheres, and follows the magisterial elucidations by Angenot (*1889*, 337-52). He stresses rightly the simultaneous or perhaps consubstantial loss of relation to a material territory and to all of its analogous symbolic or semiotic spaces—loss of purity, tradition, identity, virility, and so on and on. Alerting us to such feedbacks could be the proper use of Deleuze and Guattari.

The terms themselves of de- and re-territorialization, however tongue-twisting, cannot, I think, be dispensed with.

5. Against War: How?

In sum, capitalist civilization reposes on the insoluble contradiction between a boundless increase of productive forces and boundless economic and psychic immiseration of people, because the productive forces of labour, including technoscience, are used for exploitation of a huge powerless majority of toilers and for colossal profit and power for a tiny capitalist minority. The product that subsumes and overshadows all other multifarious products of this civilization is the production of destructive novelties, "undermining of the springs of all wealth: the earth and the worker," as Marx already told us (*Kapital. MEW* 23: 530). Capital practices "systematic robbery of the preconditions for life..., of space, air, light...," said he (ibidem 449-50), and today we could add water, silence, health in general, etc.—in fact, life liberty and the pursuit of happiness. Post-Fordist condemnation of two thirds of the adult population globally (and one third in the "rich" countries) to unemployment or piecework is a further robbery of vitality during people's youth, to be paid for in their middle and late years by defencelessness against disease and early dying. The marvellous capitalist technoscientific progress has led to one nuclear submarine carrying the destructive power of all explosives used in World War II (Virilio 161); as mentioned in Section 3, this is enough to destroy the peoples of an entire continent, and yet eight new US nuclear submarines have been made since the fall of the USSR.

Thus behind the apocalyptic Three Riders, as always, the fourth and main one advances, <u>Death</u> as this civilization's final horizon. As Benjamin exemplarily argued on the traces of Baudelaire and Balzac, the structural logic of gambling, excitement, novelty—of the commodity customer's experience and time horizon—demands that its final end be Death (for example *GS* I.2: 668). Death is the end-horizon of raping the planet by economic exploitation and ecocide, of which war is not only an illusory economic and psychological solution but also an allegorical essence. This is not the easeful death each of us has a right to: it threatens the collective death of humanity.

Whence such myopic folly, differing from any past dying empire only in its speed-of-light propagation? Probably it is intrinsic to the class thirst for power or mastery which breeds also the everlasting fear of falling behind, the ever stronger post-Welfare-State dread of not having security. When Freud speculated amid World War 1 that "the impulse of cruelty arises from the instinct of mastery" (59), we might wish to reject obfuscating terms such as instinct yet see that he put his finger on a centrally sore point. (He also rightly saw as the counterpole an "instinct for knowledge or research"—60.) This age-old impulse has never been so powerful, unnecessary, and necrophilic as in capitalism, driven by the unending "fix" of profits: most especially, in the perfectly sinful Post-Fordist age of wars, prostitution, and drugging (literal and metaphoric). It testifies to the terrible blindness of all hegemonic social theories that they have failed to factor in such lessons of war as a dominant of capitalism (cf. Kolko 464-82).

When I concluded in Section 3 that there can be no survival for humanity without strongly muzzling the profit principle and unlimited technological and financial growth, this also meant that at the latest since the mass bombings of civilians from the Nazis to the British and US airforce in World War II and since the advent of nuclear bombs, Clausewitz's famous dictum that war is the continuation of political traffic by other means must be superseded. Politics which daily use mass violence against people and have become an alternate way of economic gain and living must be stopped by self-defence for survival. Wars, armament industries, and technoscientific military research are the clearest case of such totally destructive activity.

What are we, who should still call ourselves the Left, and whose conscious core should perhaps think again about assuming communism as its poetry and prose, then to do? Vaguely and negatively put: strive to understand, and then look for articulated and organized ways to minimize and counteract the ruling-class blight of war, old and new. As a Left-wing Christian has reminded us, our horizon should be a politics that <u>consecrates</u> life (Virilio, in idem and Lotringer 144). I can supply one basic pragmatic pointer: since all major blights such as war, brainwashing, and prostitution are now semiotically and materially interwoven, the only possible response to any of them is one that does not hinder a response to any other. Counteracting war can only be done by also counteracting the IMF impositions, drugging, the procurement and spreading of arms commodities, identity politics, etc. Beside the need of achieving oppositional critical mass, in the form of Gramsci's "historical bloc" (which would itself be enough), this is what makes it necessary to shun sectarian politics like the plague, even by such potentially large groups as super-exploited women. Separatisms—the defunct *ouvrierisme* (reliance on industrial workers only, today noticeably diminished by the shift away from mass factories, for example in automation) and rural "Maoism"; macho, feminist, and generational separatism; etc.—are the worst internal enemy of radical politics. Rainbow politics could be a good name if it is understood that while the colours are separate, so that organizing around issues limited to a given "identity" may be locally useful as a first step, the rainbow is one.

Finally (the snake bites its tail): the political equivalent of this whole endeavour of mine is the fact that a segment of the "professional-managerial" class is today—as Ernst Bloch argued in 1938 for the intelligentsia in the industrialized states (343)—the one indispensable ally in any historical bloc, say with the working classes and women, which would have a chance to get off the ground. An ally is NOT a servant: it is somebody with whom one can disagree but has strategic interests in common, a community of destiny against the terrorism of capital (cf. Lefebvre, *Cybernanthrope* 56-57), which may supply criteria for resolving the disagreement. And the criteria have to be built up with contributions by each. We "professionals" are professionally trained to formulate such criteria—if we can shake off capitalist corruption and listen to political experiences from practice. For, "any erroneous understanding of truth is simultaneously an erroneous understanding of freedom" (Marcuse 147).

P.S. April 2002:

It is mandatory to update our thinking after the murderous attack on civilians of Sept. 2001 in the New York City Twin Towers, and the even more murderous attack on civilians ensuing by the US bombing of Afghanistan (best sources speak of ca. 4,000 civilians killed as of March 2002, and the count is rising), and other attacks to follow whenever and wherever the US administration so pleases. I can here only address two questions, perhaps two sides of the same question: a) Would the essay as it now reads have to be changed in some central formulations? b) What should be added to its formulations?

As to a), having lived with these formulations and their framework now for almost four years, I would hope such initial approach could be supplemented in many ways, to my mind primarily by clarifying what are the US class fractions at work in the present militarization and killings. We need a new Marx to write *The 11th September of George W. Bush.* I hope one can be found. As to b), the best supplement to this essay would be to analyze the present discourse on "terrorism" and of course actions justified by such discourse. This effort, to which I am devoting other essays,[21] could help us to decide whether the present armed struggle is a war or not, and if not then what. Here are a few preliminary though for me central points:

I believe terrorism is most usefully defined as a strategy which consists in pursuing political power by striking dread into the <u>civilian population</u> through exemplary <u>killings</u> among them. We need to focus fiercely on the two elements underlined.

---

21. See now the two Suvin items on terrorism in the Bibliography below.

If they are correct, then there is both <u>State terrorism</u> and <u>group terrorism</u> (by religious or political groups). Politically, and even corporeally or phenomenologically, there are two main ways of carrying out terror/ism or being terrorists: terror-bombing, and all other terror killings. States—such as all colonial powers in the past, and Iraq, the USA and its NATO allies or Israel in the present—can use terror-bombings (and shelling by heavy artillery), including chemical warfare; the others don't have such means—yet. That's why the Sept. 11 terrorists had to improvise flying mega-bombs by re-categorizing passenger airplanes as such.

If war is a strategy which consists in pursuing political power by "a coherent sequence of conflicts, involving physical combats between large organized groups of people, that include the armed forces of at least one State, which aim to exercise political and economic control over a given territory" (definition in my essay), then the difference between terrorism and war is that the former: a) can but doesn't have to involve large groups of people, such as the armed forces of at least one State; b) doesn't aim immediately at territorial control but at changing enemy policy so as to create preconditions for later territorial control. One should add: c) terrorism has never been even on paper brought under some code of conduct such as the Geneva or Hague conventions on war (which forbid killing civilians).

War kills as a rule both armed and unarmed people, terrorism as a rule only the unarmed. This may make terrorism morally more hateful. But inter-State and "civil" wars compensate by their sheer scale: not to mention the two World Wars, even the victims of subsequent inter-State and/or related "civil" wars often amount to hundreds of thousands or indeed millions. This does not make the al-Qaeda "airliner rammings" any better. Neither the ground nor the air terrorists blasting civilians have any justification except political calculation of the most cynical kind. When civilians are killed in wars, this is accepted as <u>war crimes</u>. The "collateral damage" excuse wears thin very quickly: as Herman and O'Sullivan concluded about Vietnam:

"Killings are not 'inadvert' [or 'collateral'—D.S.] if they are a systematic and inevitable result of calculated military policy" (51). Vietnam was then a war accompanied by massive war crimes; so were the proxy wars in southern Africa. But Indonesia, Sudan, Kampuchea or Guatemala (and others from Chile to Colombia and Mexico) were terrorist interventions by the State against its subjects. The Nazis exemplarily straddled both.

What is new in the post-September 11 world is that <u>the frontier between war and terrorism is being erased</u>—from the side of political or religious groups because they don't have airplanes or heavy artillery, but also from the side of the States (primarily the USA) adopting the methods of terrorist groups. Wars are no longer either declared or ended, prisoners are not treated under international conventions. Where Randolph Bourne famously said in 1918, "War is the health of the State," we would have to add that, more and more, "Terror/ism is the health of the State." In this sense, Hitler has won.

Bibliography

<u>General</u>: The opuses of Walter Benjamin [*GS—Gesammelte Schriften*], Bertolt Brecht, Antonio Gramsci, Karl Marx [*MEW—Marx-Engels Werke*], Friedrich Nietzsche.

Amin, Samir. *Capitalism in the Age of Globalization.* London: Zed Books, 1997.

Anderson, Perry. *Lineages of the Absolutist State.* London: Verso, 1979.

Andreski, Stanislav. *Military Organization and Society.* Berkeley: U of California P, 1968.

Angenot. Marc. *1889: Un état du discours social.* Longueil QC: Le Préambule, 1989.

—. *L'antimilitarisme: Idéologie et utopie.* Montréal: CIADEST, 2000.

—-. *Les Idéologies du ressentiment.* Montréal: XYZ, 1996.

Arrighi, Giovanni. *The Long 20th Century: Money, Power, and the Origins of Our Times.* London: Verso, 1994.

Avineri, Shlomo. "Karl Marx on Colonialism and Modernization," in Howard, M.C., and J.E. King eds., *The Economics of Marx.* Harmondsworth: Penguin, 1976, 235-59.

Baran, Paul, and Paul Sweezy. *Monopoly Capital.* New York: Monthly R P, 1966.

Bloch, Ernst. "Der Intellektuelle und die Politik," in his *Vom Hasard zur Katastrophe.* Frankfurt: Suhrkamp, 1972, 336-43.

Bourne, Randolph. *The State.* Tucson AZ: See Sharp P, 1998 (orig. 1918).

Brenner, Robert. "Uneven Development and the Long Downturn...1950-1998." *New Left R* no. 229 (1998), special issue.

Caputo, Philip. *A Rumor of War.* New York: Ballantine Books, 1977.

Castro, Fidel. "Discours prononcé à la séance d'inauguration du Sommet Sud (La Havane, 12 avril 2000)," <www.g77.org>

Chossudovsky, Michel. *The Globalisation of Poverty: Impacts of IMF and World Bank Reforms.* London: Zed Books, 1997.

—-. "It's Not Only Greenhouse Gas Emissions: Washington's New World Order Weapons Have the Ability to Trigger Climate Change." E-mail of 26/11/2000, at <chossudovsky@videotron.ca>.

—-. "Low Intensity Nuclear War." E-mail of 13/1/2001, at <chossudovsky@videotron.ca>.

Clausewitz, Carl von. *On War*, 3 Vols. Transl. J.J. Graham. London: Routledge, 1966 [orig. *Vom Kriege*, 1832-34].

Conert, Hansgeorg. *Das amerikanische Imperium.* Hamburg: VSA-V., 2002.

Creveld, Martin van. *The Transformation of War.* New York: The Free P, 1991.

Davis, Angela Y. *Women, Race and Class.* New York: Random House, 1981.

Davis, Mike. *Late Victorian Holocausts*. London & New York: Verso, 2001.

Dinnerstein, Dorothy. *The Mermaid and the Minotaur*. New York: Harper & Row, 1976.

Drèze, Jean, and Amartya Sen. *Hunger and Public Action*. Oxford: Clarendon P, 1989.

Dummett, Michael. *On Immigration and Refugees*. London & New York: Routledge, 2001.

"Éditorial" in "Comment se construit la pauvreté." *Alternatives Sud* 6.4 (1999): 1-20.

Elwert, Georg. "Markets of Violence," in idem et al. eds., *Dynamics of Violence*. Berlin: Duncker & Humblot, 1999, 85-102.

Foucault, Michel. *Power/ Knowledge*. Ed. C. Gordon. New York: Pantheon Books, 1980.

Freud, Sigmund. *Three Essays on the Theory of Sexuality*. Transl. and ed. J. Strachey. New York: Basic Books, 1975.

Fried, Morton, et al. eds. *War: The Anthropology of Armed Conflict and Aggression*. Garden City NY: Natural History P, 1968.

Gantzel, Klaus-Jürgen. "Über die Kriege nach dem Zweiten Weltkrieg," in Bernd von Wegner ed., *Wie Kriege entstehen*. Paderborn: Schöningh, 2000, 299-318.

[George, Susan.] *The Lugano Report*. London: Pluto P, 1999.

Gibbs, David N. *First Do No Harm: Humanitarian Intervention and the Destruction of Yugoslavia*. Nashville: Vanderbilt UP, 2009.

Gibson, James William. *The Perfect War*. New York: Atlantic Monthly P, 2000.

Giddens, Anthony. *The Nation-State and Violence*. Cambridge: Polity P, 1985.

Gray, Chris Hables. *Postmodern War*. New York: Guilford P, 1997.

Gray, J. Glenn. *The Warriors*. New York: Harper & Row, 1967.

Halberstam, David. *War in a Time of Peace*. New York:

Scribner, & London: Bloomsbury, 2001.

Haraway, Donna J. *Modest_Witness@Second_Millennium.* New York: Routledge, 1997.

Harvey, David. *Limits to Capital.* London & New York: Verso, 1999.

Haug, Wolfgang Fritz. *Politisch richtig oder richtig politisch.* Hamburg: Argument, 1999.

Headrick, Daniel. *The Tools of Empire.* New York: Oxford UP, 1991.

Heinig, K. *Le Prix des guerres.* Paris: Gallimard, 1962.

Herman, Edward S., and Gerry O'Sullivan. "'Terrorism' as Ideology and Cultural Industry," in A. George ed., *Western State Terrorism.* Cambridge UK: Polity P, 1991, 39-75.

Hofbauer, Hannes. *Balkankrieg: Zehn Jahre Zerstörung Jugoslawiens.* Wien: Promedia, 2001.

Human Development Report 1996. Ed. UN Development Programme. New York: Oxford UP, 1996; idem *1998.* Ibidem, 1998.

International Action Center and Tommaso Di Francesco, eds. *La Nato nei Balcani.* Roma: Ed. Riuniti, 1999.

Kaldor, Mary. *New and Old Wars.* Cambridge: Polity Press, 1999.

—-. "Warfare and Capitalism," in *Exterminism and Cold War.* Ed. New Left Review. London: NLB, 1982, 261-88.

Keller, William W. *Arm in Arm.* New York: Basic Books, 1995.

Kolko, Gabriel. *Century of War.* New York: New P, 1994.

Latour, Bruno. *Science in Action.* Cambridge MA: Harvard UP, 1987.

Lefebvre, Henri. *The Production of Space.* Transl. D. Nicholson-Smith. Oxford: Blackwell, 1997.

—-. *Vers le Cybernanthrope.* Paris: Denoël/Gonthier 1971.

Lens, Sidney. *Permanent War.* New York: Schocken, 1987.

Levidow, Les, and Kevin Robbins, eds. *Cyborg Worlds: The Military Information Society.* London: Free Association Books, 1989.

Lewin, Leonard C. "Foreword" to *Report* (below), vii-xv.

Love, Barbara, and Elizabeth Shanklin. "The Answer Is Matriarchy," in *Mothering*. Ed. J. Treblicot. Totowa NJ: Rowman & Allanheld, 1984, 275-83.

Lovins, Amory B., and L. Hunter Lovins. "Energy: The Avoidable Oil Crisis." *The Atlantic* (Dec. 1987): 22-30.

Luxemburg, Rosa. *The Accumulation of Capital.* Trans. A. Schwarzschild. New York: Modern Reader, 1968.

Mann, Michael. "Globalization and September 11." *New Left R* n.s. no. 12 (2001): 51-72.

Marcuse, Herbert. *Feindesanalysen.* Lüneburg: zu Klampen, 1998.

—. *One-Dimensional Man.* Boston: Beacon P, 1964.

Marx, Karl. "Die britische Herrschaft in Indien," in *Marx-Engels Werke [MEW]* Vol. 9. Berlin: Dietz V., 1960, 127-33.

—. *Grundrisse.* Transl. M. Nicolaus. New York: Vintage, [1973].

—. *Das Kapital, Erster Band. Marx-Engels Werke [MEW]* Vol. 23. Berlin: Dietz, 1993.

—. *Das Kapital, Dritter Band. Marx-Engels Werke [MEW]* Vol. 25. Berlin: Dietz, 1979.

—. *Selected Works,* vol. 1. Moscow: FLPH, 1969.

—. *Theorien über den Mehrwert,* 3 Vols. Berlin: Dietz, 1956-62.

McMurtry, John. *The Cancer Stage of Capitalism.* London: Pluto P, 1999.

—. *Understanding War.* Toronto: Science for Peace and Stevens P, 1989.

Melman, Seymour. *The Permanent War Economy.* New York: Simon & Schuster, 1974.

Merlo, Anna Maria. "Schiavi moderni." *Il Manifesto* Feb. 2, 2002, p. 2.

Minolfi, Salvatore. "Dominio senza egemonia." *Giano* no. 39 (2001): 13-30.

Pannekoek, Anton. *Workers' Councils.* Oakland & Edinburgh: AK P, 2003.

Parker, Geoffrey. *The Military Revolution.* Cambridge UK: Cambridge UP, 1988.

Report from Iron Mountain on the Possibility and Desirability of Peace. Intro. by Leonard C. Lewin. New York: Dell, 1967.

Rosen, Steven. "War Power and the Willingness to Suffer," in B.M. Russett ed., *Peace, War, and Numbers.* Beverly Hills: Sage, 1972, 167-84.

Rosière, Stéphane. *Le Nettoyage ethnique.* Paris: Ellipses, 2006.

Scarry. Elaine. "Beauty and the Scholar's Duty to Justice," in P. Franklin ed., *Profession 2000.* [New York]: MLA, 2000, 21-31.

Schreiber, Wolfgang. "Die Kriege in der zweiten Hälfte des 20. Jahrhunderts und danach," in Thomas Rabehl and idem eds., *Das Kriegsgeschehen 2000.* Opladen: Westdeutscher V, 2000, 11-46.

Smith, Adam. *The Wealth of Nations.* New York: Random House, 1937 (orig. 1776).

Smith, Dan. "Conflict and War," in S. George, *The Debt Boomerang.* London: Pluto P & TNI, 1992, 136-67.

Stockholm Int'l Peace Research Institute. *SIPRI Yearbook 1998.* Oxford: Oxford UP, 1998.

—-. *SIPRI Yearbook 1999.* Oxford: Oxford UP, 1999.

Suret-Canale, Jean. "Le Origini del capitalismo," in *Libro nero del capitalismo.* Milano: Tropea, 1999, 17-38.

Suvin, Darko. "Access to an Identification of >Terrorism<: Words and Actions," in his *Darko Suvin: A Life in Letters.* Ed. Ph.E. Wegner. Vashon Island WA: Paradoxa, 2011, 263-79.

—-. "Exploring >Terror/ism<: Numinosity, Killings, Horizons," in his *Darko Suvin* [see previous item], 281-305.

—-. "On Cognition as Art and Politics," in his *Defined by a Hollow: Essays on Utopia, Science Fiction, and Political Epistemology.* Oxford: P. Lang, 2012, 269-319.

Tabb, William K. "Globalization is an Issue, the Power of Capital is the Issue." *Monthly R* 49.2 (1977): 20-30.

Thompson, A.C. "War Without End." *The Nation* Dec. 12,

2001. www.thenation.com/

Tirman, John, ed. *The Militarization of High Technology.* Cambridge MA: Ballinger, 1984.

Toffler, Alvin and Heidi. *War and Anti-War.* Boston: Little, Brown, 1993.

Virilio, Paul. *Speed and Politics.* Trans. M. Polizzotti. New York: Semiotext(e): 1977.

—-, and Sylvère Lotringer. *Pure War.* Trans. M. Polizzotti. New York: Semiotext(e): 1983.

Watts, Michael. "Black Acts." *New Left R* n.s. no. 9 (2001): 125-39.

[Weber, Max.] *From Max Weber: Essays in Sociology.* Ed. and trans. H.H. Gerth and C.W. Mills. New York: Oxford UP, 1958.

Weisberg, Barry. *Beyond Repair.* Boston: Beacon Press, 1971.

Went, Robert. *Globalization.* Transl. P. Drucker. London: Pluto P & IIRE, 2000.

Wiebes, Cees. *Intelligence and the War in Bosnia, 1992-95.* Münster: Lit, 2003.

Woodward, Susan. *Balkan Tragedy.* Washington DC: Brookings Institution, 1995.

Zolberg, Aristide R., Astri Suhrke, and Sergio Aguayo. *Escape from Violence: Conflict and the Refugee Crisis in the Developing World.* New York & Oxford: Oxford UP, 1989.

4. BRECHT'S "THE MANIFESTO" AND US: A DIPTYCH (2000-01)

—For Tom Kuhn: who helped—

A. Bertolt Brecht: THE MANIFESTO
Translated by Darko Suvin

—In memory of Jochen Bunge, who first smuggled this text out to me in the 1960s, and of my father, who first gave me to read the *Communist Manifesto*, printed by a Croatoserbian partisan brigade, in 1945—

If we then in a poem now & here consider the nature
Of people, as the great Lucretius considered the nature
  of things,
It's because we too are only vouchsafed a dim break
  of day...

Brecht, On the Poem for Learning

Wars are destroying the world, & the ruins are visibly haunted
By an enormous spectre, not simply born of war.
In peace it could already be sighted, terror to the rulers
But friend to the children of slums. In scanty kitchens
Often it peeps, horrified, angry, into the half-empty pots.
Often it waits for the exhausted in front of shipyards & mines;

It visits friends in jails, passing without passport.
Even in offices it may be seen & in lecture-rooms
Heard. At times it dons a hat of steel, enters
Huge tanks & flies with deadly bombers. It speaks in many **10.**
Tongues, in all of them. And in many it holds its tongue.
It sits as a guest of honour in hovels, a headache of villas,
It has come to change all things & stay forever, its name is
   <u>Communism</u>.

You've heard much untruth about it from enemies, from friends
Much untruth also. This is what the classics say:
History books speak of great individuals, how
Their stars wax & wane; how their armies roam;
And further how empires resplend & fall. But the doubting great
Teachers examine the old writings for other lore
& they teach: history is mostly the story of how CLASSES
   STRUGGLE: **20.**
For they see all peoples split into classes struggling among
Themselves. Slaves & plebeians once, patricians & knights;
Artisans, peasants, nobility; burgesses then
& proletarians, processing the enormous economy,
Stand at daggers drawn in enormous contentions of power.
In daring subversion the partisan masters thus added
The story of ruled classes to the story of classes that rule.

Yet the ruling classes behave differently at different times,
Rome's patricians act other than Spanish grandees,
Burghers of early cities than the later cities' bourgeois: **30.**
Here, a class cleverly uses the hulking despot,
There, the despotic plurality of their own Houses;
One opts rather for bloody wars, another for slyness,
As their specific position allows, but always to strengthen
The rulers' rule, & always struggling against the ruled.
When peoples leap in slaughter on peoples, behind their battles
Other battles are raging, not so loud, steering the former.
The armies of Rome storm into the far-off icy Pontus

While back at home, in Rome, plebeians & patricians fight.
Germans are warring on Frenchmen, yet German cities, allies
   to   **40.**
The Emperor of Germans, also wage war on German lords.
When a truce unites inimical classes to counter the external
Enemy, in true danger or artificial entrapment,
Both win the fight but only one the victory:
That class returns victorious, the other rings the bells,
Cooks the victory banquet & builds the triumphal column.
For deeper & longer lasting than the wars our primers render
Are the wars of classes, open or secret, not for enemy
Cities but for their own, ending only in revolution
Or in a joint downfall of the fighters, rulers & ruled.   **50.**

Thus came about the age, which now is ending, of the bourgeois:
A fleeing serf, he became a burgher of the market town,
Then of the city, & behind its secure walls the guilds
Flourish. Cloth keeps crossing the walls, & commerce awakens
The dreaming country. Seaports build ships that sail to new
   shores,
Busily round Africa & set courageous sights
On American gold. Opening Chinese & East Indian
Markets, the New World, the accumulation of wares & moneys
Give wings to manufacture, & powerful there appears   **60.**
From feudal relations a new societal ruler, the burgher.

Industry overtakes crafts. Long will endure the distaff,
But the master crosses the market with less resounding
   footsteps
& work once divided by guilds is now by the factory owner
Divided within one, bigger workshop. & still the markets
Insatiably grow. Even manufacture can no longer fill
The new demands, & lo! machines & steam overturn
All again, & manufacturer gives way to captain
Of industry, commander of workers & financier—
Our bourgeois. The Teachers show us in detail how large   **70.**

Machine-based industry created a worldwide market
& the market in turn helped to concentrate industry
Till the bourgeoisie had fought its way to eminent rule:
State power attends to the business of the bourgeoisie now
Clothed in pomp & purple raiment, a willing executive board.

& this class has proved a hard & most impatient mistress.
With brazen cheek & iron heel it stamped out the rotten
Patriarchally still idyll, tore up the feudal old
Motley ties that bound protector & protégé,
Permitting no nexus but naked self-interest between people, **80.**
Payment in cash. The chivalric masters & loyal servants,
Love of native soil, honest craftsmanship, serving
A cause or inner calling, it has drowned in the icy jet
Of calculation, & brutally sold off dignity of persons
As small change. In place of the numberless chartered freedoms
It set up the sole Freedom of Trade. No doubt, those ties were
A natural, pious exploitation; now it is naked
& shamelessly wielded.

Physician & priest & judge & poet & researcher, in the past
Still met with pious awe, it hires as workers for wage,   **90.**
Sends to a doctor the ailing as paying customers, & he sells
His recipe, & the priest sells his consolation.
Justice may now be purchased from the watchman of property,
   the judge.
Whatever ploughs its inventor imagined, its dealer sells
For swords. Hungrily the artist glorifies, with quick
Nobilitating brush-stroke, the bourgeoisie's visage,
Versed in the artifices of art he massages for money the lady's
Languid emotions. Smirking, the bourgeois turns the poets
& thinkers into paid lackeys. The temple of knowledge becomes
A stock-exchange, & even the family's holy abode   **100.**
Hustling he stamps with the seal of unholy haggling.

Indeed, what are to us the aqueducts of Rome, the pyramids,

What a Crusade, & what even the Great Migration of Peoples,
To us who have seen the titanic buildings & expeditions
Made by this all-upsetting class, that always & wherever
It breathless reaches replaces what it created, living
On upset? Without pausing it alters machines & all products.
Formerly unimagined forces it hauls from air & water,
Creates new materials, never seen on this planet:
Thrice in one generation it changes the cloth of one's
   clothes,   **110.**
The hold of knife & fork frequently alters its feel
In the hand, & the eye is always faced with new formations.
So too are people changed, peasants are into factories
Driven, craftsmen driven in droves to new savage shores.
Villages shoot up & cities where this class digs for ore,
Dead & unpeopled in a flash when it moves away. So quick
A boom was never seen before, nor so quick a bust.

Retaining unaltered the way of production was always the first
Business of the classes that rule—this class is the first that erects
The upset as the sine qua non of society. Building its
   buildings   **120.**
On permanently quaking soil, fearing nothing
So badly as rusting & moss, it enforces daily change
On the force of existing relations, all that was stable habit.
The steady & solid is pulled down, the sacred desecrated,
& people stand unsafe, the Earth rolling beneath their feet,
Finally forced to examine their living with sober sight.

& all of this happens not in one country or two
For an unquenchable urge to sell off the bulging commodities
Ceaselessly drives the bourgeois class across the whole
Worldwide expanse of the Earth. It must everywhere look
   around,   **130.**
Build upon, settle in, everywhere tie the sticky threads.
It makes consumption & production cosmopolitan.
It is at home everywhere & nowhere. It destroys the rich

Crafts & indigenous arts, & fetches its raw materials
From furthest-off places. Its factories service fashions & needs
Brought forth by the most diverse climates. High amid
Clouds the feverish commodities climb up the mountain pass.
They trample on rotting toll-bars that have stood for a thousand
years.
Their password is CHEAP! & who are the white-bearded
geezers there,
Priests come to curse the blasphemers? Not a chance, they are
buyers.   **140.**
& those walls there, never conquered?—The agents smile
& with bales of lightest calico batter soundlessly down
The Chinese walls. Mountains make way, islands regroup,
Peoples start needing each other. Spiritual wealth too becomes
A commonwealth of spirit. The Roman scholar avidly reads
A formula from Poland, lines penned by an English hand are
completed
By a Japanese hand, & together scholars all over the world
Design an image of the world. Literatures of various peoples
Become the world's literature.

Panting, the coolie hauls from entrails of foreign vessels   **150.**
Products never before beheld, & sweating behind them
The great new begetter itself, the machine. Thus the bourgeois
Civilizes the barbarians by turning them into further bourgeois.
Like joins to like & produces more likeness, the bourgeoisie
Produces a world after its own image & likeness.

Thus cities lord it over the country, & they grow gigantic
Constantly tearing people from the doldrums of rural duration.
& as cities over country, so the bourgeois nations lord it over
The peasant henceforth; the civilized rein in barbarians
& semi-barbarians, the East becomes dependent on the
West.   **160.**

Machinery & property & people, up to now scattered about

Coalesce into huge formations. Faster & faster,
Implements pile up in prodigious workshops, masses of people
Agglomerate into abundantly producing centers, & the swelling
Property piles up in the hands of a few proprietors.
New political fields are created: loosely bound regions
Separately ruled, with separate laws & separate tariffs,
Are pressed together into one nation, with one single
National interest of the class that rules over all.

Never before did such a creative ecstasy happen   **170.**
As was set ablaze by the bourgeoisie at the time of its triumph.
It created power out of steam & electricity. In few years
It cleared up, as by magic, the wildest continents of the world,
Pumped petrol out of the ground & propelled ships with it
    & cars,
Extracted coal & amassed it into heaping useful mountains,
Dug up iron untouched by a thousand generations
& forged steel into flexible bridges & heavy turbines
Milking the rivers & lakes to light up villages & towns.
It changed forests into weightless paper. Into distant prairies
The daily paper is flung by trains, good news & bad.   **180.**
In five decades, as if humans wanted simultaneously
To live in all places of the planet, the ether became a carrier
Of messages. And now the first people rise up in steerable
    aircraft
Above the earth. No dream had ever shown to humanity
That such forces slumbered in its formative womb nor such
    liberations.
This gigantic creation of goods was confined & fettered
By aristocracy's mortmain & its State of absolute kings:
Wrathfully the bourgeoisie exploded its fetters.

Like unto hurricanes arise the creative forces & shatter
Ancient power, supposed eternal. Other classes,   **190.**
Yesterday servile, tear up the property deeds, codes
Of law & ledgers of debtors, laughing at senile rights.

Ruling opinions were always the opinions of rulers, they follow
The rulers' downward path, for the flight of thinking must follow
Such tempests: they force the thoughts of people down to the ground
Or wheel them forcibly round to other flight paths.
Right is no longer right, wisdom not wise, all is other.
The temples had seen & defied a thousand seasons' change
When they tumbled down into dust, shaken by the victors' step.
But in those left standing, the gods' countenance changes: **200.**
Lo! the Old Ones wondrously look like the rulers today!
Huge are the changes occasioned by new creative forces.

But liberty equality fraternity, what happened to it?
Freedom for the bourgeois to exploit people, say the classics, equality
Before the law for the rich & poor to buy palaces
Or to be permitted to sleep under the bridge arches.

Born out of tempests that bore it to power, the bourgeoisie
Beholds the deadly tempests violent gather against it.
For now that this class, with its new property deeds & rights,
Had conjured forth forces never hereto imagined   **210.**
It seemed a conjurer who has lost control of the underground
Forces he has brought up. As rain quickens crops, but unceasing
Completely washes them out, so the rising creative forces
Multiply fortunes & powers of the class that rules, but rising
Still further, they endanger that selfsame rule.

From now on the story of commerce & mass production tells
How the forces that create the goods engage in rebellion against
The bourgeois ownership & bourgeois ways to create goods.

Colossal crises, recurring in cycles, similar to huge
& blindly groping hands that grip & throttle commerce, **220.**
Convulse in speechless rage companies, markets & homes.
Immemorial hunger had plagued the world when granaries
  emptied:
Now, nobody knows why, we're hungry when they're too full.
Mothers find nothing in the bare pantry to fill the small mouths
While sky-high mountains of grain rot behind walls.
And while bales upon bales of cloth are warehoused, the ragged
  family,
Overnight kicked out of its rented home, wanders freezing
Through emptied city quarters. He who cursed exploiters
Now cannot find exploiters. Ceaseless was his work,
Ceaseless is now his search for work. But the gate is
  locked.   **230.**

Alas, even hell functions no longer. Where now? The giant
Edifice of civil society, built with so much exertion
By so many sacrificed generations sinks back into barbarism.
Not the TOO LITTLE is threatening, the TOO MUCH makes
  it totter.
The house does not exist for dwelling, the cloth for dressing
Nor the bread for stilling hunger: they must bring Profit.
If the product however is only used, but not also bought
Since the producer's pay is too small—were the salary raised
It wouldn't pay to produce the commodity—why then
Hire the hands? For they must produce at the workbench
  more   **240.**
Than a reproduction of worker & family if there's to be
Profit! Yet what then with the commodities? In good logic
  therefore:
Woollens & grain, coffee & fruits & fish & pork
All are consumed by fire, to warm the God of Profit!
Heaps of machines, tools for entire armies of workers,
Blast furnace, shipyard & mine & iron & textile mill
All sacrificed, cut up to appease the God of Profit!

Yet their God of Profit is smitten with blindness. He never sees
The victims. He's ignorant. While he counsels believers he
  mumbles
Formulas nobody grasps. The laws of economics   **250.**
Are revealed as the law of gravity at the time the house collapses
Crashing on our heads. In panic torment the bourgeoisie
Starts cutting to pieces its goods & wildly runs with the remains
Around the globe, searching for newer & larger markets
(The plague-stricken thus flees but only carries the plague
Along & infects the places of shelter!). In new & larger
Crises it wakes up staggered. But upon the impoverished
  people—
Whose multitudes the bourgeoisie is whirling around
In planless plans, now thrown into saunas now onto icy
Streets again—it dawns that the Springtime of the bourgeois
  class   **260.**
Is over: its constricting world can't grasp the riches created.

Against the bourgeoisie the weapons are raised that once
It death-dealing swung to shatter the feudal world, for it has
In its turn brought forth a class which swings the death-
  dealing weapons
Against it. Together with it from the very beginnings there
  grew
In huge masses its inseparable servant, the proletariat,
That only lives by work but only picks up work
If it quick & abundant adds to the bourgeois's capital.

As the capitalist is selling commodities so the worker
Sells his commodity, labour-power, & is forced to
  compete   **270.**
& to share the ups & downs of the capitalists' market .
Appendage to the machine, he sells his manipulation
& gets his subsistence & what it costs to propagate
& rear his useful kind, for the price of labour-power,
As of other wares, conforms to the cost of its coming about.

These workers cohabit no more in the patriarchal workshop
Of a master of their craft. Drilled in long columns, foot-
  soldiers
Of machine trades, they stand in the wide factory halls,
Slaves of the bourgeois class, daily & hourly enslaved.

Work is divided. The workers perform their monotonous
  part.   **280.**
The hours run on killing the mind & exhausting the muscle.
What the journeyman of the crafts saw, the product of his
  hands,
They see no more, no shoe or plough which they would
  have made.
The machine is ingenious, the worker grows dull, for the
  grips are simple:
But the effort put in is still huge, the wheels revolve quicker.
No doubt, anybody can do it. Sweating women & children
Surround the workbench, gender & age count no longer.
All they are now is mere tools & living levers, producing
Commodities whose end it is to create Profit.

When they've given their exploiter more than they cost, when
  th' exhausted slumping   **290.**
Hands finally clutch the scanty pay envelope,
At factory gates new robber bands await them: landlord,
Usurer, shopkeeper, physician, all stage their raids.

No doubt, soon enough such "middle classes" as traders,
  peasants,
& craftsmen fall into the proletariat, because the small profit
Is not enough to buy new machines, or because factory
Production devalues their specialized skill—all are kicked
  out
From shop or workshop or tenant farm to the army of
  workers.

And the proletariat climbs up step by step in the war
That rages between the owners of hands & the owners of
  tools,   **300.**
A war that came to be as soon as these classes came to be.

Single workers to begin with, then workers of a single plant
Fought their bourgeois owner. They began by fighting the ways
& not the whole system of bourgeois production of goods. They
  trashed
Foreign commodities & machines, & burned factories down
To rid themselves of this new, more profound enslavement, to
  get
Back to the feudal enslavement, to arrest, despairing & tired,
The iron hand on the world clock, by themselves forged.

Still scattered all over the country, the proletarians remain
Long disunited, divided by deadly competition   **310.**
For work, & the divided workers fight first the enemy of their
Enemy, absolute monarchs & landowners, guildsmen
& clerics; for still the flag of progress flutters over
The bourgeoisie, & it's able to incorporate all victories.
But any victory strengthens also the class it needed
For winning. The growing large industries concentrate
  proletarians
Into ever huger masses. Workers grow alike:
Who may find a wave in the turbulent torrent? Past differences,
Industriousness or skill, are cancelled working the machine.
Wages are equalized too. They fluctuate & sink in crises   **320.**
Or totally cease whenever no work is to be had. All of this
Torments all at the same time. Coalitions of workers appear
Seeking to protect their wages. Open collisions begin.

Here & there, briefly, workers may win. More often they lose
The local battle for which they united. But the union stuck
& transcended localities. Trains & then phones connect places.
All over the country scattered skirmishes grow to struggles

Of classes. As a class the workers now fight the political fight.
And the class, oft sundered through competition among its
   needy members,
Always united anew through new fights fought in common, **330.**
Reaches for the letter of bourgeois law & forces the employer
To come a cropper here & there, it manages to pinch
A fleeting little hour or so off the long working day.
But it knows, & when it forgets blows will bring it back:
It has to seize hold of the law & finally break its letter.

The rising class gains much from the old classes' dissension
And constant infighting. Still the bourgeoisie has to fight
Aristocrats in army & civil service, then within
Itself as the deadly roller of progress rolls over some of it,
& above all & always it fights the bourgeoisie of other   **340.**
Countries. All these require fellow-fighters from lower
Strata, so it drags the proletariat to political struggles
As helper, & arms its own enemy in the arena.

The proletariat learned how to learn. Painstakingly
Exploited at workbench, drill & construction crane, it needed
Education & was forced into schools. Meagre the knowledge
It got & mostly falsified, but knowledge still of the power
Of knowledge & awareness about their thirst for their own
   knowledge.

Angry abuse would a Haroon al-Rashid hear on the market
Against the bourgeoisie. The failing corner-store keepers, **350.**
Owners of petty businesses as well as rentiers & farmers
Fight tooth & nail to keep their minuscule property intact.
The carpenter luridly curses furniture factories, the farmer
Big agribusiness, & all deplore our moral decline.
These good people don't want to subvert the societal structure,
   its lone
Good side they are attacking & accusing, the great production
Of goods, shaking their shattered fists in vain.

The rotting mob of our cities, formed from putrefaction
Of the old society's lowest strata, is also oft
Pulled by revolution into proletarian ranks but it is   **360.**
Only a victim, not an enemy of bourgeois rule, & easily bought
As a bestial servant to batter the proletarians down.

The only class finally that may vanquish the bourgeoisie
& shatter its fettering State is the proletariat. It has
The proper stature & position. What ensured life in the old
Society has long since been swept away & wholly destroyed
In the being of the worker. Without property, to wife & child
Neither family head nor bread-winner, discernible
Barely by nation & race, since identical servitude bound
To identical bench & machine endow him with the same
Identity from the Ruhr to Canton, the proletarian
Sees in religion & morals mere fata-morganas,
Prejudices to him behind which hides the robbing grab.   **370.**

Other classes, having come to power, protect what they got
While dictating to everybody else the novel way of getting.
This class conquers the goods-producing works by wholly
    repealing
The way they are got. This class has nothing to safeguard for
    itself.
To the contrary, any individual safeguard it has to destroy.

Mountains of machinery behind fences & walls & hidden even
    better
By laws, & on this side millions upon millions of willing workers
Terribly torn away from the means of working by fences & walls
& the State's laws, each a singleton that may be hired
By the hour to set in motion the machines, hired like
    water-power   **380.**
Or electricity, for the cost of production, but only if that
Blind God of Profit, the crazy one, nods, the gambler.

The rulers' rule was always founded on the fact that the ruled
Could somehow live from the toil: their exploitation was sure.
But now the bourgeoisie can manage no more to ensure
A servile life to their serfs. Instead of feeding off
Its proletarians, now it must feed them. It needs to employ them
But has no employment for them & yet lets their numbers swell.
And dehumanization wins, marking the victims
& victimizers, chaos results from the bourgeoisie's   **390.**
Plans, the more plans more chaos, & lack is born from
    production
Wherever it rules, death-dealing to the vast majority.
No longer can society live under its rule. The new class
It raised, the proletariat, will bring it down: it raised
Itself the giant hands that dig its grave.

The vast majority is in this movement, & when it rules
This is no longer ruling but suppression of rule. Only
Oppression shall here be oppressed: the proletarians, lowest
Level of society, must, in order to rise, smash
Into pieces the whole social structure with all its upper
    levels.   **400.**
The proletariat can only throw off its special class
Servitude by throwing off the servitude of all.

B/ ON BRECHT'S "THE MANIFESTO": COMMENTS FOR READERS IN ENGLISH[22]

> Dal principio alla fine
> è conveniente seguire ogni giustizia.
> Giampiero Neri, *L'aspetto occidentale del vestito*
> [From beginning to end/ it is proper to follow all justice.—G.N., "The Western Aspect of Clothing", ca. 1960]

> This most rich poet scattered into all he created seeds of thought destined to spring into full life only later. He was persuaded that any living work grows and works on by immanent force, that it changes with each listener and reader reached. His poems are based on this presupposition, and only the future shall make visible the full width and plenitude of his work.
> Lion Feuchtwanger, "Bertolt Brecht" [1957]

1. Some Pertinent History (Teacher of Life)

In early 1945, most probably already in January, Brecht started working on what he at some point called a "versification of the

---

22. My thanks are due first of all to the Brecht-Archiv, Berlin, and its director Dr. Erdmut Wizisla who provided crucial help both with Brecht's variants and with the secondary literature, including a preview of his planned annotated list of Brecht's library. They extend to the encouragement of Fredric Jameson and Tom Kuhn, and to productive observations, suggestions and/or queries by Marc Angenot, Johannes Angermüller, Bonnie Borenstein, Ronnie Davis, Marcelline Krafchick, Joan Roelofs, Marc Silberman, Renate Solbach and Victor Wallis; Stephen Bronner undertook the heroically kind task of giving me a line-by-line critique. The translation was first presented at a panel devoted to it in the "Marxism 2000" conference, Amherst MA, Sept. 2000, which was encouraged by Richard Wolff and helped by Stephen Cullenberg; the respondents at the panel were Ronnie Davis and Sara Lennox. Of course the remaining faults are 99% mine and only 1% Brecht's.

[Communist] Manifesto" (GKA 27: 219) but at other points also thought of as part of a vaster project, a *Lehrgedicht* parallel to Lucretius's *On the Nature of Things;* the title of that "Didactic Poem" or "Poem for Learning" was not yet fixed but could have been something like *On the Nature of People* or, more precisely, *On the Unnatural Character of Bourgeois Relationships.* Time for this venture of Brecht's in Santa Monica was found by a hiatus in co-translating his play *Life of Galileo* with Charles Laughton: Laughton had to play in the pirate movie *Captain Kidd* in order to redeem time for that translation-cum-adaptation. But the deeper impulse for Brecht was the overwhelming approach of an end to World War II that put on the agenda the future of Germany; for émigrés of Brecht's stripe this meant: will it be socialist or not (cf. Hartinger 34-38)? During his intense concentration on what turned out to be not only a versification but also a reworking of Marx's *Manifesto*—hereinafter CM—, Brecht noted in his diary on March 10, 1945: "Between the 'Didactic Poem' and the terrible newspaper reports from Germany. Ruins and no sign of life from the workers." (GKA 27: 221) Pondering on how to rediscover for German workers the obviously forgotten teachings of Marxism, Brecht concluded that "it seems to me possible to renew the propagandistic efficacy [of CM] today, one hundred years later, and to lend it new, fortified (*bewaffnet*) authority, by sublating its pamphlet character" (GKA 27: 219-20).

This was wholly in line with Brecht's central strategy, perhaps best formulated in his magisterial 1934 essay *Five Difficulties in Writing Truth* (*Fünf Schwierigkeiten beim Schreiben der Wahrheit*), where the last but not at all least quality that a writer who wishes to combat lying and ignorance must acquire was slyness: "slyness in disseminating the truth to many people" (GKA 22.1: 81). The subject-matter of the rise and fall of the "unnatural character" (this is more elegant in the German *Unnatur*, something like "mis-nature") of bourgeois rule was forced on Brecht's attention in the last years of the Weimar Republic and hugely intensified by the coming to power of

Nazism. In the "Conclusion" to the *Five Difficulties*, surely one of the great essays of the twentieth century, he wrote:

> The great truth of our epoch (which is not enough, but without which no other pertinent truth can be found) is that our continent is sinking into barbarism because violence is used to cling to the existing relations of property over the means of production.... We cannot search out the truth about the barbaric conditions without thinking about those who suffer under them, and while we, continually sloughing off temptations of cowardice, search for the true relationships because of those who are ready to use such cognitions, we have at the same time to think about presenting the truth in such a way that it could be a weapon in their hands, and also so slyly that this presentation may not be found out and cut off by the enemy. (GKA 22.1: 88-89)

But there was a further and deeper, or at least less moment-bound, reason to use the classical model of epic verse (which, for Brecht, meant the Latin hexameter) as a pedagogical royal road to the listener's understanding. In a memo perhaps to be titled "From Whom Have I Learned", written after the June 1953 rebellion of Berlin workers, when Brecht was once again intensely meditating how to renew the efficacy of Marxian tradition for the German workers, he concluded from his experiences:

> There are at least two linked reasons why it's worthwhile to study the two great didactic poems of the Romans, Virgil's *Georgica* and Lucretius's *Of the Nature of Things*. For one thing they are models how to describe in verse the cultivation of nature and an understanding of the universe; and for another, we have in the beautiful translations of Voss and of Knebel marvellous elucidations about our [German] language.

The hexameter is a verse line which forces the German language to the most fertile exertions. It presents itself as clearly "manipulated", which makes learning much easier. Like Virgil, the translator must teach versification together with agriculture...; in brief, the great artistry of the Ancients is developed by treating great contents. (GKA 23: 269-70)

Today we might wish to say either that there is a feedback between a given form and a given content which determines not only the momentary success of artful writing in its time but also its efficacy and survival for following generations—that is, its becoming and enduring as a classic. Or indeed we might wish to say that the vocabulary of form vs. content is helpful only to a limited degree and that the how is always consubstantial with the what: most obviously so in poetry. But Brecht's optimistic conclusion might serve as a first reason to inquire further into the uses of what eventually became his unfinished poem *Das Manifest (THE Manifesto)*. Discouraged by his best friends such as Eisler and Feuchtwanger, engaged in many other pressing writings, and above all unsure of who would be the poem's readers, Brecht broke off its composition in the second half (probably in September) of 1945. He cherished the project until the end of his life.

The following commentary is divided into a "technical" section and a "substantive" section. The former speaks briefly of the tradition of hexameter in English and my guidelines for translating the somewhat messy variants of Brecht's not finally revised attempt into it. It might perhaps be skipped by readers not interested in it, but they might also find that a full, understanding enjoyment would be helped by not skipping it. The longer "substantive" section focusses on relationships between poetry and history, including doctrine, memory, and associated matters. A reader skipping it might find that supposedly technical decisions—how the translation actually reads—will not be sufficient. There have been benevolent liberal attempts to "save" Brecht by sundering the poetry and the politics in his political poetry or poetical politics. This degrades both, my two sections do not fully follow this divide, and I warn the reader against it.

2. A Commentary for Technical Readers

2.1. A hexameter is a verse line with six stresses. Hexameters are in English relatively rather rare, especially longer poems in it. There are some longer English poems in hexameter, such as Tennyson's "Locksley Hall," Swinburne's "Hymn to Proserpine" or Kipling's "Danny Deever," but then they clearly lean on—often elaborate—rhyming. G.M. Hopkins wrote, I think, only one of the "terrible sonnets" ("Carrion Comfort") in hexameter, again rhymed. Unrhymed hexameters, on the Greek and Latin mould (however this mould was misread) are very rare, except for splendid single lines:

> What seas what shores what granite islands towards
> my timbers
> (T. S. Eliot, "Marina")

When hexameters are used, often it's only in conjunction with another, so to say redeeming metre, and again usually outfitted with rhyme, such as this representative first stanza of Hardy's "Afterwards," in which the final line subsides into the more normal pentameter (five stresses):

> When the Present has latched its postern behind my
>   tremulous stay,
> And the May month flaps its glad green leaves like
>   wings,
> Delicate-filmed as new-spun silk, will the neighbours
>   say,
> 'He was a man who used to notice such things'? (159)

Or perhaps more cognate to Brecht's epic intentions, the ecological protest plus technical attention to work of Hardy's "Throwing a Tree":

> The two executioners stalk along over the knolls,
> Bearing two axes with heavy heads shining and wide,
> And a long limp two-handled saw toothed for cutting
>   great boles...(204)

—but here too at the end of each stanza a new meter (the heptameter, seven stresses) breaks any fears of monotony or awkwardness, not quite absent from the first-line spondee, the two stresses in the same metric unit or foot, [nérs stálk], which I'd have never dared to use as a translator. But then Hardy's later poems are notorious for bending stress schemes to his communicative needs, see the hexameters—if they can still be called such—of "The Second Visit":

> Clack, clack, clack, went the mill-wheel as I came...
> (208)

2.2. When I decided to translate Brecht's *The Manifesto,* I found a messy manuscript situation. In the Berlin Brecht Archive, much helped by the kindness of its director Dr. Erdmut Wizisla and its staff, I found there were 10 folders pertaining to it. But the materials in those folders are partly mingled with scantier materials for that larger plan to write a "Didactic Poem on the Nature of Man," in which *The Manifesto* as it at present stands would have been one out of four parts. The latest and biggest Brecht edition, the Grosse Kommentierte Berliner und Frankfurter Ausgabe 1988-2000, prints three variant versions of it plus a handful of fragments not contained in any version (in volume 15, edited by Jan Knopf and Brigitte Bergheim with three more collaborators, pp. 120-57). The notes on pp. 386-407, which follow Bunge's path-breaking overview, claim there are four "stages" (*Bearbeitungsstufen*), dating from 1945, of Brecht's versification of chapter 1 of Marx's *Communist Manifesto*, plus one more "stage" consisting of only ten verses in 1950. The three variants printed are stages 2-4.

To my mind, however, Brecht's copious rewritings as presented in GKA fall into TWO groups of variants. The first comprises the GKA editors' stages 1 plus 2 (of which they rightly print only one, and I shall here call it draft or variant 1), and it is obviously poetically less polished. The second comprises the "stages" 3 plus 4 (printed variants 2 and 3), which are better and differ mainly in fine-tuning and in the fact that "stage" 4 is shorter—that is, its corrections were abandoned before the end.

I used as my main text the printed variant 2 (German pp. 135-48), adding however to it the ending which exists only in variant 1 (German pp. 134-35, in my translation ll. 371 on). But I took the liberty of using some formulations which I thought of as better from variant 3, more rarely from variant 1. I interpolated one fragment from German p. 157 as my ll. 203-06 ("But liberty equality fraternity...").

For my purposes of a narrative, indeed doctrinally expository, poem, I adopted Brecht's adaptation of Lucretius's hexameter, which takes for its model Knebel's 1821 German hexameter translation of Lucretius;[23] and furthermore I adopted Brecht's

---

23. For the record, the original is *De rerum natura* in six "books" by Titus Lucretius Carus, ca. 95-55 BCE; this is perhaps best translated as *On the Nature of the Universe* or...*of What There Is*. One of the first proofs of Brecht's intensive consultation of the 1821 translation by Knebel that also contained Lucretius's Latin (Brecht read both), which he must have owned from the Weimar years and which followed him in his émigré wanderings, is to be found in the essay *Five Difficulties*, where he cites "the great Lucretius" as an authoritative source for beauty of verse being used for dissemination of doctrine (GKA 22.1: 83); eight further references to and citations of Lucretius in Brecht's poems or essays about poetry from 1933 on have been found (Knopf 158 and GKA 14: 548-49 and 675). They always use and/or adapt the Latin verse in German, so that Brecht's first hexameters in the footsteps of Lucretius also date from 1933 (ibidem 171). The two other most important discussions are Brecht's cited memo "From Whom Have I Learned" and the famous programmatic essay "On Unrhymed Poetry with Irregular Rhythm" in 1939, where the irregular rhythms and

solution to use a loose "stress" hexameter. Eisler claimed it was a "jazzed-up" hexameter, which may be a bit exaggerated unless he rightly implied that it uses syncopation (which is anyway usual in some poetic traditions, such as the English one); however, this Brechtian hexameter is at the antipodes— say—of the stately and formal six-beat French Alexandrine in which some of the most splendid Racine tragedies are written. In "stress verse" (rather than syllable-stress verse) the number of syllables can vary. "Loose" also means here that I adopted several guiding principles, all based on the wish to have lines that could be read (Brecht wrote the poem to be read aloud, and I much hope this could also apply to my translation) without too much violation of usual verse rhythms: that is, without either too much stopping or too much slurring over, except for specially intended and rare purposes.

My first principle was that my hexameter can go up to but not beyond eighteen syllables, i.e. in the Classicistic parlance I didn't want to have stress units (feet) longer than three syllables—with the well-recognized exception of the final foot in any line. The second was that at the end of each of Brecht's division into sections (which follow Marx's paragraphs in CM) I allowed myself a final line—a dying fall, so to say—of anything between two and six stresses, though I tried to keep them as near to five as possible. Also, I shunned wherever I could feet

---

"gestic elements" of Lucretius testify to his openness for social dissonances and function as the ideal modern procedure. Much has been said (best in Mayer, Bunge, Mittenzwei and Knopf) about the relationship to Lucretius documented in these places, much more awaits to be said.

On Brecht's great liking for Roman themes and literature, second in importance perhaps only to an analogous affinity to the Chinese and Japanese ones, cf. at least the classical monograph by Hans Mayer. See also note 5 below.

Brecht used the The Communist Manifesto text from a selection of Marx's works published in German in the USSR 1934; the Brecht Archive conserves the photographs and films he had Ruth Berlau make of its pages in order to scatter them singly over his study room (GKA 29: 220, Bunge 184).

composed of a single stressed syllable (catalectic iamb) and even more so a foot of two stressed syllables (spondee). The third was that there should be generally rising rhythms—iambs and anapests—though amphibrachs (3 syllables with stress in the middle) were allowed; of course, as in all English rising-rhythm verse, the first foot plus one or even two more feet could be "falling"—trochees or dactyls—since this would not put in doubt the general rhythm, but I tried to keep away, with rare exceptions, from lines with a predominantly falling rhythm (more than 3 feet of trochees or dactyls).

As to syntactic choice: I chose to have a mildly Teutonic syntax. I found a fully colloquial English syntax of 2001 (or indeed 1945) both impossible to attain with Marx's-cum-Brecht's vocabulary and aims, as well as unsuited to the matter at hand: the reader is goddam well supposed to invest as much energy into it as into a dozen pages of physics or political economy. On the other extreme, I hope I've avoided the awful translationese of (as an unkind friend put it) the "flowers did I for you pick" kind. A kinder friend said my halfway house made for a mild estrangement (*Verfremdung*): my heart leapt when I read him, for that's exactly what I'm aiming at. The reader should understand that this was written in German 60 years and one historical epoch ago. It is a piece of history. It is in my opinion more than indifferently useful for today, otherwise I wouldn't have buckled down to translating it. Thus, the reader is not supposed to gobble but to enjoy while understanding (or vice versa) and come back to ponder the poem's voice and meanings; ideally, this would be done as a collective effort after reading aloud parts or the whole of the poem. It is the voice of a near and dear but by now old-fashioned grand-uncle. But fashions have not only changed, they can change again: "O change of times, thou hope of the people!" (Brecht). So we who were "born after" (Brecht again) have to invest mental energy into finding out what we can learn from this buoyant, overconfident, wise, irritating, sly, doctrinaire, flexible, and above all stimulating voice.

In sum: How much, and just where and how, in what parts or aspects, is this poem applicable to the present day? How much can its various passages as well as its overall tone and stance be of use in vitally needed present-day debates? A public discussion of these central points is the aim of this translation. I shall attempt to start it in Section 3.

A final principle of mine imitated (even if by eversion) the mythical constitution of the Anarchist Federation of Catalonia:

1. There are no obligatory rules.
2. The foregoing paragraph is not obligatory.

In practice this meant that any of the above rules could be violated if my ear and/or my responsibility to Brecht-*cum*-Marx's sense told me so and I found no other way to follow its telling. I tried not to have too many of such violations.

3. A Commentary for Substantial Readers

Most of Section 2 above might hold for any translation of a long hexameter poem into English. There are of course especially complex problems in Brecht's poem, as in any so-called didactic and/or propagandistic verse (I shall try to unpack this banal designation later). I shall first focus on the relationship of poetry to doctrine. One can imagine extreme ideal-types, not encountered in practice, where either is a means completely in service of the other: either verse as a flat rhythmical and mnemonic ploy to sweeten the doctrinal pill, or doctrine as overall, often far-off armature to organize the poet's different—compatible but richer—concerns. The best example that comes to mind of nearness to the second extreme is Dante's *Commedia,* or at least its first two parts. But in Brecht's case the danger is rather the first extreme, that is—the use of verse for the overriding or even sole purpose of enunciating a cognitive theory, a use for which already Aristotle had in the first section of his

Poetics banished Empedocles from poetry to physics. I found a wonderful example for it in a poem that was T. S. Eliot's now almost totally forgotten contribution to World War II propaganda in 1942. He seems to have attempted to show how the type of "universal" poetry he was writing then could express Britain's struggle in 1941-42, but the result is prose arbitrarily hacked into rhythmical lines:

> The enduring is no substitute for the transient
> Neither one for the other. But the abstract conception
> Of private experience at its greatest intensity
> Becoming universal, which we call "poetry",
> May be affirmed in verse.
>
> (in Harding 78)

To the contrary, a valid poem—that is, one which should have a good reason to exist beside a prose employing the same doctrinal (philosophical, religious, political, etc.) notions and argumentation—would be somewhere in the middle between the above extremes, in a semantic creative space where ends and means, sense and sensuality, doctrine and poetry remain in a more or less fruitful tension, from the Left of much Mayakovsky and Neruda or Brecht's *Manifesto* to the Right of Eliot's contemporary *Four Quartets* or indeed some of Pound's *Pisan Cantos* (the "Liberal" bourgeois center, being in saddle, has no passionate reason to compose didactic poetry, which seems—at any rate since the Romantics—born of dissatisfaction).

In the 1920s Brecht famously remarked that gasoline doesn't fit into, and therefore disallows, the five-act "dramatic tension" form; and he subsequently elaborated—together with many other dramatists and theatre people—his "epic" or dialectical dramaturgy. Analogously, the language of *The Communist Manifesto* doesn't fit the dominant forms of the English individualist lyric, which have five stresses or less. However, it would have less trouble with the popular ballad form, which often had seven stresses, for ex. in Brecht's beloved *Sir Patrick Spens* or his equally beloved urban *Moritat* (street ballad) *Das Seemanslos [The Sailor's Destiny]*, though they are usually printed as two lines of 4+3 stresses; and some ballads have even six stresses. Thus I believe Brecht's instinct to use the hexameter was sound even apart from the wonderful example of Lucretius.[24] Brecht inventively varied and enriched this language in his attempt to find a halfway house between doctrinal generalization and concrete experience, to which I'll return; but his goal was to retain the power of Marx's generalizations that construct a cognitive edifice held together by terminological rigour. Therefore *The Manifesto* frequently uses words coined for such doctrinal precision rather than for euphony (sound) or prosody (rhythm). Examples of such repeatedly found terms might have two stresses, as "commodity," which at least has the right pair of rising stresses [-'-'], or as the more difficult, but fortunately rare in Brecht, "capitalism" ['- -']. Almost as difficult is "bour-geoisie" (phonetically: boor-zhoo-ah-zee, similar to the French pronunciation, ['- -']), since—with the quite normal elision of its second syllable and stress—it will have three syllables (phoneti-cally: boor-zhwa-zee) with a principal stress on the first and a subsidiary but often used stress on the third syllable ['-'].[25] Most difficult proved to me (this says maybe something about my

---

24. A great deal of memoir literature and philological attention has been consecrated to Brecht's not using the truly classical (Homeric or indeed Lucretian) hexameter but a freer German form. I believe the correct judgment on this was given in Eisler's retraction of his strong 1945 objections (both formal and political) in the dialogs with Bunge (81-90): the objections were formally irrelevant and politically short-sighted. See the literature in GKA 27: 220 and 226, both Feuchtwanger items (to my mind mistaken), Hartinger 62-68 (whose arguments I find best), and Knopf 163-64.

25. It is much easier in the expletive two-syllable Russian "burzhuy" (boorzhoo'y), as proved by Mayakovsky:

Yesh ananasy, ryabchiki zhuy,
Den' tvoy poslyedniy prikhodit, burzhuy!
(Gulp down pineapples, chew your quails/
Your last day is dawning, boorzhooy!)

political unconscious?) "proletarian" and "proletariat" which are quite unmanageable in the full five-syllable form and must usually be, with some difficulty, elided into four syllables and two (falling) stresses (proh-leh-teh-ryat, ['-'-])—on the example of Pope's "con-gen-yal". I note that the difficulties exist also in German (indeed, Feuchtwanger took the impossibility of fitting words such as "Proletariat" into verse as excuse to cease collaborating on the project after six weeks in 1945, see his "Bertolt Brecht" 105-06 and Bunge), but given the different rhythms they seem to me smaller.

It ought to be stressed that Brecht's *Manifesto* participates in the modern (even the most modern, if you wish post-post-modern) tendencies of much in the best poetry of our age to use an "antipoetic"—or more precisely, anti-Idealist—language recuperating exact scientific or philosophical terms. This language was wonderfully defined by the Italian poet Gozzano already around 1908 as: "lo stile d'uno scolare/corretto un pò da una serva"—"the style of a scholar/ Somewhat corrected by a charwoman" (in his poem "L'altro" ["The Other"], cited in Marcheschi 13-14). This style of poetry is of a piece with Brecht's constant attempt at melding plebeian demystification from below with precise intellectual critique. Its informing horizon is that of <u>verse narration as cognition</u>, not confined to but not at all shunning conceptual cognition in feedback with behavioural information about stances or bearings (cf. essay 1 in this book). Poetry is here not only in strong opposition to the stifling superficial babbling of the reigning, totally ideologized *doxa* of the capitalist media or brainwashed common sense, but its main reason for existing is to be a "stumbling block" (formulation of the poet Giampiero Neri, ibidem 16) to the hegemonic babble—one which forces the reader-stumbler to stop and look at what is really happening at his feet. This type of poetry remains playful but it is a serious play, the young lions exercizing sudden jumps upon each other. It is necessarily fixated on the necessary complicitous reader, at the antipodes and at the expense of the narcissistic navel-gazing of most Post-Modernism. It is much concerned, as Brecht noted in his great programmatic poem "To the Danish Worker-Actors," with precise, technical, verifiable, and repeatable observation of recurring, key, and typical events and relationships. Such materialist poetry, while remaining different from the prose of precise observation, is yet also related to it by an umbilical cord—that is, the verse is in fruitful tension both with the precise observing and, as noted earlier, with the doctrinal obsessive clarity.

The poetry is therefore articulated as a rational discourse "without any inferiority or superiority complex toward natural sciences or history" (Marcheschi 17), yet never sundered from possibly discreet or hardboiled but always strong emotion. Paradoxically, it can be verified in Brecht's *Manifesto* how, at its extreme, such apparent objectivity touches upon and fuses with a functional and gnomic, almost ceremonious, ritualization, using frequent repetitions, syntactic inversion, enjambment (syntactic carry-over into the next line), and a marked rhythm. Characteristically, a rhetorical figure called "adnomination" is used, which repeats noun root in verb root or vice versa (for ex. "passing without passport" or "Slaves of the bourgeois class, daily and hourly enslaved"). This is in my opinion emblematic for Brecht's attempt to create additional verisimilitude for Marx's concepts by replunging them into the collective activity of human working classes from which they presumably sprang. This figure may serve as a good example how cognition is to be found hidden in sensual tricks of alliteration, assonance, and echo, just as in Dante's initially obscure "Amor, che a nullo amato amar perdona" which will be found, upon reflection, to carry a serious point beneath, through and by means of the virtuosity.[26]

26. Literally, "Love that pardons no beloved/lover for loving". There's a whole little library of comments on this verse from the Paolo and Francesca episode of *Inferno*. Very crudely, "Love," the allegorical figure not too far from the Greek Eros, is not sickly sweet but (often—in Dante's usual hyperbole always) merciless toward the lovers/beloved, who have to bear the consequences of this semi-divine—in some versions, dear to Dante who ends the *Commedia* with a verse on divine love "that moves the Sun and other stars," fully divine—impulse and project. Indeed Paolo and Francesca

The poetic cognitive movement is in Brecht's usage spiral, for it is both determined, in some ways even predetermined by the nature of things, and also open to human passion and struggling endeavour (in the above examples, against prisons and slavery): nature can only work for us through human nature, and Marx's socioeconomic laws through classes of embodied people. The movement of verse enacts—with the participation of the reader—a ceremony of the struggle against overweening social injustice, in which words and things are given allegorical faces and figures, again turned toward each other; and its Great Ancestor is, indeed, Lucretius *On the Nature of Things*.

Brecht's acumen is nowhere more apparent than in his full consciousness of this ancestry. His unfinished poem had the ambition to be to Marx what Lucretius was to Epicure (himself an object of Marx's doctoral dissertation).[27] Epicure's teachings survived only in some fragments—and in Lucretius's

---

are both killed for it and land in the perpetual tempest zone of the Inferno. And yet they are presented with such understanding and beauty through full sixty-two lines, their loyalty holds so fast even in that tempest, that most readers would suspect loving may be worth it, if you are truly lovers/beloved, whatever Love may do to you.

27. The following few lines from a standard handbook speak about Lucretius, but the reader may amuse herself by finding out how much of it would apply to Brecht too, and where modifications would have to be applied: "...he shows a firm intellectual grasp of what is often a complex and abstruse philosophical argument. He has the artist's intense sensory awareness of the world about him.... His moral involvement in his subject and his sense of the ludicrous make it easy for him to modulate into satire. He is a superbly endowed artist wrestling triumphantly with intractable material, writing with a vigour and gusto hardly found in Latin after the end of the republic.... He is aware of his own originality, of the difficulties involved in treating philosophy as subject-matter for poetry; he has something of the loneliness of the pioneer as well as of the creative artist. But his theme is life itself as he had realized it in Epicurean terms...." (Wormell).

The best book I know about Lucrece, and much recommend, is by Serres, who argues, most important for our theme, that both his polyphonic style and his physics are open-ended towards the flows and turbulences of always endangered freedom.

verse, where he is repeatedly praised as the great and glorious liberator of mankind from superstition and fear of death, whose footsteps the poet wishes to follow (cf. Book 5: 55). The premonition that the oblivion could happen to Marx too—practically if not literally—was never absent from Brecht (see his poems on the great exiled poets, among whom Lucretius is—unhistorically—also found, "Die Auswanderung der Dichter" ["The Poets' Emigration"] and "Besuch bei den verbannten Dichtern" ["Visiting the Exiled Poets"], GKA 14: 256 and 12: 35). Recent history gave Brecht reason to insist on his fears.

Today, such a form of cognitive poetry is one of the best ways to carry across the roaring oceans of incessantly battering brainwashing the indispensable <u>memories</u> how great hopes flourished in the twentieth century. It offers a good chance to bring about that necessary piety which entails both a repristination of familiarity with the forgotten teachings and simultaneously their "pitiless critique" (Marx). To use Brecht without criticizing him, observed pithily Heiner Müller, means to betray him. In our age this holds, of course, for every cognitive endeavour, and in particular for Marx and the whole Marxian and Leftwing tradition. The poetry is a watchman: "Watchman, what of the night?" The night is deep and dark, but not unsurmountable: "it goes on for twelve hours, then comes the day" (Brecht, *Schweyk in the Second World War*). But orientations in the thick clouds of words and tear gas, or indeed bomb bursts, are badly needed. They have to be supplied from wherever one can get them.

4. Poetry and History

What is, then, the <u>relation of poetry to history</u>? Surely, charity begins at home: poetry cannot exist without a relation to its own history. The poet—and the translator—must be cognizant of it, but not necessarily the synchronic reader who has to fry today's potatoes today. For her, the relation is basically one of poetry to what Marx and Engels called the only science they knew—the history of relationships among people, in different social formations, in the struggles of classes differently shaping each formation. There should be no special problems here for a poet as narrating *histor*, a teller of (hi)stories committed to an understanding that functions equally as his ethics and his esthetics: for each of us has debts contracted in time toward the living and especially the dead, and the poet pays those debts. The most deeply personal economy is here at one with the sciences studying human and natural economy and with the Marxist understanding of history—those commitments to truth and memory.

However, given that readers are the central reason for the poem's existence, the overriding question for a Marxist or socialist—which includes, no doubt in complex ways, a Marxist or socialist poet—is surely the relation of the poems he is writing to the synchronic history, ongoing in the flesh of these readers. (One then also hopes for the poem's long duration, its reaching future readers too, but it doesn't do to think too much about that while writing.) What has changed in that history between 1848 and 1945, and what has not? As Braudel would put it, what are its short-duration and what the long-duration elements and aspects? A brief investigation of the relation between Marx's *Communist Manifesto* and Brecht's *The Manifesto* might provide a useful link between the relation of a poem to its own textual models and antecedents and to its ongoing historical situation.

In his diary for February 1945, cited at the beginning of this comment, Brecht noted: "The [Communist] Manifesto is as pamphlet itself a work of art," but continued by postulating that its efficacy could be "today" renewed and strengthened "by sublating its pamphlet character" (GKA 27: 219-20). This implies two main points. First, that in spite of its eminent political and artistic status, Marx's *Manifesto* has been in the practice of both the Second and the Third International movements (that is, of the Social Democratic and of the Communist parties) so automatized and ossified that it no longer strikes a potentially interested and approachable reader with the freshness required for joyous perception and efficacy: as the Formalists would have said, it has to be de-automatized, or in Brecht's own coinage, estranged (*verfremdet*). Later in Berlin, he would confide to an assistant, Käthe Rülicke: "This was conceived so slyly. I thought that if the great form is found beautiful, then the content has to be accepted together with it.... Brecht laughed a lot remembering it." (Wizisla ed., 40) And of course we should not forget that the rigidity on the official Left was in great part a defense mechanism against sharp and huge physical and ideological repression. But a second point that follows from Brecht's proceeding is that the change in literary genre, from prose pamphlet to narrative poem in hexameter, was supposed to decisively intervene in this de-automatization and new perceptibility, in the renewed and (in comparison to the dogmatic idolization) strengthened efficacy of Marx's diagnosis in actual political life. Such changes may be useful to discuss, at least partly and initially, to sharpen the reader's understanding of Brecht's ways of working and intention.

My thesis is that what unites the Marxian political pamphlet and the Brechtian "poem for learning" is that they both aspire (and largely accede) to a cognitive status. If we are still to bother about them, it is because at least some of their key insights are still valid as guides for action, and others are instructive as to where, why, and how they were (are) wrong. What the social-science people could and should learn from philology is that the what is never to be separated from the how: they are consubstantial. Therefore, the cognitive dusting off melds two modes of new understanding: it means not only a notional updating but also a rephrasing in the idiom and for the imagination of the new readers. And rephrasing is never innocent, since the how intervenes in the what. This is what differentiates Brecht's from Marx's *Manifesto*.

The long duration, what has been retained here from the "classical" Marxist tradition, is, first, Hegelian metamorphic forces of constant change, reinterpreted as Marx's chthonic forces at work from the magmatic depths of society; I shall return to the strengthening of the dynamic element in the poem. The "testimonial tenacity" (Marcheschi 27) of Brecht's is a dialogue with a view how Marx's cognitions about forces of history-as-political-economy operate in the flesh of working people. Second, Marx's *Manifesto* is updated with some later insights of his, of which I shall mention only the cyclical theory of crises and the hidden fetishism of commodity economy which are reworked as the magnificent double passage about the Ogres of Crises (translation lines 219ff.) and about the blind Moloch-God of Profit (lines 242ff.). (As usual in Brecht, there are many Biblical echoes.) Brecht participates in the style of the most effective poems discussed earlier—by Neri, for example—posited "to appear as 'marginal notes' of readings in science" (Marcheschi 17), and indeed in human sciences, according to Marianne Moore's statement in "Poetry":

> ...nor is it valid
> to discriminate against "business documents and
> schoolbooks"....

Brecht always treated with contempt the antagonism of two forms of understanding and learning, the scientific and the artistic one, while insisting that they cannot be confused. However, his *Manifesto* is more ambitious (and therefore longer): for <u>it constitutes an updating of *The Communist Manifesto* for the age in which the bourgeoisie reaches for world wars in response to economic crises of its system.</u>

Thus, the de-automatization of Marx's text implies, first of all, its <u>desacralization,</u> that is, its critical updating and modification for the 1945 situation in Germany and the world. In March 1945 Brecht wrote to Karl Korsch, the heretic Marxist theoretician whom he, for all their disagreements, revered as one of his few teachers, and who was also the most prominent among his friends to enthusiastically encourage Brecht's project and indeed to praise it as a masterpiece (Korsch 54): "I have modified, as cautiously as I could, some matters in Communist Manifesto, I put instead of the immiseration theory the insecurity caused by structural unemployment, etc. Do you think this is correct?" And further about the never fulfilled plans: "I'm now getting to the second chapter of Communist Manifesto. In it [in Brecht's plan to adapt there Engels's *Principles of Communism*, a small "catechism" in question-and-answer form], the classics will answer questions. Should I smuggle in new questions? Which ones?" (GKA 29: 349)

Second, Brecht's estrangement entails the <u>historicization</u> of the earlier text. Even the title, *THE Manifesto,* indicates it is a citation, a second-order reference to a classic: "*The Communist Manifesto* was the report of its authors to the party they were founding. Brecht's hexameters are the report of a report." (Mayer 65). Brecht's usage relates the past to the present, entangling and disentangling them. The poem is a dialectics of history, both rooted in the past and going on. Therefore, Brecht very often substitutes for Marx's past tenses, which he uses in a few beginning lines, the present tense, which makes his report more dramatically immediate and more vivid, though no less historically sweeping: I shall underline in the two examples below (translation lines 15ff. and 51ff.) the explicit switch from past to present:

> You've heard much untruth about it from enemies, from friends
> Much untruth also. This is what the classics <u>say</u>: ....

or:

> Thus came about the age, which now is ending, of the bourgeois:
> A fleeing serf, he became a burgher of the market town,
> Then of the city, & behind its secure walls the guilds
> <u>Flourish</u>. Cloth keeps crossing the walls...

The present tense presents both the validity of insights from Marx's *Manifesto* and yet modifies it with new ways of seeing and the immediacy of direct witnessing. Paradoxically, in terms of German literary theory (derived from Schiller), where the epic is characterized by turning to the past and the drama by turning to the present, Marx is more epical while Brecht is epico-dramatic.

Third, as is proper of poetry, the already vivid but largely analytical argumentation of *The Communist Manifesto* is much more strongly <u>dramatized</u>. This is achieved by various means: syntactic parallelism instead of Marx's logical subordination; further use of personification, most prominent of which is the bourgeoisie, but which encompasses also the Ogre Crises or the God of Profit, and thus builds on the strong fantastic imagery already there in Marx (see Suvin-Angenot for a lengthy discussion); and dynamic action, for ex. by the much more articulated and active Spectre of Communism. The main sections of *The Communist Manifesto* begin with a general thesis, which is then discussed and validated in lengthy analytical passages, and leads to a general programmatic upshot. Brecht uses much of this, but always subsumed under a dramatic story of workers as representatives of a humanity subjected to the growing whirlpool of violence predicated on mysterious deities of Profit, and of a possible remedy to the terrible threat.

Much more could be said, for ex. about his vocabulary or his rhetorical figures such as the hyperbole (cf. Schober 145-65), but I shall close by noting that there is an overriding unnamed figure in the poem: the narrating voice, the poet-narrator. He is an anthropologist, advancing into the jungle of factories and cities with "a hot heart in a cold person" (Brecht, GKA 26: 207); and his rigour arises out of the blood, sweat, and tears of millions through centuries. Here is an example for the foregoing discussions, the first lines of the poem:

> Wars are destroying the world, and the ruins are
>   visibly haunted

By an enormous spectre, not simply born of war.
In peace it could already be sighted, terror to the rulers
But friend to the children of slums. In scanty kitchens
Often it peeps, horrified, angry, into the half-empty
    pots.
Often it waits for the exhausted in front of shipyards
    and mines;
It visits friends in jails, passing without passport.
Even in offices it may be seen and in lecture-rooms
Heard. At times it dons a hat of steel, enters
Huge tanks and flies with deadly bombers. It speaks
    in many
Tongues, in all of them. And in many it holds its
    tongue.

The discourse has shifted into 1945, that is, out of Marx's early nineteenth-century situation of the Holy Alliance in Europe. We are in the modern world of world-wide wars, of tanks, bombers, and ruins, of many languages and repression in most of them; and yet still a world recognizable to Marx, with mines, shipyards, offices, and auditoria, but—most important—with half-empty pots, exhausted workers, slums, and jails. In other passages, the most massive addition to Marx's *Manifesto* is his own crisis theory, actualized through the vivid experiences of the post-1929 crash. This fits into the poem's heroic attempt to create a productive feedback between Marx's formulations and figures (the haunting spectre, the grave-digging, etc.) and Brecht's return to the original magma of the daily experience of millions, which also lay at the distant basis of those formulations. In philosophical language, Brecht's verse actualizes this feedback between deduction and induction, between a framework pre-existing the matter of the poem (*ante rem*) and a verification plus modification within the matter (*in* re). The modification can best be seen in this breathtakingly daring opening, in the best epic tradition of beginning *in medias res*, in the thick of things: "Wars are destroying the world". The class struggle will re-emerge with a vengeance in the latter part of the poem, but to begin with it is here to arrest not simply millennial social injustice but also the by now possible smashing up (*zerschmettern*, a wonderful expression that I failed to fit into the poem's rhythm) of the world. It is my strong conviction that the wars—both the two World Wars and the perhaps 200 "local" wars since 1945—are an essential and indispensable tool of capitalism, without which the bourgeoisie couldn't survive (see the preceding essay in this book), so that the singular paucity of sustained Leftwing theorizing about war borders on death-wish. Perhaps we're just beginning to climb out of this largely self-dug pit after the Gulf and Serbian wars. Brecht can here too serve as our Great Ancestor, who prophetically indicated the way.

5. Poetry as Learning

5.1. Here we may then reopen the question of <u>didactic or propagandistic poems.</u> These terms are more than a little misleading, for to my mind all poetry teaches attitudes or bearings by pregnant example: say, Petrarch's about yearning for the ideal woman, Dante's about the political ethics of his time validated by and as cosmology, Baudelaire's about the beauty proper to the evil megalopolises of the bourgeoisie. This is almost genetically encoded into poetry, which began either as direct accompaniment to collective work (work songs) or as a moment of pause before or after the collective enterprise (hunt, cultivation, war, athletic competition) where the song with music, and most often rhythmic movement (dance), was an organizing tool: it rehearsed the reasons and modalities of action or commented on its outcome. Homer's type of epic is halfway from an oral tribal encyclopedia to a single poet writing for civic group recitals: it is still collective poetry, though by now of the aristocratic class. It takes for its scope a knowable totality: all the techniques, including those of war, of religion, of shipping, and of political oratory, the games, the geographical and cosmic knowledge, the education, the jurisprudence, etc. Its narrative agents are there-fore necessarily types, positive or negative behaviour models: Penelope of the constant wife, Achilles of courage, Thersites of the hateful plebeian.... Later non-choral, class-society verse was then shaped by such a type of occasion in which the single person of the poet was led to reveal his own aspirations and experiences—which however remained exemplary, pretending to collective validity. It remained valid even in the great change when the poetry came to register alienation, as in the lyrics of Catullus or Baudelaire, or Hesiod's epic about our iron age:

> *Eut'an ep'emporien trepsas aesifrona thumon*
> *bouleai de khrea te profugein kai limon aterpea,*
> *deixo de toi metra polufloisboio thalasses*
> (If then you set your imprudent mind to commerce,
> Wishing to flee penury and woeful hunger,
> I'll show you what is proper to the much-roaring sea...
> *Works and Days*, vv. 646-48)

The teaching versifiers were indifferently what Aristotle and his pre-romantic readers would call poets or scientists (or indeed political leaders, such as Isaia or Solon or Mao). This held in spades for the hexameter tradition running from Homer and Hesiod to Lucretius and Virgil. Contravening this immemorial foundation, the bourgeois critical hegemony decided, at some point of etiolated Romanticism, that teaching politics was not the proper pursuit of unreliable verse, and identified all didac-tics with such disallowed "propaganda": "Politisch Lied, ein garstig Lied"—"political poem, a nasty poem," said the great Philistine Goethe (in a political poem).

Yet in all significant case, such as the names just mentioned, such versifiers or poets were never simply followers of a doctrine, rather they were its shapers or reshapers (which is poetically speaking the same). They were the opposite of facile moral-izers: creators who went in for a vision of the essence of matters, cognizers. Brecht's voice is one of a teacher, no doubt, but of a peculiar one: a Socratic pedagogic facilitator, whose overriding maxim was that the learner is more important than the lesson. In other words: the Law is here for Humanity, not vice versa; the lesson is not only to be incarnated into but also modified by the Brechtian "worker-readers," just as the versifying voice has transubstantiated and modified the original *Manifesto*. This is the voice of a critical intellectual, in a Gramscian sense organic to the plebeian movement; in Brechtian terms we could call this poem the voice of an "intellectual-reader" who has found some answers reading Marx, and repeats them faithfully, that is: reworking them for the situation of mid-twentieth century.

5.2. Somewhere in his "poetics" *Ad Pisones*, Horace discusses whether the tragic poets who take their arguments from Homer are really poets, that is, creative writers. His answer is that the epic events of Homer will be transmogrified into the tragic effects of a good tragedian if he refrains from idle paraphrase and instead of being a servile imitator be a true "translator," who takes the Homeric characters and supplies them with new speeches and actions. In Book 3 of his *Scienza nuova*, Vico comments on this passage that such excellent tragedians "will be new poets in the style of Homer" (320). Vico argues else-where that "all ancient Roman law was a serious poem" or *carmen* (390), a binding social incantation (Valéry's *charme*). Thus Brecht can be called a new serious poet in the style of Marx.

For analytical convenience, we can separate his reworking into two aspects: as to the <u>what</u>, lessons that have intervened between 1848 and 1945, and in particular Marx's later work on capitalist economics and some lessons of Leninism, born and reborn out of the World Wars; as to the <u>how</u>, the new cogni-tive tool of Lucretian narrative poetry. (Of course, I have been arguing that how and what are in any corporeal reality, including very much the corporeal reality of practicing poetry or poetic practice, consubstantial.) From various other works of Brecht, it can be inferred he considered this tool to be at least equivalent, and possibly superior, to systematic philosophical discourse, which may be a good weapon but is prone to doctrinal congealment (Brecht likened it to a condensed snowball, which shouldn't be kept in one's pocket too long). It was again Valéry who, in his discussion of poetry, observed that when a lion consumes mutton it turns into lion-flesh. Unfortunately, he hasn't given us a metaphor as to what happens when a lion cannibalizes another lion from long ago. At any rate, Marx's substance is transmuted in Brecht, as Brecht's ought to be in the reader-lamb facing any new situation—keeping however unchanged and constant the determining horizon of class liberation, and the vector of desire toward it.

Brecht's poem was not finished, but it happens to end—rephrasing the end of Part 1 of Marx's—with what I see as a sufficient ending. It answers the initial, catalyzing violence of the bourgeois world wars of each against each with a healing levelling of the violent class structure:

> ...the proletarians, lowest
> Level of society must, in order to rise, smash
> Into pieces the whole social structure with all its upper
>   levels.
> The proletariat can only throw off its special class
> Servitude by throwing off the servitude of all.

While today we may have to redefine what we mean by the proletariat, I believe at the beginning of twenty-first century, amid still worse wars already upon us, we still have to absorb—and no doubt transmute—this end.

Works Cited

This list does not pretend to give an overview of the secondary literature on *Das Manifest*. A number of pioneering works, such as Spaethling 1962, Witzmann 1964, Rösler 1975, and

Ter-Nedden 1976, have for the purposes of this subject-matter been superseded by later research. This work of Brecht's is also briefly mentioned in some surveys of his work, for ex. by Esslin, Ewen and K.-D. Müller.

Brecht, Bertolt. *Werke.* Grosse Kommentierte Berliner und Frankfurter Ausgabe. Suhrkamp & Aufbau V., 1988-2000 [GKA].

Bunge, Hans-Joachim. "*Das Manifest* von Bertolt Brecht." *Sinn und Form* 15.2-3 (1963): 184-203.

—-[und Hanns Eisler]. *Fragen Sie mehr über Brecht.* München: Rogner & Bernhard, 1970.

Feuchtwanger, Lion. "Bertolt Brecht." *Sinn und Form,* Zweites Sonderheft Bertolt Brecht (1957): 103-08.

—-. "Die Zusammenarbeit der Dichter." *Berliner Zeitung* no. 301 of Dec. 25, 1958 (letter to Bunge).

Harding, D.W. *Words into Rhythm.* Cambridge: Cambridge UP, 1976.

Hartinger, Christel. *Bertolt Brecht—das Gedicht nach Krieg und Wiederkehr.* [Berlin]: Brecht-Zentrum der DDR, 1982.

[Hesiod. *Erga kai hemerai.*] Esiodo. *Le opere e i giorni* [bilingual]. Milano: Rizzoli, 1998.

Knopf, Jan. *Brecht Handbuch: Lyrik, Prosa, Schriften.* Stuttgart: Metzler, 1984.

Korsch, Karl. "Antwort an bb." *Alternative* 8.41 (1965): 54-57.

Marcheschi, Daniela. "Giampiero Neri o della coesistenza," in S. Aman ed., *Memoria, mimetismo e informazione in "Teatro Naturale" di Giampiero Neri.* Milano: Otto/Novecento, 1999, 13-28.

Mayer, Hans. *Bertolt Brecht und die Tradition.* Pfullingen: Neske, 1961.

Mittenzwei, Werner. *Brechts Verhältnis zur Tradition.* Berlin: Akademie-V., 1972.

Schober, Rita. "Brechts Umschrift des Kommunistischen Manifests," in her *Vom Sinn oder Unsinn der Literaturwissenschaft.* Leipzig: Mitteldeutscher V, 1988, 126-80.

Serres, Michel. *La Naissance de la physique dans le texte de Lucrèce*. Paris: Minuit, 1977.

Suvin, Darko. "Haltung," entry in *Historisch-kritisches Wörterbuch des Marxismus*, Vol. 5. Hamburg: Argument, 2002, col. 1134-42.

—-, with Marc Angenot. "L'aggirarsi degli spettri. Metafore e demifisticazioni, ovvero l'implicito del manifesto," in M. Galletti ed., *Le soglie del fantastico*. Roma: Lithos, 1997, 129-66.

Vico, Giambattista. *The New Science....* Transl. T.G. Bergin and M.H. Frisch. Ithaca NY: Cornell UP, 1988.

Wizisla, Erdmut, ed. *"...und mein Werk ist der Abgesang des Jahrtausends".* Catalog of the exhibition *1898—Bertolt Brecht—1998*. Berlin: Akademie der Künste, 1998.

W[ormell], D.E.W. "Lucretius," in *The Penguin Companion to Classical...Literature*. Eds. D.M. Lang and D.R. Dudley. New York: McGraw-Hill, 1969, 109-10.

5. TO LAPUTA AND BACK: A MISSING CHAPTER OF *GULLIVER'S TRAVELS* (2003)[28]

—To the memory of Edward Said, citizen-scholar—

eis érgon d'oudèn gignómenon blépete...
astoísin d'oúpo pâsin hadeîn dúnamai.
[You do not see the things which are being born...
But I know, I cannot please equally all.]

Hellenic elegiac poet

0. Leaving the Port

I'm especially pleased to give this keynote speech to the Associazione Italiana degli Anglisti, though I ask your forgiveness for being the bearer of bad news and I hope not to meet their frequent fate of lapidation. If you honoured me by inviting to tell you what might be the most useful thing to ponder today, I'm bound to be sincere with you, wherever this may lead.

---

28. My thanks go to Carlo Pagetti and Oriana Palusci, as always my guardian angels in Italian Anglistics, and Patrick Parrinder, who fulfills the same function in UK English Studies; and for particular comments on drafts to Carla Dente, Mario Domenichelli, Alessandro Fambrini, Alba Graziano, Daniela Guardamagna, Daniela Marcheschi, Richard Ohmann, Marcello Pagnini, Salvatore Proietti, Paola Pugliatti, Brigitte Scheer-Schätzler, and Sara Soncini; they gave me welcome critiques but are not even faintly responsible for my opinions.

At the AIA Conference of 1999, Professor Agostino Lombardo said: "A world of multinationals...and unscrupulous competition from which there is no escape surrounds us every day,...all the more terrible and insidious because disguised by the convenience and comfort it offers" (137), and he offered literature as "the antidote to the sway of economy" (135). Alas, my central message is that our rulers have in practice destroyed the wall that our discipline wrongly thought was existing between culture and political economy, and we better draw the consequences. And yet in a way I'm also ending with good news, for I believe that in certain circumstances we intellectuals can make an important difference, that there is an escape—albeit not the individual one we believed in.

1. Entering Laputa in the Winter of Our Discontent: Presuppositions Shaping Our Lives

1.1. Through the Spy-Glass

You'd surely like me to speak to our proper professional concerns such as methodologies and texts, perhaps in areas where I can claim some competence such as Drama or Utopian and Science Fiction, and I too would have liked this. But in this invasive world of late aggressive capitalism without a human face, what we are allowed or denied to teach by its politicians, what monies we are given or refused for research, intervenes into our daily lives in unprecedented, capillary ways. Our supposed ivory tower was anyway for most of us at best a tolerably sturdy wooden lean-to, and is now fast becoming a version of Kingston, Jamaica: corrugated tin shacks (or in the Italian version run-down and drafty stone palaces) with semi-employed wage-slaves broiling in the polluted heat. Thus we have to wake up and look at what is happening to us, our work, our pupils, and our profession with the sober eyes that Marx thought would result from the intervention of the bourgeoisie into world history. Hermeneutics or theory in general can be bracketed out in periods of long-lasting general consensus, but thank god or alas we don't live in such periods, nor have we within living memory. Therefore it behooves us to look at how we can understand what we think we understand (that is, at epistemology) and only then at what we can, with this type of tool, understand of any particular entity (say, text). I shall, accordingly, have three sections in my submission to you: the first about the presuppositions shaping our lives as citizens and intellectuals, the second about some problems of literary theory and in particular English Studies, and the third about some initial orientations how we might approach our quite serious problems.

A useful or weighty cognition in the last 30 years, among loads of (to put it politely) uselessly weak ones, has been to figure into any statement the enunciator's own <u>situation</u> and subject-position. The concept of situation lends itself to being grasped both as a static condition—itself product and precondition for what and who is situated—and as a dynamic process. It also implies, perhaps more incisively than the subject and its position or mini-situation, the <u>limits</u> as well as the <u>changeability</u> inherent in that concept: situations change by both internal and external pressures, and we change within, with, and because of them. The limits to any situation define and further, but at some point also act as restraints for, what is situated. As Said told us twenty years ago, "...worldliness, circumstantiality, the text's status as an event having sensuous particularity as well as historical contingency are...an infrangible part of its capacity for conveying and producing meaning. This means that a text has a specific situation, placing restraints upon the...interpretation...." (39). Now of course, a fictional text is distinguished from a leading article by its peculiar ability to function also, though usually in different ways, in other specific situations; as Borges spelled out for us, the same arrangement of words will not produce the same novel in the context of Cervantes's 17th and Pierre Ménard's 19th Century, since the readers' situation in a different world will slyly infiltrate every pore of the reading. The text is not a windowless monad but a traffic between Aristotle's "sequence of events" and the readers' always already begun interpretation. This necessarily implies the triad Situation-Stance-Horizon. In order to make sense of our long-duration situation, I shall foreground two major factors.

The first is the political and technological <u>multiplication of worlds at the disposal of our experience</u>. A whole literary genre foregrounding the existence of Possible Worlds sprang up as Science Fiction, at its best fusing delight with articulations verifying some such possibilities. As Erich Auerbach put it, since roughly 1917 we have been "participating in a practical seminar on world history" (11), so that "...we live the experience of historical multiplicity" (5). Beginning to figure in my personal situation insofar it may be of use to you, let me adduce an example: My grandparents lived the best part of their lives as loyal subjects within the south-western part of the Habsburg empire. My father took his spouse for their bridal travel to the Italian lakes, and he visited once London (much to his confusion), but his spiritual home was between Belgrade and Frankfurt, with its center still in a kind of ideally purified Vienna where he had studied, in spite of the fact that he became a doctor in Tito's partizans and an active participant in socialist Yugoslavia. I myself was the first family member to have lived for periods longer than one year, and in a way been at home, in Zagreb, Bari, London, Cambridge, New York-New Haven, Paris, Berlin, Rome, Tokyo, and now Lucca, as well as to have been led to theorize my parents' radical doubts about both really existing capitalism and really existing Stalinism. Finally, my grandparents already used the railway, and two of them were taken in a cattle car to be gassed in a Nazi lager; whereas I read a paper on the first Moon landing, at the Trieste SF Film Festival, the day after a good part of the world saw it on TV.

The second factor shaping our situation is the bending of all technological and other cultural innovations that impinge on everyday life and culture to the purposes of <u>capitalism as a totalizing system</u>. Ever since Gramsci, and then Raymond

Williams and the Birmingham School—or maybe since Matthew Arnold—we ought to have understood that "the real depth in the strength of the Modern Western State is the strength and depth of its culture and...[the] heterogeneous plurality [in the culture]" (Said 172). "Production of culture is production of everyday life, without which your economic system cannot implant and expand itself" (Jameson, "Notes" 67): Hobsbawm calculates that two thirds of the GNP in the societies of the capitalist North today derive from the "mental" labour of the "new middle classes," those who do not employ other people, and whose core is constituted by intellectuals, largely university graduates. Ohmann's classical book about the role of English, albeit in America, notes that "Knowledge (technical, scientific, managerial) is accountable, not only for the material triumphs of that [capitalist, DS] system, but for the all-encompassing control it has over the way we live..." (*English* 273). Through copyright and patent legislation, often through piratic plunder of non-patented knowledge, it is being more and more subsumed under exploitable property (cf. already Ohmann, *English* 316-25 and his *Politics*). We live in a "knowledge society": alas, one in which useful and perniciously fake knowledge are closely inter-twined. Knowledge as use-value for living is being evicted by knowledge as quantifiable exchange-value for profits, with its logical end in "smart" bombs for mass killings.

Therefore, our civic concerns are no longer something we may do as it were privately: indeed, I believe that we can only understand what our profession is if we understand how and why it is being shaped by given forces on a national and inter-national level. In the epistemological optic I propose to you, modestly, Suvin's First Law on Cognition: The epistemological and the political intertwine (say, as a double helix—cf. Suvin „On Cognition," and Mohanty 110 and passim). Those who do not put an explicitly defensible civic cognition at the heart of their professional cognition at best adopt the dominant episte-mology of when they were students, and at worst adapt it to the new epistemology of what Kipling might have called the economico-political Powers-That-Be.

This reminds me of an apocryphal anecdote in which Shklovsky said to Trotsky: "As a literary critic, I'm not interested in war." To which Trotsky responded: "But war is interested in you."

My first conclusion: we cannot escape being involved in the politics and economics of knowledge. Like Gulliver, in Laputa.

1.2. Mirror, Mirror on Laputa Wall

Let me then talk first about our situation in general as intellectuals in Post-Fordism, and second as members of de facto English Studies departments (whatever they may call themselves today).

What is our long-duration situation? It is one where capitalism has in quicker tempos than ever before created entire social classes, only to render them useless and disposable soon after. Both Fordism with its "hard" technology (crucially that associated with mass car transport), and Post-Fordism with its "soft" technology (crucially computer technology and biotechnology) needed more "software" or "human engineering" people than before. One of the twentieth century's earmarks was therefore the enormous multiplication and enormous institutionalization or collectivization of the earlier independent artisan and small entrepreneur—and one such institution is the school, in particular the university. The growth in our numbers culminated during the Fordist Welfare State, in both its Leninist and Keynesian variants; this growth has been stopped and reversed since the 1970s, with a tendency of back toward small artisan-entrepreneurs but without the economic independence they might have had in Dickens's time. We are back at computerized Gradgrinds, only the taboos have shifted from the sexual to the political totem-field. To the reserve army of workers has now been adjoined the second reserve army of intellectuals and indeed middle managers.

It follows that we exist in a deeply contradictory situation, impacted in the sense a split tooth is impacted. We are the name-givers of categories and alternatives; yet we have in the 20th Century been largely complicitous in the creation of "the masses"—an alienated consumer-blob out there analogous to the dispossessed producers stripped of self-determination and expertise, only in relation to which can there be cultural and financial elites. We are essential to the policing of workers and learners, but we are ourselves workers and learners. On the one hand, as Marx famously chided, "the bourgeoisie has stripped of its halo every occupation hitherto honoured and looked up to with reverent awe. It has turned the physician, the lawyer, the priest, the poet, the scientist, into its paid wage-labourers." On the other hand, the constitution of intellectuals into professions is impossible without a measure of autonomy, of corporative self-government which allows control over one's classes or artefacts. This constitution was enabled by the fact that salaried men and women are "the assistants of authority" (Mills 74), but no authority can abide without our assistance. Henri Lefebvre concluded that "[The middle class] individuals live or attempt to live an elite life, evading through 'culture,' while their knowledge serves capitalism.... They live a double life...in a *jouissance* half real and half illusionary." (32-33) Our professionalization secured for the best paid of us sufficient income to turn high wage into minuscule capital: but even the poorest intellectual participates in privilege through her "educational capital." We are essential to the production of new knowledge and ideology, but we are totally kept out of the strategic decisions about universities or dissemination of artefacts. The list of such variants to Dr. Dolittle's two-headed Pushme-Pullyou beast, between self-management and wage servitude, could be extended indefinitely.

The ever more brutal conflicts of the capitalist age have created a huge sociopolitical turbulence in which our lives are lived. At the latest since the World Wars, we have had to learn the lesson of what Gayatri Spivak nicely calls "an acknowledgement of epistemic fallibility" (18): nobody is monolithically fit for the angel with a flaming sword at the exit and entry of Eden— neither our rulers nor those of us who are their critics. Epistemic fallibility is a translation into Greco-Latin of what Nietzsche announced to us 125 years ago as the Death of God. The trouble with many of us is that we behave as a symmetrical inverse of most Christians: we believe in the Death of God on our Sunday, the day we make official ideological commitments to tolerance, but we all too often proceed based on 19th-Century episte- mology of certitude during the six days we teach and research; most prominently, so do all the orthodox Post-Modernists who proclaim the new godhead of absolute relativism. Let me say this with the Nietzsche you won't find cited in De Man: "...to see differently, to <u>want</u> to see differently, is no small discipline and preparation of the intellect for its future 'objectivity'—under- stood...as the ability <u>to control</u> one's Pro and Con and to dispose of them, so that one knows how to employ a <u>variety</u> of perspec- tives and affective interpretations in the service of knowledge" (555). This means to me: for any one precise interest, purpose or stance there <u>IS</u> an "objective"—or better, pertinent and useful, albeit even then most probable rather then infallible—inter- pretation of a text, and indeed of a necessary action; for other interests or situations, which enforce a different context of the hermeneutic circle, there are other most probable interpreta- tions. They ought to be themselves evaluated according to our stance toward the situation which shaped them; and a reason- able variety of interpretations compatible with, or at least inter- esting for, one's own interpretation should be held in mind when propounding it. If you'd allow me, I'd like to call these shifting strategic totalities a strong historicising thought.

We have come up hard against the limits of usefulness of relativism, including what partakes of relativism in the no doubt welcome focus on otherness. Otherness becomes an alibi for exoticism and evasion unless it is, first, collective and not only individual, and second, a boomerang returning to help us see ourselves in a different light, as the other of the Others, and often at that as the powerful other (say the Europeans) against the powerless, humiliated and exploited Others (say the "extra-communitarians" of Africa and Asia drowning off our shores or inside our society). This return of the repressed has a technical name inside epistemological theory, it is first the Russian Formalist and then more completely the Brechtian effect or device of making things strange (*V-Effekt*). I wish to speak here, on the traces of Elaine Scarry, of beauty as a kind of Brechtian estrangement-effect alerting us to aliveness.

Scarry argues that "one's daily unmindfulness of the aliveness of others is temporarily interrupted in the presence of a beautiful person, alerting us to the requirements placed on us by the aliveness of all persons, and the same may take place in the presence of a beautiful bird, mammal, fish, plant." We may take this as the extension of the epistemological argument for art by Viktor Shklovsky in 1917, "Poetry is what makes the stone stony": "Beauty seems to place requirements on us," continues Scarry optimistically, "for attending on the aliveness...of our world, and for entering into its protection" (90)—in the double or biunivocal sense of being protected by beauty and in return protecting it. If we do so, we are then tacitly entering into a relationship of solidarity, an overarching collocation in a new field of force, a pact, the root of which, Scarry reminds us, is the same as the root of *pax, pacis* (92): peace in the sense of dynamic contentment. Beauty presents us with the possibility of a new compact, which may be actualized if we learn to truly see it and let it change us in the process of being changed by us. It is a new covenant or contract for enhancing life with the beautiful object of our sight and feeling. Or, more cautiously, perhaps we better say beauty presents us with the possibility of a new compact, which may be actualized if our perception de-alienates us and we learn to truly see it and let it change us in the process of being changed by us. Such a life-furthering potlatch competition is best known to us, of course, from the experience of love, and is inconceivable to the capitalist squeezing out the juices from other people and beings, where production for profit is diametrically opposed to creation.

This would then be an attempted undoing of what Marx called alienation of labour, Lukács reification by the imperialist world, and Weber disenchantment by bureaucratic rationalism. It is most deeply personal and yet in the same breath necessarily distributive; it partakes of the supreme civic virtue of justice—"fair and free" (this phrase is, alas, glossed by the OED as "obsolete or archaic," last noted while qualifying a city in Shelley's *Cenci).* Scarry fortunately argues her case by way of the specifically English semantic cluster around the term "fair," whose original meaning is "beautiful" or "fit" (91-92). Let me add further OED instances to her argument: said of conduct, actions, arguments or persons, "fair" means "free from injustice" as in "fair and square," "a fair wage"; the *Pall Mall Gazette* in 1886 defines "fair houses" as "firms where the rules of the Union are followed" (671/562). "Fair play" partakes perhaps most clearly of equity, in the most general sense it means "equitable conditions of actions," and so does "a fair field (and no favour)." "Fair" is also both an index and a factor of civilizing ways where oppositions may be settled without violence, as in "fair means [not] foul" (OED 672/562). The very frequent fair vs. foul opposition shows how considerations of beauty and justice fuse in an as it were cosmic chord where the personal is the political, the untuning of which means chaos—as we know best from the witches' ditty in *Macbeth.* Beauty's deeply personal and necessarily distributive aspects meld in a "cognitive event that affirms the equality of aliveness...an inclusive affirmation of the ongoingness of existence, and of one's own responsibility for the continuity of existence" (Scarry 92).

I'd like to conclude this first section by suggesting that we must strictly differentiate the sociological from the axiological definition of intellectual, even at the cost of having our axiological group encompass a single-digit percentage of the sociological one (maybe 3%, let's say optimistically?). The best sociological definition I found is by Wright Mills: intellectuals are people who "produce, distribute and preserve distinct forms of consciousness" (142)—images and/or concepts. But it seems to me a <u>use-value or axiological</u> definition would be something on the order of: "people who interpret the past and the ongoing flow of cultural production as articulations of a beauty that keeps alive the necessity of justice." This is not the only way to arrive at justice: most rebels have perhaps arrived at it from what Brecht called the socially very productive passion of indignation, but it seems to me <u>our</u> privileged professional-cum-civic way, and incidentally also the most delightful one. And so I propose to you, again as modestly as I can, <u>Suvin's Second Law of Cognition: Whoever is not fruitfully alienated from our murderous norms and their enforcers is in our historical epoch to that degree not a creative intellectual</u>.

2. Visiting the Word-Machine:
Some Aporias of Literary and English Studies

2.1. The Populace and the Women
Doubt the Project-Makers

How does this look in the field of literary and cultural studies? To my mind it is centrally a matter of how the necessary specialization was handled—that is, in what relationship it stood to ongoing history and to what constituency it spoke.

Toward the end of the Weimar period, Walter Benjamin inveighed against separating literary history from general history and against its celebration of "the eternal values" of "word art". He identified as the "seven heads of this hydra of academic esthetics: creativity, empathy, transcending the moment, re-creation, identification, illusion, and art appreciation" (286). His essay ends in the famous call: "The point is not to present the written works in the context of their time, but to present in the time that they arose the time that is cognizing them—our time. In that way literature becomes a tool of history..." (290). In optimal criticism "the cognitive use of books would be identical with their literary 'evaluation'" (295). The crisis of literary studies was to him part of a general crisis of *Bildung* (education or acculturation) out of synch with the actual production and reception of books. This time of crisis, roughly the two decades from 1917 on, was the most acute moment of civilizational discomfort prior to the 1990s, except that we lack their hopeful aspect and therefore ought to hearken back to it. At the time, similar pioneering conclusions were arrived at by Brecht's reflections on the function of art (for example the notion of copyright) arising out of his court case about *The Threepenny Movie*, as well as by Gramsci writing in prison.

However, such dissident and radical European origins of literary and cultural theory, ranging from Paris-Berlin Dadaism and Surrealism to Russian Futurism, Formalism, and Bakhtinian dialogism, were after the two World Wars buried under a rigid separation of academic specialties. I shall return to this when I speak of English Studies, but wish to note here one central matter. For all its enrichments, the upshot of critical innovations in France and the USA was that literary theory had by the late 70s—at the time of the ascent of Reaganism, increased militarism, and a massive turn to the Right—"retreated into the labyrinth of 'textuality'," purged of anything worldly—that is, purged of history. The quintessential work of literary art, the poem, became "an urn or icon..., a spatial figure rather than a temporal process" (Eagleton 48). Criticism had thereby updated the doctrine of old-fashioned German *Geisteswissenschaft*, with its sharp ontological division between the reality of art and the reality of life. <u>Professionally</u>, this precluded an understanding of the texts' full import, since "...texts are worldly, to some degree they are events, ...a part of the social world, and of course of the historical moment in which they are located and interpreted"; indeed, "The realities of power and authority—as well as the resistances offered by men, women, and social movements...— are the realities that make texts possible, that deliver them to their readers." (Said 3-5) Surely there were countervailing tendencies, in the work of such radicals as Said and Jameson who Americanized the great European dissident tradition, in non-separatist Feminism or in the semi-demi Marxism without class conflicts of New Historicism, but on the whole the US packaging of French Post-Structuralism was a disaster of major proportions, as anybody who has taught graduate classes on that continent from the 1980s on can testify. It succumbed to "the extraordinarily Laputan idea that...everything can be regarded [only] as a text" (Said 173).

Most important, the retreat into esotericism and poorly masked despair in the bulk of literary criticism after the mid-1970s meant <u>civically</u> that it "retreated from <u>its constituency, the citizens of modern society</u> [underline DS], who have been left to the hands of 'free' market forces, multinational corporations, the manipulators of consumer appetites" (Said 4; cf. also Lombardo). Given the US global cultural hegemony, this was exported and dumped into the United Kingdom, in spite of the splendid tradition of Raymond Williams, Stuart Hall, and many others. Indeed the England of Thatcherism could claim to have pioneered the Post-Fordist turn to the Right.

2.2. Our Word-Machine: Building and Operating It

In order to test this, I now focus on English Studies. I wish to draw some brief lessons from its well-travelled history and to make a few proposals to you how to think further about its present state.

<u>2.21. Some History</u>: English was taught in grammar schools since Elizabethan times, and then in dissenting academies and training colleges. What we could call with Michael "secular English literature" (379) or belles lettres entered into it slowly, mainly as poetry, fables or proverbs, with some snatches of prose and rarely *Robinson Crusoe* or *Gulliver's Travels*. Within such secular matter, school anthologies at end of 18th Century gave pride of place to Pope, Thompson and Cowper; after the Romantic impact, Shakespeare advanced from fourth to first

place and Milton was rediscovered, while education in schools through drama also started (cf. Michael 198, 236, 269, and 382, and Parrinder). It is only in mid-19th Century that history of literature entered this teaching (Michael 381). A second impulse for university English studies came from the semi-colony of Scotland, which contributed the notion of "British literature," and from India. In the latter subcontinent, the 1835 English Education Act made English the medium of instruction and required the study of English literature. It turned the acculturation into bourgeois values of the Raj's Indian subjects from the frontal onslaught of Christian proselytizing to an enablement in the language of the conquerors and their official values (cf. Viswanathan). "The idea that the study of English literature was a 'civilising force'...brought the subject back to Britain" (Eaglestone 10-11) to educate the "British savages": the petty bourgeois, city poor, and above all the workers (cf. Eagleton 27). There it met the burgeoning Mechanics' Institutes and other working-class self-help institutions, which used heavily Shelley's *Queen Mab*, Shakespeare, and non-fictional writings (cf. Altick, and Suvin, *Victorian* 271 and 294-5). The status of such English was of course not comparable to the Classics taught at Oxbridge, but it was steadily rising through the extension of franchise, mass literacy, and arguments such as Arnold's *Culture and Anarchy* (1869).

The introduction of studying English/British literature can thus be seen not only as lying "in many different soils" (Michael 135) but centrally as a tug-of-war between the contending liberatory interests for self-help and understanding from below and the co-optation from above, as in the case of voting franchise and literacy. The university change from studying English language to stressing literature came about after World War I and the Russian Revolution, that is, with the obvious entry of the lower classes into political confrontations. We know perhaps better the young Tillyard's and Richards's program for English literature in Cambridge after 1917, but it became feasible and extensive only after the 1921 Newbolt Report to the British government.

The Report pleaded for English literature to become "[an education that] would form a new element of national unity, linking together the mental life of all classes [underline DS], experiences which have hitherto been the privilege of a limited section" (para. 10). It claimed that English, as a subject and a method, was the only basis possible for a "universal, reasonable, and liberal" national education (para. 57). The implementation of this report between the two World Wars led to the instauration of the remarkable hegemony English, and English literature in particular, speedily achieved within humanities, at the expense of classics and religion.

Already in Arnold our best selves "carry us beyond the ideas and wishes of the class to which we belong" (95). English literature became a substitute humanist religion (cf. Eagleton 22-23), with all the paraphernalia of sects, acolytes, and the esoteric/exoteric divide. But the Newbolt Report advanced from Arnold's cultural classes with a minority of the elect to an inclusive national "democracy," bridging the dangerous gulf between "the mind of the poet, and that of a young wage-earner" (para. 148). Their common denominator was "the contemplative individual self,...a view equivalent in the literary sphere to...possessive individualism in the social realm" (Eagleton 196-97). In Brian Doyle's adamant conclusion, "The major development between two World Wars was the establishment of English studies as a bulwark against, rather than force for social change and cultural innovation" in the guise of professional scholarship which applied a model of masculine gentleman to colleagues and authors (*English* 70-71, underline DS). We may wish to nuance this a bit and call English Studies perhaps a force for careful co-optation of the non-ruling population through change and innovation that updated this model but stayed within it (for example the addition by the somewhat maverick Leavisites of the hotly contested D.H. Lawrence and T.S. Eliot to the teachable canon or "great tradition"). Nonetheless "literary study both in the UK and in the USA developed during the 1930s as a means to deflect the contemporary challenge of Marxism" (Easthope

7). I can report to you that when I was in the 1950s studying in Bristol under L.C. Knights, and wrote my first paper for him on the medieval Robin Hood play-fragments, he politely looked askance at my Marxist approach, assuring me that *Scrutiny* had demolished that in the 1930s...

The profession's model of a masculine gentleman implied what I would call, taking off from Norman O. Brown's characterization of Swift (612), the domestication of the tigers of English literature. In particular it implies: first, the exclusion of many women, and the housebreaking of those that could not be excluded, for to my mind Austen is at least a lynx and Emily Brontë surely a full-fledged panther. Second, the exclusion of popular culture and lower classes as well as lower bodily functions: much of Swift was deplored, More and Morris's utopias banished into political science, and it was the end of the 20th Century before the British Council asked me to write a report on the two existing M.A. programs in Science Fiction in the U.K. (both now on their last legs, in spite of my recommendations). Third, the downgrading and/or co-optation of writers who were rebels, or from the lower classes, or "Celts" as they are nowadays called: Blake did not make Palgrave's *Golden Treasury*, hugely popular until today; J.S. Mill was part of Eng. Lit. but Adam Smith, who wrote about such uncouth things as production, was not; Milton's *Areopagitica* was readmitted into the great tradition but Shelley's *Mask of Anarchy* was not; Byron was a minor womanizer; poor Oscar Wilde was tolerated as a court fool but not as an accuser; Shaw, the accuser, had to play the fool all his life; and so on. Fourth, the exclusions concerned all the domains that a Victorian gentleman would consider infra dig: reconciliatory politics of the Walter Scott type were OK, but not Swift's defence of Ireland or Wollstonecraft's rights of women or Morris's revolution, however peaceful; sciences, as C.P Snow reminded us causing a huge stir, were definitely ungentlemanly, even if they were of as huge epistemological significance as the laws of thermodynamics. Finally, work, what most readers and even writers do most of their waking time, was woefully under-represented, not only by critical exclusion but in the actual fiction. I must sorrowfully conclude with Eagleton that "[l]iberal humanism is a suburban moral ideology, limited in practice to largely interpersonal matters....stronger on adultery than on armaments..." (207).

2.22. Some Lineaments of the Present: In the mid-1970s, just before the onset of The Great Reaction, Richard Ohmann concluded his book *English in America* by what Said (229) will call admiringly in the '80s a devastating observation:

> In English departments I see a moderately successful effort by professors to obtain some benefits of capitalism while avoiding its risks and, yet, a reluctance to acknowledge any link between how we do our work and the way the larger society is run. Always[, in] our talk about literature and teaching...[w]e either look too narrowly at the givens of daily work or cast our eyes upward to the transcendent realm of timeless human values and the healing force of literary culture. (304)

Let me try to begin updating this for another continent and the more dire times in which we find ourselves.

The astonishing success of the discipline of national literatures, and English Lit. in particular, as the central arts subject within the Keynesian or Welfare State, resulted in a constant demand for undergraduate places—quadrupled in the UK in the thirty years after the 1940s—and career opportunities (Doyle, *English* 121). The price paid for it was a boosting of national cohesion on Newboltian lines and a retreat into innocuous specialization. Doyle's book on "Englishness" registers that the *TLS* 1972 survey into the state of English, while evidencing a loss of faith in its power to exert a civilizing influence, also found a firm belief in "an unchanging literary essence which is taken to inhere within [some canonic] selection of English texts" (*English* 123). The supposedly greater "flexibility" being introduced by some new methodologies did not lead the new "pluralist consensus," that treated English as "high culture" (cf. the Kingman Committee in 1988 and Doyle, *English* 136), to articulate a clear set of aims and principles for it. Yet at the latest since the 1981 Cambridge crisis about "structuralism," which showed that the Right was on the offensive demanding "submission to greatness" embodied in the canon as against weird Frenchie pluralism (Doyle, *English* 130-32), the lack of a clear rationale for the existence of English—say its value for a critical public opinion in civil society—meant leaving it naked unto its enemies should the tacit contract with our financial and legal bosses change.

This is exactly what happened in the last quarter century, as a gathering landslide well described by Docherty: his 1999 book *Criticism and Modernity*, he wrote, was penned partly from rage at the government of the day, and its slogan "how can you justify your existence and your privileges?" (2) As we know, this has become the prayer-mill mantra we unceasingly hear from all governments between Thatcher-Reagan and Blair-D'Alema-Berlusconi, including the so-called Left, following docilely if a little bit less openly and less rapidly. However hypo-critical when orated by people putting billions into bombing poorer nations back into the Stone Age, the question is, to my mind, <u>very</u> well put, and it behooves us to think how to answer it. Savage capitalism is going about its proper business, having shed the pretence of caring for culture, useful during the Cold War, along with other sops to not strictly, hugely, and immedi-ately profitable activities. What would going about <u>our</u> proper business, not split between civic and professional interests, mean?

One answer is of course to transform literary into cultural studies. I shall not usurp the role of the other keynote speaker slated to deal with cultural studies, but only remark that as most Marxists, "in culture and scholarship I am often in reasonable sympathy with conservative attitudes" (Said 22), if they are truly such—in Swift or in Shakespeare or in Aeschylus—and not liberalism of a past century. I still believe there is a humanizing and liberating factor, not found elsewhere, in narration, with its agents, chronotopes, and the choices articulated therein (and I see poems and plays as special cases of narration). This is conveyed in the artefacts' form: "A little Formalism turns one away from History...a lot brings one back to it" (Barthes, quoted in Easthope 177). But as a materialist I also believe that we should follow and understand (or even stand under) our material. This means, to begin with, two things: First, that narrations in Science Fiction, comics, films or soap-operas also exist and must be understood—indeed, they are what most people really attend to when trafficking with culture. Second, as shown magisterially by Williams's *The Country and the City*, that the principal narrative relationships cannot be fully understood without all the other relationships explicit or implicit in the narration—and principally those dealing with acquisition, appropriation, and power. Thus my ideal image of literary and cultural studies would be that of two only partially overlapping but mutually fully illuminating circles.

The other answer is to divide Eng. Lit. into Scottish, Welsh, English proper (and possibly Ulster, Manx, and Channel Island?) literature. You will not expect from somebody who has been offered Croatian citizenship, while his wife was refused it as not being ethnically pure enough, to say too much about this. I am in favour of such self-determination of nations as will foster liberation rather than ethnic cleansing. I am in favour of noting the strong element of "upper-class, imperialist, metropolitan discourse" (Crawford 11; cf. also Doyle "Hidden") in English literature, on condition of not forgetting the plebeian and anti-imperialist counter-discourses (cf. Lucas 39, Eaglestone 107-12). I fully agree, against the chauvinist fantasies of Leavis and Co., that there is no fixed, unchanging entity called Englishness, and that his Englishness "replaces the ethical regard for others within the community with an ethnic regard for self-identification" (Docherty 244). But then, not only is there also no unchanging entity called Scottishness, Irishness or Welshness, but I further believe there do exist historically shifting and multiple strategic totalities, and I see no difficulty in recognizing an Englishness of the Lockean upper-class, based on property, and another of the radical Romantic poets, based on personality untrammelled by State and upper-class pieties. There is little Englishness that Spenser's and Swift's stances toward Ireland have in common. In sum, if Scottishness means that Muriel Spark's *The Prime of Miss Brodie* (and the splendid movie thereof with Maggie Smith) ought to be attacked for fouling the national nest, as it was, I am against Scottishness; if it means recognizing, as Crawford generously put it, that Spark shows how "tendencies in Scottish cultures could be linked to the darkest side of fascism" and that she is "exemplary for us at this moment in Scottish cultural history precisely because of her internationalism" (328-29), I am in favour of it. For the great Hugh MacDiarmid, Aleksandr Blok and Vladimir Lenin were in his tradition.

A third answer, which would be my favourite, is interdisciplinarity. As Marx and Engels said, "We know only of one science—the science of history" (*German Ideology*). Auerbach has fleshed this out: "History is the science of reality that affects us most immediately, stirs us most deeply and compels us most forcibly to a consciousness of ourselves. <u>It is the only science in which human beings step before us in their totality</u>." (4-5, underline DS) To talk about *The Beggar's Opera* without music, or of Mary Shelley without Castruccio Castracani, or of modern poetry and novel without the positive US influx, or of J.R.R. Tolkien without his being shelled in the trenches of World War 1, or of John Arden without Bertolt Brecht, or of Williams without Gramsci, is to sin against our matter. And I was much tempted to extol the good aspects of Comparative Literature which I have taught for a third of a century, but in spite of the vogue of the name I see little prospect of this becoming a key notion in the coming years or decades. Much more money would be needed to implement its study, primarily on the doctoral level. Our problems are elsewhere, and so I have resisted the temptation.

In conclusion to this section, we have to take stock of both our Arts Faculties' and our profession's failure to defend the humanist ideology they claimed as their raison d'être. As Ohmann told us in the less virulent Vietnam War crisis, "Humanist, humanize thyself!" (*English* 67) We have to build on a lot of cognition that has, from Brecht, Bakhtin, Kenneth Burke, Empson, and Barthes on, related texts to strategies of acceptance. Literature and culture obviously cannot today be an oasis sheltering us from the desertifying simooms of capitalism. Rather, we have to engage in attempts at climate control. Thus I propose to you Suvin's Third Law on Cognition (drawn from Vico): Only when the body intervenes, the mind can understand.

The women of Laputa, cuckolding the project-makers, seem to have understood this well.

3. How to Leave Laputa

3.0. In *Bringing English to Order*, Goodson and Medway argue: "English has been the means through which powerful groups, especially governments, have sought to achieve ends which were...not neutrally 'educational'"; English is a "battleground" of "groups with agendas" (cited in Eaglestone 117, underline DS). We may object English is not only that, but we have seen how it was moulded and determined by the different agenda of liberal-cum-social-democratic inter-class education, an idea dominant from World War 1 to Thatcher, that is, coeval with a response to Leninism. What, then, might our agenda be?

3.1. First of all, who is entitled to shape English Studies? Surely not only, nor even primarily, the private corporations and their political stooges: we have to strongly resist what Gramsci called the bourgeois ideology of a hegemony of economics over the civic and political society. Let me cite two diagnoses of American studies, the negative complaint by Paul Giles and the wonderful positive horizon by Djelal Kadir, while substituting

"English" for their "American":

> "The academic profession of English literature has consistently aspired toward a rhetoric of self-allegorization, whereby the integral spirit of the nation would manifest itself synechdochically in a series of classic texts, from which a naturalized affiliation could be adduced between nation and narrative..." (Giles 74).
>
> "The best hope for English studies as an area for knowledge...is for it to cease to be English and an instrument of official state policy, [a national and nationalist project,] and become, instead, <u>an independent, international field of inquiry and teaching</u>....[that is,] an exogenous discourse on England" (Kadir 11 and 13, underline DS).

Such an exogenous discourse would take a leaf out of the book of U.K. culture itself, where the exogenous discourses of Stuart Hall (from Black Jamaica) or Raymond Williams (from the Welsh working-class) have even preceded what happened in literature with Rushdie, Mo, Ishiguro, Kureishi, and so on. English literary history is no longer only about the fate of the English nation or British nations; it is a global phenomenon (cf. Greenblatt 53), which therefore has to be judged globally, equally by those of us in Italy as in the USA or India. As the antifascist exile Auerbach concluded, "our philological home is the Earth: it can no longer be the nation" (17).

Would this downgrade the importance of English language, literature, culture and their studies? Not at all, in my opinion: but it would provide another horizon and use for them. I say it as a Comparatist: few literatures can so justly pride themselves on the cultural continuity, on such an intra-literary dialogue about life and happiness, as is found in English; and I could cite you an admiring note of Brecht's, surely not suspect of bourgeois Anglophilia, saying so. Shelley's great poem against the Blair of his day, Premier Castlereagh, beginning "I met Murder on the way/ He had a mask like Castlereagh," could perhaps be matched in many other literatures, but his position in a line leading from Langland and Milton to the poetry of, say, Owen, Auden or MacDiarmid would find very few parallels elsewhere (except in China and Japan, for analogous reasons of safe national development).

3.2. Secondly, what might be a useful horizon for English Studies in my initial sense of fusing professional and civic aspects? "How can there be art after Auschwitz?" (whose *Kommandant* liked to play Haydn, it seems), asked Adorno. "Will there be poetry in dark times?" asked Brecht, and answered: "There will be poetry about the dark times."

I shall pick out only what I believe may grow today to be two strategically central orientations for us, the international and the national one. In both cases, the orientations take into account Bourdieu's famous definition of intellectuals as "a dominated fraction of the dominant class" (319ff.).

The first orientation possible for us has to do with the second "A" in AIA, with the relation of "English" studies—the understanding of fiction and other writings from England, Scotland, and Wales—to the total warfare globalization carried out primarily by the US government, always buttressed by a truly Orwellian misuse of English language and often buttressed by the domination of the dark side of US culture. As Jameson has argued in a remarkable article on globalization as a philosophical issue, "There is a fundamental dissymetry in the relationship between the United States and every other country in the world,...even Japan and those of Western Europe" (58). Film and TV belong equally to economics and culture: along with weapons and agribusiness, they are the principal export of the USA and an enormous source of profit. They are owned and pushed by huge mega-corporations based on the monopoly of the relevant information technology and on the politics of copyright: "ideas are private property and designed to be sold in great and profitable quantities" (60-61). One of US government's principal aims is to further this ideological and economic hegemony by insisting on dismantling any national protection of culture by means of subsidies and quotas, and as a Canadian I could sing you a little song about what this has done to Canadian culture. Jameson's well-taken example is the English 1990s' wave of movies around Channel Four and the British Film Institute, which "would not exist without the government and its older BBC and socialist traditions." The sharpest conflict is, however, with western Europe—Germany and most notably France. The success of these untiring US efforts would mean "the tendential extinction of new national artistic production elsewhere" (61).

This might have central consequences for a discourse on English literature. The triumph of Hollywood and US TV is no doubt, to begin with, economic and formal. But let us realize that the addictiveness of its breathless editing, consubstantial with the dominant US sensationalism and violence, the domestication of mass killing as right and enjoyable, leads to destruction of critical distance and other cultural ways "people live in their bodies and use language as well as the way they treat each other and nature..., [traditions] which are rather recent and successful accommodations of [their] old institutions to modern technology" (Jameson 63). US cultural production mostly wipes out or transforms beyond recognition local film, TV, music, thus everyday life, and therefore even the highest of High Lit. However, I have absolutely no wish to revive a defence of highbrow as against lowbrow, or of English as against American, literature or culture. The fault-lines lie <u>within</u> both, not between them. What we must always look out for is whether a given genre or text, high or low, allows for "practices of consumer choice and personal autonomy that train the otherwise subaltern individual" in preparing for civic responsibility (70), as Stuart Hall and Martin Jacques have argued about musical culture helping to overcome the subalternity of Black minority groups in Britain. The death of the 1960s-70s film experiments in England and the rest of Europe, from England to Hungary and Yugoslavia to Sweden, is a death of the modern and the political "possibility of imagining radically different social alternatives" (Jameson 62). Hollywood and US TV are, magically enough, both a profitable business and a <u>fundamental late-capitalist cultural revolution</u>—exporting a training for or indeed brain-washing into consumerism by means of images of consumption (cf. Jameson 63-64, Sklair, and Suvin "Utopianism"). And yet it is by now crystal-clear that market-bound affluence <u>cannot</u> be made available to most people on the globe.

Jameson's conclusion is that French resistance to US pressure "...sets a fundamental agenda for all cultural workers...and may be an adequate focus for reorganizing the...notion of cultural imperialism and indeed of imperialism generally, today, in the new late-capitalist world-system" (Jameson 59). The more or less democratic arms'-length institutions of the Welfare State, for example the initially admirable socialist or at least Keynesian British institutions of Arts Council funding and university funding, must be protected against the Right-wing attempts to dismantle it and empower private business. For Jameson, "...the defense of national autonomy can take the form of defending the [humanizing] powers of arts and high culture, the deeper kinship between such artistic modernism and the political power of collectivity itself, now however conceived as a unified political power, a collective project rather than a dispersal into democratic multiplicities and identity positions" (73). Surely, I'd add, without such public support the great UK dramatur-gical renaissance after 1956, with Arden, Pinter, Wesker and so many others—a part of the last great world season of classical drama theatre—would not have existed. We come therefore to the somewhat paradoxical conclusion that tactically, "...nation-states and their national cultures are [here] called upon to play the positive role [as against Americanization as the standard-ized ideology and practice of consumption]" (74).

All of this does not mean shutting English Studies even more tightly off against American Studies, but on the contrary learning from them how to use the proper antitoxins.

The second, national orientation possible for us has to do more with the "I" in AIA. In the as highly endangered 1930s Walter Benjamin concluded that the producer of an intellectual work is impelled <u>by his professional or class interest</u> to exercise solidarity with the producing workers. This was largely forgotten after the 1950s, as the welfare-and-warfare State epoch saw the culmination of the "cut" from the global surplus we "middle" 10-15% were getting; and "the shouts of triumph of this 'middle' sector over the reduction of their gap with the upper one per cent have masked the realities of the growing gap between them and the other [85-90%]" (Wallerstein 104-05). But today, our immediate interests are oppositional because capitalism is obviously engaged in large scale "structural declassing" of intellectual work (cf. Guillory 134ff.). There are few matters more humiliating than the experience of being pushed to the periphery of social value—measured by the only yardstick capitalism knows, our financing—which all of us have undergone in the last quarter century, with our students increasingly condemned to part-time piecework without security. Intellectuals never had power over productive relations, but now we are bit by bit losing our relatively large autonomy.

Thus, I think our liberatory interests as intellectuals are twofold and interlocking. First, they consist in securing a high degree of self-management, to begin with in the workplace. At this particular moment, this means, to my mind, a defence of the professionality of education as a public service, of meaningful democratic participation in the control of both production and distribution of our own work. But second, this defence will certainly fail unless we enter into such strategic alliances with other social groups as would consent to fight the current toward demagogic and finally militarized browbeating, present in all our States, from our sweatshops and fortress neighbourhoods to universities. Here the boundary between our as it were dissident interests within the intellectual field of production and the overall liberation of labour as their only guarantee becomes permeable. I have neither the knowledge nor the authority to speak about Italy, but from my attempts to understand its cultural history, it would seem this might be done under the banner of defending the Constitution still officially in force.

Both of these orientations, the national and the international one, would mean advancing from Gramsci's "national-popular" strategy to a "national-modernist" one, and returning to the absolute necessity of a great collective or national project, his "civic humanism" *(umanesimo civile)*—a Modernist People's Front so to speak. It would be both an integral defence of literature not sundered from culture and language, and yet one with some chance to succeed.

Can this be our agenda? Morally, professionally, and politically I have no doubts it ought to be. Do we have as teachers, researchers, intellectuals, and citizens the energy to coalesce around some such program in spite of and against all the major political parties, say from Blair to the extreme Right? I cannot answer it, and if I could it would not be my situation both as an "extracommunitarian" and as your keynote speaker to tell you so. I can only pose some alternatives and say that either we do something of this kind, or we shall be reduced to the neo-medieval status of a begging order, perpetually threatened with overwork and underpayment, precariousness and extinction. In either case, as the governments all over the world are making clear, the road back to Keynesian humanist disciplines—the English Studies I knew as a student of L.C. Knights—is barred. But the choice how to go forward is still ours. The poets have always known this: "Do not go gentle into that good night," said the earlier Dylan; and "If Winter comes, can Spring be far behind?" asked the greater Shelley.

And if we need a Great Ancestor, we can still find him in English Studies. You might have wondered about my title, but you can perhaps see that I have all the time been talking about disembarking from Laputa and allying with Lindalino. So allow me the final (im)modesty to propose <u>Suvin's Fourth Law on (Applied) Cognition: The paragon we as intellectuals ought to follow in today's jungle of cities is Jonathan Swift</u>.

Edward Said told us so in 1983 (cf. 27-28 and 54ff.).

Works Cited

Writings on and immediately around "English Studies" (mainly pertaining to Section 2) are marked by an initial asterisk *

* Altick, Richard D. *The English Common Reader.* Chicago: U of Chicago P, 1967.

* Arnold, Matthew. *Culture and Anarchy.* Cambridge: Cambridge UP, 1960.

* Auerbach, Erich. "Philology and *Weltliteratur.*" Transl. M. & E. Said. *Centennial R.* 13 (Winter 1969): 1-17. [Orig. 1952 in *Weltliteratur: Festgabe für Fritz Strich.* Eds. W. Muschg & E. Staiger.]

* Baldick, Chris. *The Social Mission of English Criticism 1848-1932.* Oxford: Clarendon P, 1983.

Benjamin, Walter. "Literaturgeschichte und Literaturwissenschaft" and "Wie erklären sich grosse Bucherfolge?", in his *Gesammelte Schriften*, Frankfurt: Suhrkamp, 1980, III: 283-90 and 294-300.

Bourdieu, Pierre. *In Other Words.* Trans. M. Anderson. Stanford: Stanford UP, 1990.

* Brown, Norman O. "The Excremental Vision," in R.A. Greenberg and W.B. Piper eds., *The Writings of Jonathan Swift.* New York & London: Norton, 1973, 611-30.

* Colls, Robert, and Philip Dodds eds. *Englishness, Politics and Culture 1880-1920.* London: Croom Helm, 1986.

* Crawford, Robert. *Devolving English Literature.* 2nd edn. Edinburgh: Edinburgh UP, 2000. [orig. 1992]

* Docherty, Thomas. *Criticism and Modernity: Aesthetics, Literature, and Nations in Europe and its Academies.* Oxford: Oxford UP, 1999.

* Doyle, Brian. *English and Englishness.* London & New York: Routledge, 1989.

*—-. "The Hidden History of English Studies," in P. Widdowson ed., *Re-reading English.* London: Methuen, 1982,

17-31.

* Eaglestone, Robert. *Doing English: A Guide for Literature Students.* 2nd edn. London & New York: Routledge, 2002.

* Eagleton, Terry. *Literary Theory.* Oxford: Blackwell, 1983.

* Easthope, Antony. *Literary into Cultural Studies.* London & New York: Routledge, 1991.

* Giles, Paul. "Transnationalism and Classic American Literature." *PMLA* 118.1 (2003): 62-77.

* Goodson, Ivor, and Peter Medway. "Introduction" to iidem eds., *Bringing English to Order: The History and Politics of a School Subject.* London & New York: Falmer P, 1990, i-xv.

* Greenblatt, Stephen. "Racial Memory and Literary History." *PMLA* 116 (2001): 48-63.

Guillory, John. "Literary Critics as Intellectuals," in W.C. Dimock and M.T. Gilmore, eds., *Rethinking Class.* New York: Columbia UP, 1994, 107-49.

Hall, Stuart, and Martin Jacques, eds. *New Times.* London: Verso, 1991.

Jameson, Fredric. "Notes on Globalization as a Philosophical Issue," in idem and Masao Miyoshi eds., *The Cultures of Globalization.* Durham & London: Duke UP, 1998, 54-77.

* Kadir, Djelal. "America and Its Studies." *PMLA* 118.1 (2003): 9-25.

* [Kingman Committee.] *Report... into the Teaching of English Language.* London: HMSO, 1988.

Lefebvre, Henri. *La Survie du capitalisme.* Paris: Anthropos, 1973.

* Lombardo, Agostino. "The Value of Literature," in *The Economy Principle in English. Proceedings of the 19th AIA Conference.* Ed. G. Iamartino et al. Milano: Unicopli, 2002, 129-38.

* Lucas, John. *England and Englishness.* London: Hogarth P, 1990.

Marx, Karl. *Manifesto of the Communist Party,* in idem and Friedrich Engels, *Collected Works.* London: Lawrence & Wishart, 1976, Vol. 6: 475-519.

* Michael, Ian. *The Teaching of English: From the Sixteenth Century to 1870.* Cambridge: Cambridge UP, 1987.

Mills, C. Wright. *White Collar.* New York: Oxford UP, 1953.

Mohanty, Satya P. *Literary Theory and the Claims of History.* Ithaca & London: Cornell UP, 1997.

* [Newbolt Report.] *The Teaching of English in England.* London: HMSO, 1921.

Nietzsche, Friedrich. *On the Genealogy of Morals*, Third Essay, in *Basic Writings of Nietzsche.* Transl. and ed. W. Kaufmann. New York: Modern Library, 1968.

* Ohmann, Richard. *English in America*, New York: Oxford UP, 1976 [rpt. with new retrospective Introduction Middletown CT: Wesleyan UP, 1996].

*—-. *Politics of Knowledge: The Commercialization of the University, the Professions, and Print Culture.* Middletown CT: Wesleyan UP, 2003.

* Parrinder, Patrick. "Shakespeare and (Non-Standard) English."' *European English Messenger* 5.1 (1996): 14-20.

* Said, Edward. *The World, the Text, the Critic.* London: Vintage 1991 [orig. 1983].

Scarry, Elaine. *On Beauty and Being Just.* Princeton: Princeton UP, 1999.

* Scholes, Robert. *The Rise and Fall of English.* New Haven: Yale UP, 2002.

Sklair, Leslie. *Sociology of the Global System.* Baltimore: Johns Hopkins UP, 1991.

* Spivak, Gayatri Chakravorty. *The Postcolonial Critic.* London & New York: Routledge, 1991.

Suvin, Darko. "On Cognition as Art and Politics: Reflections for a Toolkit," in his *Defined by a Hollow.* London: P. Lang, 2010, 269-319.

—. "Utopianism from Orientation to Agency: What Are We Intellectuals under Post-Fordism To Do?" in his *Defined...* [see previous item], 217-67.

*—-. *Victorian Science Fiction in the U.K.: The Discourses of Knowledge and of Power.* Boston: Hall, 1983.

* Viswanathan, Gauri. *Masks of Conquest: Literary Study and British Rule in India.* New York: Columbia UP, 1989.

Wallerstein, Immanuel. *Geopolitics and Geoculture.* Cambridge: Cambridge UP, 1992.

6. IMMIGRATION IN EUROPE TODAY: APARTHEID OR CIVIL COHABITATION? (2006-07)[29]

—To the memory of Ernst Bloch—

aspice agedum hanc frequentiam [sub] urbis immen-
sae tecta...: maxima pars istius turbae patria caret....
vix denique invenies ullam terram, quam etiamnunc
indigenae colant; permixta omnia et insiticia sunt.

29. Like my earlier essay on "Exile," this one does not cover most of the central questions. It omits the properly economic-cum psychological, or if you wish anthropological, mainsprings of migration today: poverty and the yearning for a better life. I attempt here only to approach some striking new phenomena arising from immigration and a possible horizon for dealing justly with them.

Preliminary approaches to Section 1 were tried out at the Symposium "Between Home and Host Cultures" hosted by Collegium Budapest, Sept. 2006, and at a lecture for the Dottorato in Letterature e culture dei paesi di lingua inglese at the Univ. of Bologna, Oct. 2006. My thanks go to the organizers, Prof. Sorin Antohi, Prof. John Neubauer, and Dr. Zsuzsana Török in the first and Prof. Silvia Albertazzi and Dr. Rita Monticelli in the second case, also to Prof. Emilio Santoro for counsels about critical literature and to Marcelline Krafchick, Joan Roelofs, Zs. Török, and Richard D. Erlich for critiques leading to improvements. All responsibilities are mine alone.

Thanks go also to the libraries at Uppsala and Central European universities.

(So look at these masses under the roofs of our metropolis: a major part of this disordered multitude has
no country.... You will scarcely find a single country,
finally, that is still settled only by natives; all are intermixed with and engrafted upon each other.)
Seneca, *Ad Helviam matrem*, 42 C.E.

No longer foreigners nor immigrants in a foreign land,
but fellow-citizens with God's people....
Saul of Tarsus, *Ephesians* II.19-20. ca. 60 C.E.?

Whilst I realize that what I have been saying...is im-
practicable and unpolitical from the point of view of
[a politics in the traditional sense of the word], I still
want to claim that any politics which fails to sustain
some relation to the principle of unconditional hospitality has completely lost its relation to justice.
Derrida, "The Deconstruction of Actuality," 1990s

0. A Retrospect

In an earlier essay about this field ("Exile"), I accepted some
fundamental lessons of Edward Said: not only his broad vision
and incorruptible lay humanist value-judgments, but specifically
the insight that any more or less forced displacement of people is
irremediably secular and historical, that displaced persons and
personalities are as a rule wilfully produced by some classes
of humans in power from among other classes of disempow-
ered, suffering, wronged, and damaged humans—who then
cannot be fully comforted by any transcendental mission as
saviours for other people and other times to come. As a totally
laicized Christian-born Palestinian intellectual, Said was well
placed to understand the need for social solidarity, perhaps I
should say brotherhood and sisterhood or just dignity. I propose
to pursue this strand, which constituted the first part of that

essay, in its different recent dilemmas (where the problem of my earlier essay's second part, "The Displaced Intellectual as Creative Interpreter," seems to me not uninteresting but rather secondary).

My former essay was centrally an attempt at a rectification or purification of our tribal terms by adding some new tools to the pioneering historical semantics of Raymond Williams in *Keywords* (cf. Suvin, "Comparative"). It pretended to no more than a first orientation, leaving out such key depth-factors as the world market of commodities and labour-power, demographic trends, wars, and other causes of mass displacement (which shall, alas, also be slighted here). It proposed a typology of division into expatriates (largely expecting to come back to enhanced status, and therefore marginal to my concerns), political exiles, and then émigrés and refugees, the first mainly single people or families leaving for economic reasons and the second mainly large groups leaving because of political persecution including war. It addressed itself only to the modalities and consequences of people getting more or less reluctantly from an original society to a new and strange one.

I now wish to develop matters of the (im)migrants position in and treatment by the "target" society, which is today our principal problem. Even in the first essay I noted that most immigrants have the basic economic problem of surviving. This engenders a temptation to engage in officially illegal activities— such as prostitution, dope-dealing and other black-market activities, or simply petty crime—which is strongly helped along and often rendered inevitable when the ill-advised "target country" government pushes them into the position of second-rate inhabitants, denied insertion, training, working permits, etc. In that case, immigrants are often forced to fulfill the prophecies of chauvinists who see them as threats, so that I concluded: "A runaway feedback loop of mutual resentments is not difficult to set up. [This] alternative is a qualitative leap toward militarization and Police State, which is the not-so-hidden agenda today behind the hyped-up terrorist scare (that is real but marginal and to be fought in the hearts and minds of people by removing the causes for its mass appeal). The coming about of forbidden zones barricaded at will by the State and even by private entrepreneurs would divide people into humans and sub-humans. This would also render obsolete all talk about displaced persons: we would all live in an *univers concentrationnaire* without an outside, a universal ethnic-cum-class apartheid."

This negative feedback loop and the slide toward apartheid States may be prevented by affirmative action from an alliance of enlightened citizens' and immigrants' organizations within the "target countries." What may the horizon and orientations of such an alliance be is the theme of the present essay. It will focus on the political and epistemological aspects, touching only here and there on the probably crucial economic aspect since it needs separate (if converging) treatment.

1. Changes in Mass Displacements: Are Non-Citizens People?

<u>1.0.</u> Today we are in a situation of rapidly growing voluntary or semi-voluntary displacement, a rush toward economic survival and betterment which the British Black scholar Gilroy calls "purposive vagrancy" (88-89 and passim). It is moved by a deep wish for enhancement, and often even for a salvation, of lives. The last quarter of a century has perhaps revealed the deep springs of all mass migrations: the push to pass from zones of poverty to zones of (relative) richness; the pull of capitalist need for cheap labour. Such springs flowed during the Cold War too, but they were overlaid by the ideological conflict which stressed political exiles. The standard introduction to migration by Castles and Miller, reprinted and updated many times, concludes: "The refugee regime of the rich countries of the North has...shifted from a system designed to welcome Cold War refugees from the East and to resettle them as permanent exiles...to a >non-entrée< regime designed to exclude and control [immigrants]

from the South" (107; cf. also Zolberg).[30] This is of a piece with many indications of deep changes in mass displacements of people across borders during the last fifteen years. I shall list a few of the changes, all of them coinciding with or intersecting and reinforcing the economic push-and-pull suggested above.

1.1. A first difference is the impact of <u>wars</u>, and the ensuing mass immiseration superadded to the "normal" economic immiseration of global capitalism, in Africa, ex-Yugoslavia, and Iraq. The migration waves from Africa have mainly remained on that continent (less than 1.5% of Sub-Sahara Africans who leave their native countries go to the European Union, cf. Liberti), while those from ex-Yugoslavia have in large part (but not wholly) returned to its successor States. The estimated 1,200.000 or more refugees from Iraq are mainly in Jordan and Syria, just as the earlier ones from Afghanistan went across the porous borders with Pakistan and Iran. Thus Europe and North America have not yet seen many consequences of this wave (or of the earlier Palestinian refugees).

A second one is the growing <u>feminization</u> of immigration: the UN Fund for Population report of Sept. 6, 2006, estimates immigrants at ca. 200 millions, half of them women. This might look normal, as it almost reproduces the average global gender relationships (not quite, as women are globally a majority). However, economic emigrants were traditionally young and middle-aged men whom families might then follow (cf. Willcox ed.). They are now often women—not only in the USA, where over half the immigrants have been women since the 1960s,

30. Note, though, that most displaced persons in these years still go South-South, for example within African countries or from the Indian subcontinent to affluent Arab countries, or that they go from China and East Europe to the countries of metropolitan capitalism, rather than in the classical exodus from Europe to overseas. Unfortunately, this essay of mine is, like its predecessor, enforcedly focussed on Euro-Mediterranean experiences. However, I think the problem of denizen rights vs. two-tier societies has by now also been globalised. It clearly obtains, for example, in China's refusal of basic rights to rural migrants into cities.

but also, say, in Italy, where domestic help is usually Filipino or Romanian women while prostitutes were first Albanian but now are often Nigerian (and in Japan immigrant prostitutes have for the last decades been Filipino and Thai). Feminization is—as in non-migrant situations—a correlate of badly paid work (cf. Castells 2: 170ff., Apitzsch-Jansen eds., and Lutz ed.). A considerable part of it is what Sassen (in "Women's") calls a "feminization of survival": survival of people and families through labour of millions of women zigzagging between legality and illegality—as a rule strongly abetted by the "source" States such as the Philippines, Thailand, and the successors of the USSR—and subject to extra exploitation but often self-chosen as a lesser evil.

A third change is the beleaguered fortress mentality: the orientation of the richer part of Europe and North America toward a Fortress Europa and Fortress Amerika (Japan has always been Fortress Nippon as far as immigrants' treatment is concerned). Its hypocritically hidden motive is not an interdiction of illegal immigration, economically most undesirable for the capitalist profit-makers and pragmatically quite impossible. The real end of all vexations and deaths (a reasonable estimate is that 30,000 immigrants have died trying to penetrate Fortresses Europe and Amerika each) is to keep the legal as well as illegal immigrants from receiving civic rights such as unionization and the vote, and thus the same payments as "native" ones (cf. the works by Wood, Altvater, Sassen's *Losing* and *Mobility,* Cohen *New*, and especially on the treatment of workers' mobility in function of exploitation Moulier-Boutang's by now classical *De l'esclavage au salariat)*. I shall devote a separate sub-section to this knot of problems.

Thus, politically, the main problem of immigration has replaced that of emigration (though at least the brain-drain is also a major problem for the poorer South). While there are still many politically persecuted exiles denied protective rights both where they come from and where they arrive to, the millions of people surging across the Rio Grande, the Mediterranean, and the ex-Warsaw-Pact borders into more affluent metropolitan loci are all trying for a better life. The negative part of today's experiences is not their movement, nor the epicyclical one of us intellectuals, but the undignified and self-defeating ways (even worse in Europe than in the USA) in which national and international authorities are meeting this real problem.

Some studies point to the growing number of migrants from the ranks of highly skilled professions, usually also from affluent countries, who can often choose where to go, and are numerous around the new "global cities." The richest among them are "bi-local," the family may indeed be multi-local (cf. Papastergiadis 44-45). This is an important development but I shall slight it here. Not only does it seem difficult to quantify, though it's clearly a minority among migrants; it is also often undertaken for the purpose of a temporary experience aimed at enhanced status upon return home. The experience of such expatriates, discussed in my "Exile," is largely different from that of the rest of migrants.

1.2. In the age of Fordism and the Cold War migration was as a rule tolerated, sometimes fostered and co-organized, and at any rate often politically welcomed by the "target" States, and thus predominantly legal. The above factors amount to a sea-change to Post-Fordist globalized and often illegal migration. Its underbelly is the consolidation of transnational networks—communicational and financial, ranging from beneficent to utterly degrading—between migrants and source countries. The pull of capital sucking in cheap labour force and the push of poverty from the "South" has spawned a huge "migration industry" of middlemen for illegal human border-crossing, "a vast unseen network underpinning a global labour market...boring through the national fortifications," which can be divided into people-smuggling and people-trafficking. Smuggled migrants are moved illegally for profit, as unequal partners in a commercial transaction; trafficked migrants are deceived and coerced for naked exploitation through the sale of their sexual services or labour.[31] There are few organized counter-measures to illegal migration, none efficient—nor can they be unless root causes for migration were to be addressed by a drastically changed trade and investment policy (119). There is no mystery about the root causes: the classical case study by Thomas about migration from the UK to USA showed that, under conditions of free trade, emigration rises with the economic gap between classes, the lack of upward mobility, and of course demographic pressure. As mentioned, the root cause is poverty (cf. Kane): the impossibility of gainful work in capitalism either because of land scarcity (as in Rwanda), water scarcity (as in China) or job scarcity (in most cases).

Migration that is not overtly political has a major financial impact on the "source countries." The World Bank report of Dec. 2006 for the year 2005 has immigrants' remitting to the home countries US$ 232.5 billion (the biggest flows are to China and India, followed by ca. nineteen billion to Mexico and ca. fourteen to the Philippines), to which should be added the huge illegal remittances. But in this epoch, what in my earlier essay seemed monadic State societies are rendered porous by dense networks of periodic home visits, frequent phone or internet communications, etc. (cf. Bauböck, Cesarani-Fulbrook eds., Hannertz, Faist, Ong, Leggewie-Münch eds.). Classical one-way migrants are increasingly giving way to so-called "transmigrants"—say from the Caribbeans or the Philippines, Mexico or Turkey, not to speak about the Balkans and eastern Europe, or about the old Chinese diaspora which pioneered the toing and froing. Ties with the "source" countries, including religious and other indoctrination from them, remain stronger. In countries where reception is particularly rigid or hostile, such as Switzerland, this also works against the desire for assimilation, particularly in the younger migrants from economically

31. See Castles-Miller 115. The traffic in migrants doesn't seem to be run by what can properly be called mafias, i.e. highly organized international criminal groups, which at least in the 1990s preferred smuggling drugs, arms, and toxic waste (Palidda 220-21).

comparable "source" countries.

All such processes, going on with undiminished scope, have redrawn the population map of most countries. Many countries have switched from being emigration to immigration ones: the UK, Italy, and Spain to begin with, but also Poland and the Czech Republic in relation to Ukraine, Hungary to Romania, Slovenia and Greece to rest of Balkans; a witty book about emigration in Italy was titled *Quando eravamo Albanesi (When We Were the Albanians)*. Globally, UN statistics count over 190 million people (3% of the 6.5 billion world population) as born outside of the present State of permanent residence. Not only is the number growing rapidly, but the percentage is much higher in richer "Northern" countries. Thus, as of 2006, in the European Union forty-one million people of 462 million were "foreign born," or ca. 9% (as opposed to 13% in "Northern America"). Or: in Sweden 20% of the population has one foreign-born parent, and the situation is similar in the USA, Netherlands, and probably also in France (the statistics vary from State to State in part because of incompatible definitions, but US estimates show official statistics are as a rule underrated by 40-50% due to illegal immigration). In Italy, for all the political clamour, the percentage seems much lower (cf. Colombo-Sciortino).

1.3. The political correlative of the "beleaguered fortress" mentality is a rebirth of apartheid-type racism. It is at its strongest in those European Nation-States—and parts of the USA—which are proceeding as swiftly as political discontent among popular masses will allow it (e.g., more slowly in France and Germany than in the rest of western Europe) to dismantle the economic and social guarantees of the Welfare State. This savage privatization has resulted in mass transmutation of jobs into precarious, stressful, and much worse paid employments, as well as in sharp downgrading of health services, pensions, and all accompanying social safety nets for the great majority of the population. Life has become much more insecure, the comfortable succession of generations and narrowing gap between genders of the 1945 to mid-'70s epoch are being reversed and the resulting tensions hugely exacerbated, the gulf of proletarization yawns ever more widely and threatens more people more nearly. The capitalist reliance on both transfer of work into poorer countries with much lower wages and the import of such super-exploited labour into the metropolitan States has been ideologically recoded into an earnest threat to the "autochthonous" population, since it is easily identifiable in everyday life as foreign-speaking people of different behaviour. It has thus allowed the capitalist media and politicians, as well as the revived racist parties of the semi-fascist Right, to shift the blame for insecurity from the economic policies of super-exploitation to the immigrants.

While there are welcome exceptions in some stances and some countries (cf. beside the titles adduced earlier also Balke ed., Bielefeld ed., and Rea ed.), on the whole we are assisting at a complex hierarchization, setting the native workers first against the foreigners hailing from the European Union and then against the legal, semi-legal, and illegal *"extracomunitari"*—while in the background there always hovers the opposition of Whites vs. Blacks or Asians. Both on the global scale of North vs. South and in the mass import of such imperial or colonial relationships into all metropolitan cities and agribusinesses (as argued by Balibar, *Nous* 77ff.), the spectre of a racist division into humans and sub-humans, so ably perfected by the Nazis, has returned (cf. Wallerstein's essay in Balibar-Wallerstein). The sub-humans can live in slums and favelas, their function is to be an ever-present threat to the legally exploitable jobs of the precariously employed. Castel, who induces from the French example, speaks of this as a disaffiliation, which entails the dismantling of social citizenship and public control over conditions of living that had in the Welfare State generation brought about the abatement of chronic insecurity and rise of autonomous personalities. This abrogation of the compromise between the ruling and the working classes leads to the reproletarization of entire societal groups and classes, a regime of legalized violence, and a massive production of asociality or antisocial individualism (see also Balibar, *Nous* 299-300 and passim).

1.4. A first conclusion: It is striking that what has remained constant for the last ca. 200 years—with the partial exception of the extraordinary gap of Keynesianism plus Cold War in ca. 1945-75, which in some ways favoured directly or indirectly political migrants—is a contradiction at the heart of national capitalisms. All of them rely on the State for their existence, while not only poor-mouthing it ideologically but also as soon as possible riding roughshod over any constraints it might impose on immiseration and ecocide. The contradiction has not at all been abrogated by today's transnational globalization, since today's borders are free for the rich and the finances, less for commodities, even less for information, and most restrictive for poor people and workers: as a witty remark put it, capitals are exported, workers and the poor deported. The inhuman use of Nation-State borders is openly to be seen by the effects of mass migrations across them, very often because of their intolerant rise (the clearest example being perhaps in the '40s Pakistan and in the '90s Croatia). It is most elegantly phrased when Giorgio Agamben asks whether in the 1789 *Déclaration des droits de l'homme et du citoyen* "the two terms are to name two distinct realities or whether [Man] is actually always already contained in the [Citizen]" (162; cf. Balibar, *Nous*).

It was Hannah Arendt, looking back at the 1914-45 period, who formulated the great insight that the real truth of the Nation-State is giving certain rights to its <u>citizens</u>—rather than to <u>people</u> or human beings in general, regardless of their birthplace and/or descent; and that this logically leads: either to expulsion, which statistically doesn't work; or to "naturalization," a revealing bureaucratic term implying that an official seal of citizenship, bestowed by the country of arrival, cancelled the aliens' "unnaturalness"; or—overwhelmingly—to a neglect that leaves the immigrants in a limbo of full or semi-illegality, where often "the only practical substitute for a non-existent homeland [is] an internment camp" (or today often a ghettoized enclave). If Arendt concluded that refugees had "attached themselves like a curse to all the newly established states on earth which were created in the image of the nation" (284), we have to conclude that in our age of Never-ending Holy Warfare we ain't seen nothing yet.[32]

But, mindful of Epicure's great maxim "Vain is the word of a philosopher which heals no human suffering," I have now to go beyond phenomenology and ask at least in initial ways "what is to be done"?

2. Criteria and Value-Orientations: A Possible Epistemologico-Political Alternative

2.0. A Right to Rights

In quite general terms, the question whether and how far immigrants can and will be admitted to citizenship is part of the problem of popular sovereignty. Are the people sovereign, and subject only to the laws they participated in making, *de nobis non sine nobis*? Is a democracy a State in which all citizens, as

---

32. In this light, the concept of a diaspora grows as dubious epistemologically as it often is politically ambiguous. This concept (instead of migration or similar) is meaningful only in juxtaposition with and in fact derivation from a closed ethnic political entity—as its very name, meaning "dissemination" or "seeding forth," shows. It was pioneered by emigrants from ancient Parsees or Israelites, and globalized by those leaving an existing or potential cultural "homeland" (Armenians, Black Africans, Irish, Italians, Indians, etc., later from Palestine and other "Arab" States, and today from all peripheral and semi-peripheral States in Africa, eastern Europe, Asia, and increasingly Latin America). Diasporas differ from colon(izer)s, say from Phoenicia, Hellas or England, who leave richer and more powerful States, by being movements towards potentially richer loci by people who originally have small or no power and/or scant economic means beyond their labour power or trading and artisanal skills. Beside the works cited in 1.2, cf. Ang, Cohen *Global*, Harris ed., and my "Exile," also the periodical *Diaspora* 1991ff.

Aristotle put it, in turn obey and are obeyed: "...the citizen must know and share in both ruling and being ruled?"[33] If we transform the lip-service to democracy to our abiding beacon, the answer is yes. Who then might be the people or the citizens on whom democratic sovereignty rests? As suggested earlier, the 1789 French *Declaration of Rights*, though a huge breakthrough at the time, is still ambiguous. Nonetheless, we can proceed from its most useful sections. Its article 1 proclaims that "Men [i.e. every person, not only citizens of a country, DS] are born equal in rights," and article 2 that Man has "natural and inalienable rights," such as "liberty, property, security, and resistance to oppression." This is a far cry from today's citizenship in the more affluent North,

> "[which] represents the final privilege of status, the final factor of exclusion and discrimination.... To take these [human] rights seriously...would mean that they should subsume the only two rights to freedom today reserved for citizens: the right to residence and the right to circulation in our privileged countries" (Ferrajoli 288-89, from whom I cite also the 1789 *Déclaration;* see also his discussion of the UN Universal Declaration of the Rights of Man of 1948 and the two Pacts on Human Rights following it in 1966).

In particular, article 4 of the 1793 French Constitution establishes that all adult foreigners resident in France for more than one (!) year and living from their work or property are admitted to all the rights of a citizen (Santoro 105). If we care about freedom, which means the chance of autonomous self-realization for each and for all, we cannot have a good part of the denizens of any particular place or country consist of a free group and an unfree one (be the latter workers, women or immigrants).

---

33. Aristotle, *Politics* 1277a 31-32 in *Selections* 470; cf. also 1275a. Roman law, valid for many centuries, formulated this as *quod omnes tangit ab omnibus approbari debet* (what touches all must be approved by all).

Half a century ago, T. H. Marshall noted that citizenship is to a large degree an instrument of social stratification; today, if we exclude most or even a large part of immigrants, we are adopting the horizon of a two-tier or apartheid State and society, necessarily developing its ghetto "bantustans" and enforced by omnipervasive and militarized "security" forces. I wish to discuss refusing such a horizon.

To avoid the Police State, our only alternative is simultaneously epistemological: to change our understanding of this problem; and political: to set up and enforce, in accordance with our changed understanding, reasonable and equitable political rules for people's living together. It centrally amounts to extending the Rights of Man to (almost) all people living under the same sky, in a community of fate: to making citizens out of denizens.

These rules have a granite foundation in the notion of people's inalienable rights, which might be thought of as centering around the concept of living a life of dignity. To do so, we need some fundamental and universal rights or entitlements:[34] a solid minimal material basis is needed, but also a legal status that empowers the person to have serious rights against the political authority whose subjects they are, and the societal status of a recognized and esteemed member of the place's community. All of us need to eat, be secure, and make sense to ourselves, to value ourselves and be valued.

2.1. Epistemology: Images of People's Life

On the epistemological level, what is happening in the age of globalized commodification can perhaps be understood as the

---

34 The term "entitlements" has been popularized by Held (20-21). The eminent theoretician of law Ferrajoli speaks even of a sphere of legal indecidability, that is, of the individual and social rights which are in principle prior and higher to legislation. Such an approach would require serious revisions in Marshall's trichotomy of civil, political, and social rights (see Zolo ed.).

struggle between enforced privilege and equality of opportunities. Privilege creates a manichean dichotomy of more valuable vs. less valuable lives, with the final horizon of valuable vs. valueless lives (*lebensunwertes Leben*, as the Nazi doctrine for the "under-people" so well put it). The Cold War dichotomy of "us" vs. "them," rendered obvious from a glance at the map and the heavily armed borders around the "Soviet camp" and all its offshoots, had collapsed after 1989 leaving a seemingly united world of triumphant capitalism. But after a brief lull, accompanied by economic recession in the USA when arms procurements fell off, a new dichotomy was constructed, in a quintessential Post-Modernist move, by the interaction of the US State as hegemon with various reactions to the inhuman face of capitalist globalization, themselves more or less inhuman according to the situation of their arising. Against them various "wars" were proclaimed, such as the (failed and deadly) "war on drugs," but eventually the biggest and most inhuman reaction, dubbed "Al Qaeda," was elevated by the US establishment to the status of the Enemy, happily restoring the dichotomy. Globalization here means, whatever the slogans, a hierarchy with certain nations and classes ("us" again) on top and everybody else more or less (in most cases, much more) on the bottom. The founding and quite inescapable structural dichotomy had shifted from a seemingly horizontal one into a vertical one. Capitalist globalization functions by daily digging an ever deeper trench of inequality between the upper third (if not upper 5-10%) of the rich North and the rest of the world: the geographico-economical South of poorer States and continents and the imported or at any rate produced South of all the slums and impoverished areas of the North.

The upper-class politics of enforcing inequality, always by threat of hunger and other indignities and where need be by mass killings, were blared in sanitized form around the clock by the world media. But in the mute depths of the increasingly dispossessed working masses, two main counter-politics arose: criminality and migration. The criminal classes can be thought of as illegal capitalists who claim their cut or share of the spoils. Impeded from direct competition with the "legal" capitalists by economic weakness and existing laws, they largely prey on the little people (workers, peasants, small traders, and similar) to whom they, however, present themselves as helpful or enabling middlemen against the common upper-class and rich-nation oppressors (and in certain situations, such as organizing migration, really so function). The epistemological horizon of the lower classes involved, who embark upon migration whenever they can, is truly and sincerely global: *ubi bene ibi patria*, home is wherever one can live better than where one is at. They are daily voting with their feet for Marx's slogan "the proletarians have no country." What was in the Cold War called the "Third World" has englobed most of the former "Second World" (the "Soviet bloc") and turned from an entity visible on the map to a substratum visible almost everywhere in daily life but acknowledged in the reigning capitalist and racist ideology only as a criminal menace. The periphery has infiltrated the center.

These two epistemological orientations, borne by the rulers and the ruled, center on opposed views of people or persons. For the ideal-typical image in capitalism man (they usually favour the aggressive males) is a predator or prey in the jungles of competition where the abler wins and the weaker rightly fertilizes the grounds. The transcendental fetish of this view is the Invisible Hand of the Market, bolstered by very visible aerial bombings, marines, borders, and police. For the ideal-typical image by the plebeians, people—while clearly unequal—have equal rights to life, liberty, and the pursuit of happiness. True, in the lower classes such an ideal type is often inflected by strong hegemonic ideologies from capitalism and crime, including hierarchic religions and "identitarian" resentments in which somebody lower than you (by gender, race, ethnic appurtenance, and so on) must be found on whom to vent your frustration. It is therefore difficult to find, after the demise of utopian radicalism, a clear synthetic image for it which could be opposed to the Social-Darwinist jungle of the Market, but some quasi-Kropotkinian lineaments may be found in plebeian self-help collectives of all kinds.

In this state of affairs, how can we avoid apartheid State and society? I think: by rejecting the capitalist view and practice, and by differentiating the wheat from the chaff in the plebeian views and practices.

2.2. Toward Politics: A Right to Citizenship as a Human Right

I shall proceed by way of five concatenated axioms.

My first, so to speak anthropological axiom is that the right to people's displacement across any and all borders is a central human right, and should today be foregrounded. As Kant told us in *Zum ewigen Frieden (Toward Perpetual Peace)*, people should be seen as citizens of a general Nation of Humanity (*Menschenstaat*). This is not philanthropy or charity but a "hospitality, according to which a foreigner has the right not to be treated inimically because of his arrival to the soil of another person (*eines andern*)" (54). It is a right of visiting (*Besuchsrecht*) based on the right of common possession of the Earth's surface, where originally nobody has more right than anybody else to be at a given place. The powers that prevent this, and also wage and prepare wars, Kant concluded, "drink injustice (*Unrecht*) like water" (60). Marx probably remembered this when he wrote that nobody, not even all the nations put together, has property rights on the Earth surface, that each generation is only a steward with usufruct, whose duty it is to leave better conditions for coming generations (MEW 25: 784). Put positively by a prominent exile, "From wherever the line of sight is equally raised toward heavens, the divine matters are at an equal distance from the human ones" (Seneca 8,5).

This is a utopian horizon, but there is no abiding realism without firmly advancing toward it.[35] The Nation-States may

---

35. Cf. also Kant's "Idea for a Universal History from the Cosmopolitan

become useful manifestations of popular sovereignty and societal democracy, but today their overriding function is policing labour to ensure its cheap availability. The immigrant countries gain cheap labourers without the "reproduction cost" of having schooled them (sometimes to a high skill), and omitting largely or fully the ongoing social costs for native labour. In order to do so, "the immigrant must have as little security as possible, even when s/he has been legalized or naturalized, in sum the immigrant must be such forever or at least for a long time, with the unlimited possibilities of exploitation which arise from this" (Balibar, *Nous* 108). In the rest of this subsection I propose some difficult, but not impossible, ways to advance from repression to cohabitation.

The following two axioms mediate between epistemology and politics. I draw one from van Gunsteren's formulation of a "community of fate." In the wake of Arendt's discovery that human rights are consubstantial with citizenship rights, he proposes three theses, which I shall adapt to my language: 1/

Point of View." Derrida (21) sees a limitation of Kant in his choice of the right to a *Besuchsrecht* instead of the right to a *Gastrecht*, which Kant glosses as becoming somebody's *Hausgenosse* (household member) for a given time. I have two comments. First, Kant's founding this human right on the right of common possession of the Earth's surface and on the equal right of all people to be at a given place on Earth is already a huge, decisive improvement over the nationalist, and *a fortiori* the racist *Blut-und-Boden* stance dominant in our day; thus a Kantian stance furnishes a very good starting point for further adaptations. Second, however, his distinction between visitor and household member—who are, I think, differentiated by both the intimacy offered to newcomers and the duration of their permanence—points to a real difficulty that can only be overcome in the blue utopian distances of an evolving cosmopolitan contract and of a settlement which would build on the nearer and more evident right to visitation (cf. Stanton 637). A lengthy visitation with full civic rights may get very near to a membership in a locality's (or nation's) extended "household."

And it would behoove us to remember ancient wisdom: " When a stranger resides with you in your land, you shall not wrong him. The stranger who resides with you shall be to you as one of your citizens; you shall love him as yourself, for you were strangers in the land of Egypt...." (*Leviticus* 19:33-34).

that we all belong, at different levels, to communities of people who have not necessarily chosen to live together but find that they are inescapably interdependent, and thus have to choose between coexistence or an apartheid whose ultimate horizon is genocide; 2/ that we cannot have pure or perfect citizenships (for example, ethnically pure States) but only imperfect ones, and what matters in them is how to facilitate access to human rights to the greatest number of people; and 3/ that for each person on this globe there must be at least one locus or territory in which s/he has citizen rights, and thus also human rights. Thus my second axiom is that each State—or analogous community, such as the European Union—should foster the maximum of economically and politically possible human rights for all its denizens by giving them the maximum of economically and politically possible citizen rights.

The great precedent to follow here is the (incomplete, and increasingly threatened) integration of women and the working classes into a very incomplete but still worthwhile political society. The integration of the working poor is more difficult because there are globally many more of them, so that it also demands a global approach; I shall return to this.

My third axiom follows from the first two. It is based on Hammar's distinction between immigration policy and immigrant policy (in his *Democracy* and *European*). Immigration policy regulates the flux of immigrants, taking into account (one hopes intelligently) the needs and possibilities of the State effecting it. Immigrant policy concerns the life of immigrants in what should be—but rarely is—a host society, which is new and strange to the immigrant. The axiom is that our value focus ought to be on immigrant policy, which supplies criteria for any acceptable immigration policy. Immigration policy is primarily limiting and focussed on control: it is the domain of border controls and police. Immigrant policy is primarily enabling and focussed on integration: it is the domain of participation by both the civil society and the immigrants, singly or in associations. From the stance of valorizing both human dignity and civic amity or civility, what happens to immigrants in relation to other people with whom they share a common destiny is the overriding end, and all legal and economic policies must be adjusted accordingly. Of great practical importance is here that there be no Chinese (or Berlin, or Rio Grande, or Israeli) Wall dividing liberal political rights from socialist economic rights: they intertwine, and must be negotiated according to necessity and merit in each case.

In the Cold War era, relatively liberal immigration policies in the richer countries were offset by restrictive integration policies (through such categories as the *Gastarbeiter* who could be sent home at will). Today, when God and Communism are dead, both immigration and integration are as a rule increasingly restrictive, with a few exceptions for needed specialists (e.g. computer programmers). It should be noted, however, that there is a whole spread of integration attitudes (cf. Boucher ed.), from the liberality of Sweden or Canada to the rigidity of Switzerland and Greece, with Japan, Germany, and Italy near to the rigid pole or *ius sanguinis*. Countries following these old rigidities of the racist kind may be the vanguard of structural precarization, with native workers to follow.

My fourth, properly political axiom follows Kant and the much maligned Enlightenment, and in particular what Bloch calls (in *Naturrecht*) dignity, to consider what human rights might today entail. It is perhaps most consistently suggested by Marx's reading of the categorical imperative as a refusal of "all conditions in which people are degraded, enslaved, forsaken, contemptible beings" ("Toward the Critique," 257–58; see Balibar *Nous* 188 and passim, also Richmond). The condition of most migrants has been compared to other forms of "unfree labourers," ranging from slaves and forced labour, through bonded labourers to workers in illegal sweatshops and prostitution (cf. Papastergiadis 58). An elementary minimum human right is today the refusal of any such apartheid—and finally of caste society, soon perhaps to be genetically enforced. This right is politically formulated as "one person, one vote." There are in principle no second-rate people, and there should be no second-rate denizens of any country or territory (in monotheistic terms, there are no second-rate souls).

In Jefferson's words, each person has a right to "life, liberty, and the pursuit of happiness." This seems innocuous enough, but the observance of this axiom would put paid to almost all immigration policies on the Earth today. It points to the fact that all class privileges in post-feudal times, say from Locke on, refuse the status of full (that is, juridical) personhood to the groups they want to discriminate against economically and existentially—women, workers, foreigners, et al.—by infantilizing and/or criminalizing them, turning them into non-persons or sub-persons.[36] The Nazis were here again most consistent by using the overtly racist terminology of "subhumans." Obversely, this means that the original and quintessential European migrants, Gypsies (Roms) and Jews, were then among their favourite extermination groups. The Gypsies still have no State to speak for them, and can therefore function as a good meter for identitarian, pseudo-racist (there are no races within Homo sapiens) discrimination toward migrants.[37]

------

36. See Dal Lago, as cited in note 5, and note 27 in Suvin "Exile" for a first bibliography of citizenship discussions, to which I shall now add Dal Lago ed., Layton-Henry, Palidda, Simmel, and Zolo ed. As Dal Lago points out, further differentiations between non- and sub-persons are to be found in Bourdieu's splendid *Weight/Misère*.

Among the banalities and wooden language of the UN there may be found some useful nuggets, such as: "The benefits of international migration... not only for migrants themselves, but equally for receiving societies— are contingent on the protection of migrant rights. Labour rights are the mainstay in the prevention of exploitation and ought to be safeguarded." (*International*, point 13)

37. The other categories of the Nazi "democidal" mass murders were communists, homosexuals, some uncompromising religious sects such as Jehovah's Witnesses, the psychically damaged poor, and some Slavic populations (Soviet war prisoners, Serbs in Ustashi Croatia). The last two categories seem due to the Nazi ideology of race purity; the common denominator of the others seems to be a loyalty overriding Nation-State boundaries. It would behoove us to meditate deeply on this, for the Nazi

Of course, one should realistically add that any society has the right to defend itself by means of penal law, and such a right obviously extends to immigrants, whatever their cultural differences. Yet it can by no means follow that all, or most, or even very many, potential or real immigrants must be targeted under such law. Balibar calls this "the reign of institutionalized racism, of daily contempt and abuse of power which is, bit by bit, extended to all 'immigrants' or those held as such" (*Nous* 109). Unless we agree to sliding toward a permanent state of emergency with practically unchecked police powers, the basic principle of law that each case is to be examined on its merits must strictly be followed. Treating whole groups, sight unseen, as potentially dangerous is a clear case of discrimination and usually of racism. This is also what the mushrooming detention centers in practice mean, as well as expulsions as a means of ordinary administration rather than as a consequence for individual proved crime. Such practices are not only unethical, they are inefficient and integration-preventing instruments. Our energies and finances should rather be directed toward finding out intelligent forms of humane reception acceptable both to the immigrants and the majority of the native civil society. This begins with the allocation of resources to people rather than camps and prisons: for example, a paid interval for obligatory language courses and citizenship courses.[38] It carries on with legal and financial help for total integration into public schools, rather than paying for group private schooling, and into normal job training programs.

I do not primarily refer here to those "especially protected" against expulsion, such as political asylum seekers, minors

---

instincts were often unerring.

38. In Québec, a political unit anxious and thus careful about integration, such language and citizenship courses last six months. Let me add that it is quite clear from linguistic investigations, in Canada and Europe, that children learn the "target" country language better and faster if also given instruction in their mother language, so that bilingualism is pedagogically (and politically) not a problem but a resource.

and seniors, the sick or pregnant, or family members of those already in a country; to which I strongly believe those who have been regularly living and paying taxes in a country for X years, should be added. I am talking about normal, non-criminal adults, for whom I would invoke my fifth, politico-economical axiom, to be phrased in a US revolutionary way as "no taxation without representation." This means that a vote should be automatically extended for local elections (up to region level) to all those residents having paid one year of taxes, and for national and European elections after, say, two or three years of residence with some proof of work or property, of language knowledge, and of participation by eventual children in obligatory public schooling.

3. Some Prospects for Civil Cohabitation

3.1. In conclusion, "We have to admit, realistically, that there is in the long run no alternative to wars and terrorism but the effective universalization [of basic human rights]" (Ferrajoli 289). In the case of European countries this would mean, simultaneously, two radical changes.

First, a quite different foreign economical policy, aimed at what Balibar calls "co-development" between at least our portion of the global North and South should be adopted:

> Only such a project would enable us to find an equilibrium between a security-oriented Europe, that violently represses the migrations it has itself brought about, and a borderless Europe open to "savage" migrations (that is, entirely directed by the market in humans as instruments). Only this would enable us to deal with the conflicts of interest and culture between the "old" and "new" Europeans, the "legal" and "illegal" ones, [usually called] "the "communitarians" and the "extra-communitarians." ("Pour l'Europe," Thesis 11)

It should not be forgotten, even if I had to neglect this in the present essay, that all (im)migration is also emigration. As Sayad has rightly insisted, the study of the social relationships which lead to emigration and of their continuous dynamism, is a precondition for a full understanding of all migrations, which has three centrally concerned factors: "the society of emigration, the society of immigrations, and the emigrés/immigrants themselves" (18, and cf. 14-19).

The politico-economical precondition of such co-development is no European participation in wars (except in defense to a clear and present aggression against Europe). I noted above how wars are a major source of immiseration and therefore migration. But furthermore, history shows that wars cheapen the price of people and favour despotism and a drift toward subjection and slavery (cf. Weber 6-9).

Second, co-development on the basis of equal rights of denizens would imply at least two matters. To begin with, restricting admission and treating all those admitted (in the classical French tradition) as prospective citizens. Until the change of economic policy described above bears fruits—the only long-term solution to migration quandaries—it is in the present distribution of affluence among different parts of the world unrealistic to open borders for population transfer beyond what can be economically and psychologically borne by the present citizens (but this is elastic and should be judged by direct consultation of the people/s involved). However: once admitted, the immigrants must be treated by the criteria advocated in Section 2, as other citizens or "almost citizens." This implies to my mind as full an integration as possible but without imposing a "melting pot" assimilation.[39] No doubt, integration is a two-way street,

---

39 I adopt here Zincone's definitions of integration as "the capacity of both the old and the new members of a community to accept common rules of civil cohabitation" and of assimilation as "the transfusion of a different cultural identity" (*Da sudditi* 243). Beyond the civil duties, such as those I mention, the extent and pace of assimilation should be left to the new citizens themselves.

requiring that the immigrants observe some central human duties, which go hand in hand with the conferral of rights. I believe that no society can be asked to admit people who do not approve of such duties and tenets: popular sovereignty, gender parity, religious tolerance in a lay State, avoidance of significant violence (including clitoridectomy) except for self-defense... Separate schooling (as opposed to separate provisions for aiding immigrants and their children to begin learning) is to my mind incompatible with these goals.

Unless we go in for such radical, but I think reasonable and to my mind not at all extreme changes, how can civic integration, as against sectarian or chauvinist group involutions on both sides, be even begun? And how can we have civic peace, preventing both racist persecution against and potentially terrorist sympathies within the migrants, without a careful, multiculturally respectful yet robust integration? Without offering most immigrants more practical democracy and civility than the regimes they come from? (Democracy for the poorest and most vulnerable groups in a society is, notoriously, the only guarantee of democracy for the great majority.)

3.2. In support of this stance, let me recall some further, most pertinent statistics. First, official EU analyses predict that Europe needs the employment of twenty more millions of immigrant workers in the next twenty-five years, which with families means perhaps 60-80 millions! But second, perhaps just as explosive, a rapid "greying" of West-Central Europe is proceeding apace, followed somewhat more slowly by some parts of East Europe and even of North America. There, low native fertility must be compensated by either longer work years or, for the most part, by immigration of younger people in order to satisfy not only present work demands but also future pension funds (cf. Schödlbauer). Balancing pension funds—as a part of general national revenue and allocations for the social infrastructure of roads, schools, hospitals, etc.—without major social injustices will quite clearly require many more immigrants.

Immigrants are thus economically a blessing in disguise, yet they are politically everywhere a bone of contention if not a main excuse for revived racism and crypto-fascism. Shall immigrants then be pariahs or helots, as one study calls them, or at best "hands" and labour-power (cf. Sayad 61) in a dangerous vacuum of political rights and duties, or shall they be citizens? Shall they be people with more or less equal rights as their co-sharers of fate or with few rights except to be exploited both as labour power and taxpayers: harbingers of civic equality or of an apartheid society? In other words, can they be dealt with primarily as a security (or "law and order") issue, pertaining mainly to the ministry of the interior and the police, or as a complex but central issue determining the future of our societies? This is the problem that incides most deeply on all of us, immigrants or present citizens of the richer parts of the world.

For one example, Schödlbauer draws a scenario for Germany—based on the most probable forecast from the official statistics—of a "four quarters society": two quarters beyond working age, largely in old-age institutions, one quarter "native" employed citizens, one quarter of "'foreigners,' people with minor participation rights, living under the tutelage of laws aimed at good behaviour or expulsion, less educated and affluent..." (17). For another, we have ghettoized communities at the outskirts of most major cities, approaching conditions already fully realized in today's internment camps.[40] At the current rate of immigration without integration we are moving toward an apartheid where liberty, equality of chances, prosperity for a major part of the population, and equality of all other human rights, "the founding pledges on which the legitimacy of present-day States rest" (Schödlbauer 18), would be trampled down.

In tiered societies, that is, precapitalist tribes and States, the stranger is not only a political but also a religious alien. Today

---

40 To the rich literature on internment camps, touched upon in my "Exile," Agier and the latest issue no. 4 of *Conflitti globali*, "Internamenti," should be added.

the growing gap between the rich and the poor is leading either toward permanent armed conflict or back to a tiered society, probably to both. It is something we close our eyes to at great peril. Just what form such apartheid might take depends centrally on how strongly will economical and ecological pressures increase political conflictuality, and is thus today unclear. However, if the richer powers and classes of the globe continue on the present course, the probability of violent conflicts in the streets will go on growing.

<u>3.3.</u> This growing threat must be met by what Balibar has untranslatably called *droit de cité*, a system of public rights that entails refusing the amalgamation of different degrees of illegality (such as entry by contravening existing laws) with outright crime; it means condemning all administrative arbitrariness towards a supposed second-class (immigrant) citizenry, and establishing democratic representations by those who work and pay taxes to the same authority *(Nous* 108-09). In sum, I argue that every human being has "a right to rights" (cf. both titles by Calloz-Tschopp). This constitutes civility or *droit de cité*, not too dissimilar from Machiavelli's republican *vivere civile* (Balibar, *Nous* 209) but in a context of world pluralism and multiculturalism. The life of equal rights in "a common thing" is the only alternative to the existing covert and growing overt violence, from above and from below.

I can see at least four objections to this horizon. The first three are, in theory though not at all in practice, easily dealt with within my present framework. The fourth may indicate its limits.

First, the supposedly free market, as it is now, seems diametrically opposed to this horizon: "the problem of democratic citizenship is...whether there is space for an experience of democracy and of a State based on law which would not be totally subordinated to the market model..." (Zolo, "Strategia" 14; cf. also Santoro). The more reason to tame the inhuman face of the capitalist globalization, while preserving the great capitalist achievement of high productivity as a precondition for human rights.

Second objection: it contravenes central ideologies of the Nation-State as a "pure" and autarchic, self-enclosed unit. But the time for such dangerous myths and enclosures is clearly passing.

Third, the objection might be that the European Union, as it is now, is diametrically opposed to the civility and right to rights it often hypocritically invokes. The more reason to change the present Europe of banks and police forces into a Europe of its sovereign people(s)—meaning all those people who in it really dwell and upon whose labour it has rested and rests. It is also the only stable precondition for Europe's civil and even friendly relationships with peoples from other parts of the world, such as those proposed by Balibar. As the foremost Italian expert on the matter remarked: "It has not been grasped how essential are migrations for the coming about of a dynamic European space, capable of dialogue with the rest of the world and of using societal resources" (Dal Lago, *Polizia* 119). Beside the need of asserting the primacy of democratic society over its executive organs, he is speaking here of the need for tackling misery at the root, i.e. by means of a different economic policy towards poorer countries. This would also mean denying present-day mantras blindly propagandizing the unregulated market (ibid. 120-21), ideologies to which the unceasing interventions of strong governments and bodies such as the IMF ceaselessly and amply give the lie.

A cautionary note: in a not too distant future we shall see increasing numbers of "climate refugees," displaced by rising waters and, in a symmetrical development, by desertification. The thousands leaving New Orleans after Kattrina may soon become millions leaving Bangladesh and other poorer countries. Indeed, a report of Christian Aid from Spring 2007 calculates their number up to 2050 at one billion (one thousand millions)! In that case, our window of opportunity for democratic regulation of migration, before the climate exodus, may be <u>less than a</u>

quarter century.

But the fourth, and final, objection to my horizons may be that all the unemployed, illegally employed, and precariously employed, all those subjected to increasing and it seems boundless exploitation and domination, constitute the new global proletariat. In a Marxist analysis capitalism cannot exist without such a pole of misery because it draws its profits from its living labour; hence, whatever minor amendments to that status are within such a social formation possible for this or that smaller fraction, the status itself is unchangeable, and further immiseration inevitable. If this is true, if capitalism truly condemns a growing majority of humans to a life of psychophysical misery and (for hundreds of millions already) premature death, then we are most probably facing both apartheid and mass revolts including terrorism and urban guerillas. My proposals bet on the chance, even if small, of a radical democracy. But we cannot close our eyes to the alternative.

3.4. Castles and Miller noted early on that the global migration process is relatively impervious to official restrictions both in the source and the target countries. It is wishful thinking to deal with it by police and armed forces: it won't go away. They reasonably conclude their book:

> Exclusionary models of immigrant rights and nationhood are questionable, because they lead to divided societies. Similarly, assimilationist models are not likely to succeed, because they fail to take account of the cultural and social situation of settlers. The multicultural model is [the most viable set of responses] to the needs of settlers, and a statement about the openness of the nation to cultural diversity.[41]

---

41. Castles and Miller 253-54. There are many tensions and possibly aporias in the concept and/or practice of multiculturalism, which ought to be divorced from separatist and patriarchal "identity politics" in favour of both the personal right to secede from any community and rainbow-

However, our economic and political rulers today rarely follow reason, they rather ride the tiger of unbridled exploitation by means of xenophobia and panic-mongering:

> There was a young lady from Niger
> Who smiled as she rode on a tiger
> They returned from the ride
> With the lady inside
> And the smile on the face of the tiger.

Since the horizon of this essay is one of a radical democracy, as codified in philosophy by an Enlightenment that to my mind goes from Spinoza to Marx, I quote at parting a passage from the former, not in order to return to his terms but to advance from them:

> For it is certain that seditions, wars, and contempt or breach of laws are not so much to be imputed to the wickedness of the subjects as to the corrupt constitution of the State. For men are not born citizens but must be made so.... [I]f wickedness more prevails and more offences are committed in one State than in another, it is certain that the former has not sufficiently pursued harmony nor framed its laws with sufficient

---

like amity-in-unity of various coexisting communities. There is a voluminous debate, surveyed in Dal Lago *Non-persone* 167-77 not only for or against multiculturalism but also between "responsible" and "happy" multiculturalists, cf. at least Cohn-Bendit and Schmid, Sassen *Guests*, Todd, and the Zincone titles.

While "communitarian" identity politics—rooted in small polities, and today reactualizable only as separatisms (cf. Walzer), right up to murderous chauvinisms—may at times be unavoidable, and sometimes helpful (cf. for women Phillips), for modern citizenship under globalization I would subordinate them to the right of each person's self-determination, including dissent from phony closures. To be against is just as integral a part of liberty as to be with.

forethought, and therefore failed to acquire its absolute right as a State. (212-13)

Works Cited

See also the works cited in my essay "Exile" (below), where I discuss Arendt at more length. I found the best introductory overview to the present situation in Dal Lago's *Non-persone*, multi-faceted, vivacious, and freedom-loving, with a very rich multilingual bibliography. All unacknowledged translations from non-English sources are mine.

Useful internet sites (all http://www.): asylumlaw.org, displacement.org, esclavagemoderne.org, gisti.org, internalremi.revues.org, migreurop.org, noborder.org, picum.org, remisis.org, statewatch.org, united.non-profit.nl

Agamben, Giorgio. "Beyond Human Rights," in P. Virno and M. Hardt eds., *Radical Thought in Italy*. Transl. C. Casarino. Minneapolis: U of Minnesota P, 1996 [Italian in his *Mezzi senza fine*, Torino: Bollati Boringhieri, 1996].

Agier, Michel. *Aux bords du monde, les réfugiés*. Paris: Flammarion, 2002.

Altvater, Elmar. *Der Preis des Wohlstands*. Münster: Westfälisches Dampfboot, 1992.

Ang, Ien. "Diaspora," entry in Tony Bennett et al. eds., *New Keywords*. Malden MA & Oxford UK: Blackwell, 2005, 82-84.

Apitzsch, Ursula, and Mechtild M. Jansen eds. *Migration: Biographie und Geschlechterverhältnisse*. Münster: Westfälisches Dampfboot, 2003.

Arendt, Hannah. *Imperialism*, part 2 of her *The Human Condition*. New York & London: HBJ, 1973, 267-302 [written in 1945-49].

Aristotle. *Selections*. Transl. and ed by T. Irwin G. Fine. Indianapolis & Cambridge: Hackett, 1995.

Balibar, Étienne. *Nous, citoyens d'Europe?* Paris: La

Découverte, 2001.

—-. "Pour l'Europe altermondialisatrice." www.lautrecam-pagne.org

—-, and Immanuel Wallerstein. *Race, nation, classe.* Paris: La Découverte, 1997.

Balke, Friedrich ed. *Schwierige Fremdheit.* Frankfurt: Fischer, 1993.

Basch, Linda G., et al. *Nations Unbound.* New York: Gordon & Breach, 2000.

Bauböck, Rainer. *Transnational Citizenship.* Aldershot: Elgar, 1994.

Bielefeld, Uli ed. *Das Eigene und das Fremde: Neuer Rassismus in Europa?* Hamburg: Hamburger Ed., 1998.

Bloch, Ernst. *Naturrecht und menschliche Würde. Gesamtausgabe* Bd. 6. Frankfurt: Suhrkamp, 1961.

Boucher, Manuel ed. *Discriminations et ethnicization.* La Tour d'Aigues: Ed. de l'Aube, 2006.

Bourdieu, Pierre, and Loïc Wacquant. *An Invitation to Reflexive Sociology.* Chicago: U of Chicago P, 1992.

—-, et al. T*he Weight of the World.* Tr. P.P. Ferguson. Cambridge: Polity P, 1999 [orig. *La Misère du monde*, Paris 1993].

Calloz-Tschopp, Marie-Claire. *Les "sans-État" dans la philosophie de Hannah Arendt.* Lausanne: Payot, 2000.

—- ed. *Hannah Arendt, les Sans-État et le "droit d'avoir les droits,"* 2 Vols. Paris: L'Harmattan, 1998.

Castel, Robert. *Métamorphoses de la question sociale.* Paris: Fayard, 1995.

Castells, Manuel. *Power of Identity. The Information Age*, Vol. 2. Oxford & New York: Blackwells, 2004 [cited from *Das Informationszeitalter,* 3 Vols. Opladen: Leske & Budrich, 2001-2003].

Castles, Stephen, and Godula Kosack. *Immigrant Workers and Class Structure in Western Europe.* Oxford: Oxford UP, 1985 [orig. 1973].

Castles, Stephen, and Mark J. Miller. *The Age of Migration.*

3d edn. Houndmills & New York: Palgrave Macmillan, 2004 [orig. 1993].

Cesarani, David, and Mary Fulbrook eds. *Citizenship, Nationality and Migration in Europe.* London & New York: Routledge, 1996.

Cohen, Robin. *Global Diasporas.* Seattle: U of Washington P, 1997.

—-. *The New Helots: Migrants in the International Division of Labour.* Aldershot: Gower, 1987.

Cohn-Bendit, Daniel, and Thomas Schmid. *Heimat Babylon.* Frankfurt a/M: Hoffman & Campe, 1992.

Colombo, Ascher, and Giuseppe Sciortino. *Gli immigrati in Italia.* Bologna: Il Mulino, 2004.

Dal Lago, Alessandro. *Non-persone.* Milano: Feltrinelli, 2004.

—-. *Polizia globale.* Verona: ombre corte, 2003.

—- ed. *Lo straniero e il nemico.* Genova & Milano: costa & nolan, 1998.

Derrida, Jacques. *On Cosmopolitanism and Forgiveness.* Tr. M. Dooley and M. Hughes. New York: Routledge, 2001 (*Cosmopolites de tous les pays, encore un'effort!* Paris: Galilée, 1997).

Faist, Thomas. *The Volume and Dynamics of International Migration and Transnational Social Spaces.* Oxford: Oxford UP, 2000.

Ferrajoli, Luigi. "Dai diritti del cittadino ai diritti della persona," in Zolo ed. [see below], 263-92.

Gilroy, Paul. *After Empire.* Abingdon: Routledge, 2004.

Gramsci, Antonio. *Quaderni dal carcere*, Vol. 2. Ed. V. Gerratana. Torino: Einaudi, 1975.

van Gunsteren, Herman. *A Theory of Citizenship: Organizing Plurality in Contemporary Democracies.* Boulder: Westview P, 1998.

Hammar, Thomas. *Democracy and Nation-State: Aliens, Denizens, and Citizens in a World of International Migration.* Aldershot: Avebury, & Brookfield VT: Gower, 1990.

—- ed. *European Immigration Policy.* Cambridge & New York: Cambridge UP, 1985.

Hannerz, Ulf. *Transnational Connections.* NY & L: Routledge, 1996.

Harris, Joseph E. ed. *Global Dimensions of the African Diaspora*, 2 Vols. Washington DC: Howard UP, 1993.

Harris, Nigel. *The New Untouchables: Immigration and the New World Worker.* London: Tauris, 1995, & Penguin, 1996.

Held, David. "Between State and Civil Society," in Geoff Andrews ed., *Citizenship.* London: Lawrence & Wishart, 1991.

International Migration and Development [résumé of the report presented by the UN Secretary-General to the General Assembly in June 2006]. UNDESA Population Newsletter. www.un.org/esa/population/unpop.htm

Kane, Hal. *The Hour of Departure.* Washington DC: Worldwatch Institute, 1995.

Kant, Immanuel. "Idea for a Universal History from the Cosmopolitan Point of View," in L. White ed., *On History.* Tr. R.E. Archer and E.L. Ferkenheim. Indianapolis: Bobbs, 1963, 11-26.

—-. *Zum ewigen Frieden/ À la paix perpetuelle.* Paris: Vrin, 2002. [Texte allemand de l'Académie de Berlin, Vol. VIII: 343ff.]

Kritz, Mary M., et al. *International Migration Systems.* Oxford: Clarendon P, 1992.

Kyle, David, and Rey Koslowski. *Global Human Smuggling.* Baltimore & London: Johns Hopkins UP, 1991.

Layton-Henry, Zig. *The Political Rights of Migrant Workers in Western Europe.* Newbury Park: Sage, 1990.

Leggewie, Claus, and Richard Münch eds. *Politik im 21. Jahrhundert.* Frankfurt: Suhrkamp, 2001.

Liberti, Stefano. "Migrazione dall'Africa...." *Il Manifesto* 23/11/2006, p. 6.

Lutz, Helma, et al. eds. *Crossfires: Nationalism, Racism and Gender in Europe.* London: Pluto P, 1995.

Marshall, T.H. "Citizenship and Social Class," in his

Sociology at the Crossroads and Other Essays. London: Heinemann, 1963.

Marx, Karl. "Toward the Critique of Hegel's Philosophy of Law: Introduction," in W*ritings of the Young Marx on Philosophy and Society*. Ed. and trans. L. D. Easton and K. H. Guddat. Garden City NY: Doubleday, 1967, 249–64.

Marx, Karl, and Friedrich Engels. *Das Kapital*, Vol. 3. *Marx-Engels Werke [MEW]*, Vol. 25. Berlin: Dietz, 1979.

Moulier-Boutang, Yann. *De l'esclavage au salariat*, Paris: PUF, 1998.

Ong, Aihwa. *Flexible Citizenship*. Durham & London: Duke UP, 1999.

Palidda, Salvatore. "La conversione poliziesca delle politiche migratorie," in A. Dal Lago ed., *Lo straniero e il nemico* [see above], 209-35.

——- ed. *Délit d'immigration*. Bruxelles: Migrations, 1992.

Papastergiadis, Nikos. *The Turbulence of Migration*. Cambridge: Polity P, 2000.

Phillips, A. "Citizenship and Feminist Theory," in G. Andrews ed., *Citizenship* [see under Held].

Pries, Ludger ed. *Zwischen den Welten und Zuschreibungen: ...Arbeitsmigration im 21. Jahrhundert*. Essen: Klartext V, 2004.

Rea, A. ed. *Immigration et racisme en Europe*. Bruxelles: Complexe, 1998.

Richmond, A.H. *Global Apartheid: Refugees, Racism and the New World Order*. Toronto: Oxford UP, 1994.

Santoro, Emilio. "Le antinomie della cittadinanza," in Zolo ed. [see below], 93-128.

Sassen, Saskia. *Guests and Aliens*. New York: New P, 1999.

——-. *Losing Control: Sovereignty in the Age of Globalization*. New York: Columbia UP, 1996.

——-. *The Mobility of Labor and Capital: A Study of International Investment*. Cambridge & New York: Cambridge UP, 1988.

——-. "Women's Burden." *J. of International Affairs* 53.2 (2000): 503-24.

Sayad, Abdelmalek. *L'immigration, ou les paradoxes de l'altérité*. Bruxelles: De Boeck, 1992.

Schödlbauer, Ulrich. "Bevölkerung," in *IABLIS: Jahrbuch für europäische Prozesse* 5 (2006): 9-54.

Seneca, Lucius Annaeus. *Ad Helviam matrem de consolatione*. Stuttgart: Reclam, 2001.

Simmel, Georg. "Der Mensch als Feind." *Aufsätze und Abhandlungen 1901-08*, Bd. 2. Frankfurt a/M: Suhrkamp, 1992, 335-43.

Spinoza, Baruch. *Tractatus politicus*, in his *Opera*. Ed. C. Gebhardt. Heidelberg: Winter, s.a. [1925].

Stalker, Peter. *Workers without Frontiers*. Boulder: Riener, & Geneva: ILO, 2000.

Stanton, Domna C. "On Rooted Cosmopolitanism." *PMLA* 121.3 (2006): 627.40.

Suvin, Darko. "Exile as Mass Outrage and Intellectual Mission," in Maria Teresa Chialant ed., *Viaggio e letteratura*. Venezia: Marsilio, 2006, 69-95.

—-. "Comparative Literature and the Power/ Violence of Terms: From Historical Semantics to Political Epistemology," in P. Mildonian ed., *It Started in Venice: Proc. of the International Comparative Literature Conference 2005*. CD, Venezia: Libr. Ed. Cafoscarina, 2009: 67-78.

Thomas, Brinley. *Migration and Economic Growth*. Cambridge: Cambridge UP, 1973.

Todd, Emmanuel. *Le destin des immigrés*. Paris: Seuil, 1994.

Walzer, Michael. *Spheres of Justice*. New York: Basic Books, 1983.

Weber, Max. *Soziologie—Weltgeschichtliche Analysen—Politik*. Stuttgart: Kröner, 1964.

Willcox, W.F. ed. *International Migrations*, 2 Vols. New York: Gordon & Breach, 1969 [orig. 1929].

Wittgenstein, Ludwig. *Philosophische Untersuchungen*. Frankfurt: Suhrkamp, 1967 [cited from *Philosophical Investigations*, 3d edn. Tr. G.E.M. Anscombe. Oxford: Blackwell, 1999].

Wood, Ellen Meiksins. *Empire of Capital*. London & New York: Verso, 2005.

Zincone, Giovanna. *Citizenship: Between State and Society*. S. Domenico di Fiesole: European Univ. Institute, 1999.

—-. *Da sudditi a cittadini*. Bologna: Il Mulino, 1992.

—-. *Uno schermo contro il razzismo*. Roma: Donzelli, 1994.

Zolberg, Aristide R. "Wanted but not Welcome: Alien Labor in Western Development," in W. Alonso ed., *Population in an Interacting World*. Cambridge MA: Harvard UP, 1987, 36-73.

Zolo, Danilo. "La strategia della cittadinanza," in idem ed. *La cittadinanza*. Roma & Bari: Laterza, 1994, 3-46.

7. BRECHT AND COMMUNISM: REFLECTIONS ON AND AT A TANGENT FROM A SYMPOSIUM

—To the memory of Helene Weigel—

I cannot write this review in any other tone than first-person singular, for if I had known of the Berlin 2006 conference I'd have tried to participate: it deals with two matters at the centre of my interest in these years, namely Brecht and Communism. I'd have noted with joy how Manfred Wekwerth and I have had the same impulse to go back to Brecht's versifying of Marx in *Das Manifest* by making out of the various versions a coherent and highly interesting text (his is usefully printed at the end of the volume, while my English translation in jazzed-up hexameters, with commentary, may be found as essay 4 in this book), and how we ended up with a very similar text. I'd have noted with less joy some sectarianisms also present at the conference, which is now available as issue no. 1 (2007) of *Marxistische Blätter*, that looks like, and was, advertised as a book title but has not been given an ISBN number. Furthermore it's not clear whether one of Brecht's definitions of communism, "Es ist das Einfache das schwer zu machen ist" (It is the simple thing which is difficult to do), should be the title, as on the first inner page, or

"*Bertolt Brecht und der Kommunismus*" (BB and Communism) as on the title page. The result is that it is unavailable in any catalogue or electronic bibliography, and after months of writing around I had to get it through a friend in Germany who contacted *Marxistische Blätter* (they don't answer e-mail). I do not detail this only as a justified gripe but mainly because it speaks to some parlous organizational—and thus political, and of course imaginative—gaps of the Marxist Left, which are a good introduction to my theme.

There is a minimum common denominator to this book. All of its contributors would agree with, and several cite, Marx's categorical imperative: „To overturn all situations in which a human is a humiliated, an enslaved, an abandoned, a contemptible being ("Alle Verhältnisse umzuwerfen, in denen der Mensch ein erniedrigtes, ein geknechtetes, ein verlassenes, ein verächtliches Wesen ist"—MEW 1: 385). This is the monster that the Perseus (or St. George) of communism must slay: on pain of extinction—for communism but also for our Andromeda, humanity as we know it. Further, all the contributors find this imperative grows much more urgent in today's perfectly sinful society of "turbocapitalism." Insofar, the volume is to be applauded. But this doesn't by itself go far enough.

For the rest, the volume seems rather similar to a group of small crabs at the sea's edge, groups and singularities scuttling energetically sideways from each other. Even within the same paper, some contributions seem to be going into all directions at once, which doesn't help in arriving anywhere. My personal interest is in what I can get out of this volume to facilitate thinking about communism today. But before I get to this, I shall briefly consider two other themes. Some minor notes and discussions, as well as the interesting report by Klaus Höpcke on the CD resulting from federal German politicians reading their favourite Brecht poem, will remain unconsidered.

The first is "What did Brecht mean for my communist education?", represented by the articles of the Cuban filmmaker Juan Garcia Espinosa and the graduate student David Salomon (but echoing in a number of other articles). Both testify, in these times of suppression of historical memory, what our author meant to people outside of what we know in Euro-America and in the generations up to 1989. He is situated quite rightly as a paragon, a model, a delightful teacher. This is a role known to us, before the German "art worship" (say the *Kunstverehrung* of Goethe), in the Fathers of the Church(es) and in love poetry from Sappho and Petrarca on. Some other time it would be interesting to compare such models.

The second theme is "What did Communism mean to Brecht?" This question is not so easy to delimit from the third theme, my main theme, because a number of contributors use its philologico-historical *ductus* to point out how we can learn from Brecht for the dark future coming at us today (this was before the financial crash of 2008). I shall begin with a subsection that deals with Brecht and the "really existing" Communist parties, well represented in one of the five sections within the W.F. Haug article and in the contribution by Sabine Kebir. Their overviews both come to the conclusion he was an "independent communist intellectual" (Kebir's title) whose attempt at dialogue with the SED failed as "intervening thinking" (Haug). Particularly welcome is Kebir's use of little known archival data, for example, about his contacts with Soviet authorities who in 1941 tried to engage him in collaboration with the KGB (he refused politely). I have always thought the best encapsulation of his politics was given by a friend in Los Angeles (I forget the name) who characterized him as "a one-man party, in close alliance with the communists."

Some central points of "What did Communism mean to Brecht?" are dealt with by Hans Heinz Holz and Jost Hermand. The latter's paper does so by means of a detour through a, to my mind persuasive, central stance identifying Brecht as "teacher of *Unbürgerlichkeit* (non-bourgeoisdom)." His hate of bourgeois individualism and corrupt liberalism induced him to stress achievements in literature and the arts, as well as in ethics, before capitalism (Medieval and Baroque works, China) and putatively after it (Gorki, Picasso, Eisler). This historical sequence should not really be taken as merely temporally "progressive"; as Hermand also notes, Brecht's roots were in the plebeian forms of poetry, theatre, narration, and language, so it is largely a class scheme. The fixed point remains the hate of the bourgeoisie. Calling Brecht a materialist and radical applier of Marxism, Hermand does not mention communism at all (nor does the paper by Dieter Dehm). Twenty plus years ago I'd have been enthusiastic about his paper, which is as always excellent at what it does. But with today's interest horizon, it reminds me, as do a number of other articles here strongly arguing for some Leftist ideology, that even the best German philological tradition is still firmly based on the Idealist doctrine of "two realities": there is art and then there is life...

Holz writes about the *Parteilichkeit* (taking sides, with a pun on the [Communist] Party) of Brecht's lyrics, where the tenderness about the little plum-tree crippled by the capitalist city courtyard implies by contraries a deep protest. He ends with a polemic against Haug's call to "refound" communism, arguing that while the Party is nothing without us, we are, so far as power goes, nothing without the Party. I read him as arguing also that this would be Brecht's position, for he cites the *Lob der Partei*: "The individual can be destroyed, the Party cannot be destroyed." It remains unclear what this means today, after it has been falsified.

This second theme can be rephrased as "How Do We Read Brecht's Opus after the Collapse of the 'Really Existing' Socialism?" It is pursued at length by Ernst Schumacher with respect to theatre, who ends with some reflections of what might its "mole" function be today.

This leads to my final and most important theme: What can somebody like me, who takes Brecht also as paragon for present-day existential politics, get from this volume for understanding what should and could be a proper, communist stance *(Haltung)* and activity today? This may mean, first, "What can I get out of Brecht's refraction of Marx's and Lenin's tradition for understanding the present-day horrors of capitalism?" I take it that this is the point of Hermand's and Holz's contributions, too. But then, as a young man named Ulyanov wrote more than 100 years ago, "What Is To Be Done?" There is no way around the crucial question of a vanguard Party after the experiences sparked by that young man. I observe a curious blockage, almost a taboo here: it is again (with one partial exception, to which I shall come to at the end) dealt with obliquely, through esthetico-philosophical discussions rather than overtly politico-economic and organizational ones. *Politisch Lied, ein garstig Lied (*"Political poem, a horrid poem"): Goethe seems to have even on the Left won out against Brecht; and economics surface perhaps in 2 out of the 17 papers.

Such a discussion is implicit in the views that Brecht was really an orthodox realist by Thomas Metscher and Reinhard Jellen, or an orthodox Marxist by Werner Seppmann, and in all three cases argued as being not so far from Lukács's views and a dialectics of possibility plus intervention. Surely such positions—insisting that beside clear divergences between them, strongest during the Hitler-Stalin period, they also held some premises in common, so that their confrontation cannot be simply reduced to Stalinism or Socialist Realism against (say) Luxemburgism and Modernism—are a welcome corrective to "western Marxist" simplifications. These articles stress clarity and Lukácsian humanist dialectics; they all love Descartes and abhor Derrida. Again, having written against the Post-Modernist vulgate—than which the later Derrida is much better—I would accept a number of such insights as useful; and many terms they use (such as realism) can be stretched so that only connotations without denotations remain. But the connotations of some of the terms and turns that peep out in these polemics are strange, and remind one of the 1930s-40s Lukács, not the late "humanist" one (which they sometimes confuse with the early "reification" one). Strangely enough, Seppmann, for example, categorically states that Brecht cannot be called a Modernist (arguing this by means of one quote from Duchamp that Modernism doesn't pose the question of truth!). Jellen, the most apodictic of them, says that Brecht was a follower of Lenin's mirroring theory in epistemology and esthetics (p. 119), which I think cannot be defended in any form, and that the Brecht-Renaissance after 1968 (he means in West Germany) was a fatal turn for the worse. In brief, Brecht and Lukács were one as far as content goes, but differed about who was a Formalist (pp. 119-20). Both were for catharsis too, as Lukács misleadingly explained in his late *Eigenart des Ästhetischen* (and Metscher repeats on p. 14). This ante-diluvian aesthetics using content versus form, which can at best be called Kantian (that is, pre-dialectical) and at worst Zhdanovian, was of course in practice allied with police enforcement, even if much less bloody in the GDR than in the USSR. Aesthetics thus segues seamlessly into politics and the worst errors of "really existing communism." It significantly contributed to its defeat, brought about by TV images (commodity aesthetics) and banks, not tanks.

This problem was identified by Brecht in early unflinching verses after the 1933 defeat (smaller than today's) "To Him Who Hesitates" (*An den Schwankenden*). I cannot cite all of it, as I should, but will use the verse that Seppmann does:

> Wir aber haben Fehler gemacht, es ist nicht mehr zu leugnen.
> Unsere Zahl schwindet hin.
> Unsere Parolen sind in Unordnung. Einen Teil unserer Wörter
> Hat der Feind verdreht bis zur Unkenntlichkeit.
>
> Was ist jetzt falsch an dem was wir gesagt haben
> Einiges oder alles? (GKA 12: 47)
>
> [But we have made mistakes, it cannot be denied./ Our numbers shrink./ Our slogans are in disarray. One part of our words/ The enemy has twisted out of

recognition.// What is now false in what we were saying/ Some or all?]

The last two lines to my mind open up from politics towards epistemology: How do we know what (we think) we know? Is there not a strong probability that the Progress-Science paradigm (of clear bourgeois origin in both cases!) has led us astray, as Gramsci clearly realized? Isn't it then obligatory to get rid not only of the Kantian but also the Positivist dichotomies such as Nature-Culture (Metscher still argues for a dialectics in Nature waiting only to be discovered by humans, I suppose since the sabre-toothed tigers)? In that sense, all of us ought today to rightly hesitate and renew ourselves.

Thus I got most out of the essays by Heuer and Haug for my project of understanding a possible movement toward communism. Uwe Jens Heuer begins to talk epistemologically when he notes that possibilities or probabilities are more useful to think with than determinism. But he gets only as far as statistical possibilities, old stuff going back to thermodynamics at the beginning of the 20th Century. The whole revolution in physics since Einstein and Planck (never mind electronics, warfare, and finances, never mind Kafka, Joyce and Dos Passos) seems to have passed our Kant-Zhdanovians by, as if 100 sensational and horrible years were nothing: a fine ostrich "humanism!" To the contrary, today it is quite normal to say that the reality described by quantum mechanics is "composed of many worlds" (Castoriadis 161), or that in several of its branches "a whole battery of models" are regularly used, and "no one thinks that one of these is the whole truth, and they may be mutually inconsistent" (Hacking 37)! Models, that is what Brecht is about, and while Lukács reached for types, which are a kind of model, he didn't quite make it (I argued this in "Lukács"). Most interestingly, however, Heuer has arrived at the necessity of a faith for Marxism that would not be religious belief but would "cover that field" (76) and thus co-opt its energies. Those who have read my "Inside the Whale" will readily understand that

I am fully sympathetic to this opening, as I would say towards salvation.

The most useful essay for me is the one by W.F. Haug. Here I must confess to some embarrassment as I occasionally participate in his Inkrit conferences and write in *Das Argument* of which he's an editor. But those who frequent Inkrit meetings will remember occasions when I have disagreed, publicly and somewhat sharply, with him. So I'll conclude by focusing from his rich overview on the gist of his position, beyond what I have already mentioned. Haug discusses Brecht and Marxism and repeats his meritorious position that Brecht was an original Marxist thinker on a par to, and with, "selective affinities" (unknown to both) to Gramsci—and I can only hope he will at some point discuss Benjamin, too. This entails warnings against a too total totality and in general against too clearly outlined images of the world and "world views" dear to the German philosophical tradition and Lukács (in all of his phases). To the contrary, Brecht latched on, directly and through Lenin, to Hegel's contradiction and to a pleasurable, indeed witty, Marxist dialectics, with practical twists and turns which would be as much art as science. Much before Derrida, Brecht deconstructed the unsplittable atom of Subject, Ego, and Personality into oscillating and recombinable quarks and charms of attitudes and relationships. He applied Heisenberg and the Copenhagen School from physics to relations between people, affirming that "what we investigate has been changed by the investigation" (GKA 22.2:730, cited by Haug, p. 63). A series of such soundings allow Haug to affirm that "these proposals, if taken seriously, would suffice to put out of joint the whole view of the world taken by many communists in the 20th Century as being Marxism, and would give an orientation toward a reconstruction which amounts to a refounding" (*Neugründung*, p. 71) This proposal put the cat among the pigeons, and occasioned strong rejoinders from the Holz-Jellen wing. One can only suppose they felt their world view was being challenged.

My own view is that the metaphor of refounding is somewhat

slippery, as the fate of Haug's reference to Rifondazione comunista in Italy testifies to: it has since split into quarrelling *groupuscules* without real political, never mind intellectual, impact. Maybe reconstruction on the medieval model, where old Roman buildings were quarried for large blocks out of which to build Christian churches, is less ambiguous. Haug has of course used large blocks of Marx in erecting his own building, but I don't think even he has yet come (in writing, at least) to terms with Lenin's legacy.

If I'm allowed a final, *sotto voce* complaint: some Teutonic navel-gazing may also have been at work in this conference. Nobody seems to have reflected on, say, Jameson's redefinition of utopia or indeed of Brecht as centrally a transmissible method; or on Žižek's rereading of Lenin. Derrida is sneered at, while Balibar or Badiou do not exist. This sits strangely with a Brecht who knew some aspects of England and the USA very well, and whose greatest success was arrived at in Paris.

* * * * * * *

At the end, I shall go off on a tangent to summarize some insights I believe have to be added to those in this volume in order to BEGIN making sense of Communism, and how Brecht may be supremely useful to understanding what this might be. First of all, we would have to unpack the term "communism," used without much differentiation in this volume. I would phrase this as: communism can be a locus, an orientation for a movement, and a horizon. Puzzlingly, each of these somehow implies and needs the others.

Communism as <u>horizon</u> is the future Earthly Paradise of a classless society, a society where oppositions will not be dealt with antagonistically, through murder and hunger: not by pistol but by pencil, as Brecht says in the nearest approximation to it he allowed himself to pen, the Prologue to the *Caucasian Chalk Circle* (which also, as Haug remarks, sketches the ideal role of the intellectual in Arkadi Cheidze, the singer-narrator). As all horizons, it is orienting, often inspiring, and always unattainable, for it moves with the viewer and pursuer oriented toward it.

Communism as <u>locus</u> is any real society claiming to be largely or even asymptotically utopian or non-antagonistic (harmonious, as the Chinese Communist Party hypocrites today say). It could be, as Lenin and Brecht and all classical socialists and Marxists believed, a first absolutely necessary step towards a disalienated life of people in a community, IF (and only if) it, a/ was not stifled by poverty and aggression, and b/ did not pretend to be the oxymoron of a finally reached horizon, an illusion that also necessarily grows into a religion and a lie (Nietzsche can be used here, as Brecht used him: nobody in this volume mentions his work, I think).

Today, bereft of locus, we still might have (if we don't lose the faith Heuer and Derrida speak of) the <u>orientation</u>, a vector leading from our quite dystopian and catastrophic locus of capitalist barbarism towards the utopian horizon (in the positive sense of eutopia, *pace* Engels). Orientation means, etymologically, turning toward the Orient of the rising Sun, the source of light and warmth, indeed of all life. Orientation toward a communist horizon is the subspecies of Brecht's bearing (*Haltung*) proper to Brecht's philosophico-political followers. It would be at piece with Brecht's permanent eager receptivity to better ways of thinking, which Wekwerth so engagingly transmits in his introduction, and Schumacher confirms: maybe it's naivety we need as a tool? Maybe sympathy too? Let's try it out and see.

This orientation is today our minimum requirement, without which all talk of communism should cease. But for a proper collective orientation, that is, a movement with this orientation, we need a cultural revolution, a rebuilding on the basis of an updated Marx for a cybernetic age and a most dangerously rotting capitalism, as well as a clear idea how to organize, that is, what to take from Lenin and what not. Anarchism, noble as it is in many ways in people like Kropotkin, will get us nowhere:

as we have seen in these last 10 years.

Thus, when Holz and other comrades say a Party is necessary, I agree—though we'd have to see just how to modify even the original Lenin precepts. When Haug says a Cultural Revolution is necessary, I also agree—possibly first of all. It would mean we had a political collective which can accommodate Kebir's autonomous communist intellectuals within the Cause. Then indeed we could get back to Brecht's "Lob der Partei" (Praise of the Party): "Wir sind sie" (We are her).

Works Cited

Brecht, Bertolt. *Werke.* Grosse Kommentierte Berliner und Frankfurter Ausgabe. Suhrkamp & Aufbau V., 1988-2000 [cited as GKA].

Castoriadis, Cornelius. *Crossroads in the Labyrinth.* Transl. K. Soper and M.H. Ryle. Brighton: Harvester, 1984.

Hacking, Ian. *Representing and Intervening.* Cambridge: Cambridge UP, 1983.

Marxistische Blätter no. 1 (2007): "Bertolt Brecht und der Kommunismus" special issue. www.neue-impulse-verlag.de/mbl/archiv/year-2007.html

Suvin, Darko. "Inside the Whale, or *etsi communismus non daretur*," (2007), in his *Defined by a Hollow.* Oxford: P. Lang, 2010; German in *Das Argument* no. 271 (2006): 383-98.

—-. "Lukács: Horizons and Implications of the 'Typical Character'." *Social Text* no. 16 (1987): 97-123.

8. ON THE HORIZONS OF EPISTEMOLOGY AND SCIENCE (2008-09)

—for Gene Gendlin—

One basis for life, and another for science is in itself a lie.

Karl Marx (1844)

...Because the lust for profit of the ruling class sought satisfaction through technology, it betrayed humanity and turned the bridal bed into a bloodbath. The mastery of nature, so the imperialists teach, is the purpose of all technology. But who would trust a cane wielder who proclaimed the mastery of children by adults to be the purpose of education? Is not education above all the indispensable ordering of the relationship between generations, and therefore mastery, if we are to use this term, of that relationship and not of children? And likewise technology is not the mastery of nature but of the relation between nature and humanity.

Walter Benjamin (1928)

1. Central Orientation Points for Epistemology[42]

> I wish first to speak of how I ought to speak, and only then to speak.
>
> Agathon, in Plato's *Symposium* (C4 BCE)

1.1. Against the Unique Truth (Monoalethism)

> *Ein Führer, ein Volk, ein Reich!* (One Leader, One People, One Empire)
>
> Powerful Nazi slogan

Towards the end of the *Critique of Pure Reason*, Kant raises three vital questions for human reason: How can I know? What shall I do? What may I hope? The sequence of the questions is very interesting: first comes what interests the philosopher or critical intellectual in general, which would be fair enough for his purposes except that he pretends they are universal, and only second the practical applications of properly gained knowledge. The horizons of hope come last (while faith and love, the other components of the classical Christian triad of virtuous values, are nowhere to be found).[43] To the contrary, there are good arguments that for most less specialized people as well as for all

---

42. My understanding of epistemology has been much shaped by the tradition of Brecht's and Marcuse's dominating vs. emancipatory science on one hand and on the other by Merleau-Ponty and some of his French contemporaries in psychology and philosophy, by Vygotsky, Wittgenstein, and too many others to mention. I have to single out my discussions for 20+ years with Gene Gendlin, that go much beyond what I could say in a note but can be glimpsed in "On Cognitive."

My thanks also go to Rich Erlich for much textual help and editing.

43. Kant practically created the focus on epistemology, see Rorty 134-48. At the end of his *Logik* (Introduction, A 25), he seems to have subsumed these three queries under a fourth: "What is Man?"

For useful historical overviews see Suchting and Laugstien, esp. the former on Marx and the latter on Brecht and Gramsci; neither mentions Nietzsche.

collectives (groups, classes, societies) first come the pragmatic and value horizons determining why bother to think and do something, while the epistemological question of <u>how does one, or how do we, know what (we think) we know</u> is subordinated not only to them but also to practical action with which it is in continuous feedback, and thus on the whole would come last. Nonetheless, for orientation in periods of great confusion and/or for limited purposes, epistemology remains important, and will in this essay (which partakes of both) be my beginning, though not my end, since I want to go on into science as politics.

I am not aware of a systematic basis for epistemology (gnoseology, theory of knowledge in the wider sense) we could today use, but it seems possible to glean some central orientation points for it. I postulate that our interpretations of what is knowledge or not, a proper or improper one, is largely shaped by the "framework of commitments" we bring to them. I take this term and my subsequent initial discussion mainly from Elgin, who summarizes one widespread kind of agreement by formulating what I would call a strategic "soft" skepticism, which still allows action and value-horizons:

> Philosophy once aspired to set all knowledge on a firm foundation. Genuine knowledge claims were to be derived from indubitable truths by means of infallible rules. The terms that make up such truths were held to denote the individuals and kinds that constitute reality, and the rules for combining them...were thought to reflect the real order of things.—This philosophical enterprise has foundered. Indubitable truths and infallible rules are not to be had. (183)

Instead, thinking always begins with working approximations based on "our best presystematic judgments on the matter at hand" (ibid.) or by "the general fundaments of our orientation in the world" (Weber 323). As we advance toward a larger whole of understanding, we often discover they are untenable or insufficient, and at any rate have to be both tenable and modifiable to accommodate breadth and coherence. As Mark Martial said about a book of his verse, some are good, some bad, some so-so—there is no other ensemble to be had.

Some scientists (usually not strong on theory) like to discourse on evidence, in the sense of proof. However important this may be, what counts as evidence is "theory-laden," determined by "our conception of the domain and...our goals in systematizing it..." (Elgin 184-85).[44] The *New York Times* claims it brings "All the news that's fit to print": discounting the hyped "all" and the bad grammar, who determines how what is fit? There may be some internal rules wedded to novelty (dog biting man is not news, but man biting dog is), but even novelty as criterion is an invention of fast-moving times with worldwide commerce and industrial production, not to mention the capitalist scramble for profitable niches. Alternative presuppositions and goals would always find alternative ways of organizing the domain of what is worth knowing—say, all the news of interest to anti-capitalists (which would, for example, disbar calling the mass killing of civilians "collateral damage," or the present Iraqi and Afghan regimes "democratic"). Choices between these alternatives are, in all interesting cases, not arbitrary but of a piece with our interests and goals, which steer the categories that cut up our world (cf. Weber 323-25). In a dispute, they depend on the available background of agreement as to which category is relevant to judge an event. Of course, if we are loyal to the enterprise of understanding or cognition, we shall often fine-tune these, and sometimes modify them drastically: all hypotheses are fallible. Nor is experiencing something a magic wand: any police constable or UFO reports' investigator will tell you that our beliefs and expectations largely steer that too.

---

44. I am attempting in this paper an as clear as possible overview and summary without too much technicality. Even when I'm in sympathy with some intricate arguments, they often, alas, get short shrift, so for example those in Barnes-Edge eds., Hesse's "Theory and Observation" in *Revolutions*, Longino...

The horizon I am sketching is in a subsequent book by Goodman and Elgin characterized as "reject[ing] both absolutism and nihilism, both unique truth and the indistinguishability of truth from falsity" (3). The difficulty is that, when we construct however open-ended a system of interpretations, we employ—knowingly or not—multiple standards of rightness beyond consistency: appropriateness or relevance, accuracy, scope, entrenchment in previous discourse (this is discussed by them at length in 11-23), and the standards may conflict with each other and/or with our practical goals. Adjudication between them, giving the various factors different weightings etc., will often lead to a solution, but it remains that, as a rule, "A number of independently acceptable systems can be constructed, none of which has a claim to epistemological primacy" (24). A univocal world—the fixed reality out there—has been well lost, together with the Unique Final Truth (divine or asymptotically scientific) and other Onenesses of the monotheist family. This is both encapsulated and symbolized by Gödel's theorems, which are a rigorous proof that any non-trivial formalized system of a certain richness necessarily includes undecidable propositions and that the non-contradictory nature of such a system cannot be demonstrated within its own terms. In other words, deduction can very well get to apodictically necessary ("true") propositions, but who shall deduce the deductions or terminate the terms? A sense of panic at the loss of this clear world, at the loss of theological certitude, not only permeates dogmatists of all religious and lay kinds, but has also engendered its symmetrical obverse in the absolutist relativism, which often claims to be authorized by (say) Kuhn or Feyerabend—who have at any rate, I would add, great liberating merits. How is a third way possible beyond this bind?

It can begin by recognizing that right and wrong persist, but that rightness can no longer be identified with correspondence to a ready-made, monotheistic Creation, but must be created by us, with skill and responsibility: "Having been ordered to shoot anyone who moved, the guard shot all his prisoners, contending they were all moving rapidly around the sun. Although true, his contention was plainly wrong, for it involved an inappropriate category of motion." (Goodman and Elgin 52). Thus, truth in the strict logical sense is subordinate to rightness or correctness (cf. Aronowitz vii-xi and passim), in Hellenic terms to *orthotes* rather than *aletheia*. Truth is too solidly embedded in faiths and certitudes of monotheistic allegiance, Goodman and Elgin think, while categories as well as argument forms and other techniques within continual human cognition are better instruments for practical use, testable for situational rightness. The rightness is also dependent on our various symbol systems. One consequence is that science loses its epistemic primacy: "[it] does not passively inform upon but actively informs a world"— as do in different ways and with different standards of rightness the arts and everyday practices of other kinds (Elgin 53). As Bruner argues, the arts are differently entrenched: they implicitly cultivate hypotheses, each set of which requires a Possible World but not the widest possible extension for applying that set in our World Zero, that is, testability in the scientists' sense; rather, they must be recognizable as "true to conceivable experience" or verisimilar (52 and passim). Both arts and sciences finally repose on intuitions, which are however for science buried in their axioms (Aristotle and Frege agree on this) as indubitable certainties. Whether you prefer Marx's or Balzac's description of nineteenth-century France will depend on your general or even momentary interests, but they're in no way either incompatible or subsumed under one another. It is not the case that one is cognitive and the other is not.

Sketching an operative epistemological way can further proceed by recognizing that there are still some logical ways if not of defining truth then at least of defining untruth: "if p is false, one cannot know p; knowledge then requires truth. Moreover, one cannot know that p without being cognitively committed to p; knowledge also requires belief or acceptance." (Goodman and Elgin 136) As Orwell might have put it, all opinions are constructed and relatively wrong or limited, but some are more wrong than others. This holds first of all for those whom I shall call <u>monoalethist</u> (from *aletheia,* truth): all those which—from monotheists through Laplace's scientific determinism[45] to lay dogmatists such as the Fascists, Stalinists, and believers in the Invisible Hand of the Market—hold they have the Absolute Truth, including Post-Modernists who believe relativism is absolute. Only belief in the absolute right—Haraway's "God-trick" ("Situated" 589)—is absolutely wrong.

William Blake's poetic Jehovah put this monomania perhaps best:

> Let each choose one habitation,
> -
> One command, one joy, one desire,
> One curse, one weight, one measure,
> One King, one God, one Law.
>
> *(The Book of Urizen,* ll. 79, 81-84)

Nonetheless, even Goodman and Elgin cannot quite manage without the term truth. They offer a strong argument against using as a main instrument of evaluation "truth" in the strict logico-theological sense, inside a closed circle of verbal statements, and in favour of using rightness (cf. the long discussion 150ff.), but I wish to continue using the term truth by redefining it to include rightness. What is in that sense, say, the truth of the atom bomb? Depending on the categories and interests chosen, it may (among a multitude of other possible answers) be the instantaneous liberation of a given high quantity of energy for a destructive purpose, or the proof for a

---

45   I am referring to the famous statement in Laplace's *Essai philosophique sur les probabilités* of 1825:

"The present state of the system of nature is evidently a resultant of what it was in the preceding instant, and if we conceive of an Intelligence who, in a given moment, embraces all the relations of the beings in the Universe, It will be able to determine for any instant of the past and the future their respective positions, motions, and generally their affections." (cited from Wallerstein, *End* 206)

given inter-atomic structure of matter, or finally the effect on the lives of hundreds of thousands of inhabitants of Hiroshima and Nagasaki. The first answer is military, the second pertains to "objective" theoretical physics (it was "sweet physics" for Fermi and Oppenheimer, see Haberer 185-216), the third to the horizon of a not yet existing humanized science. The formal difference between them is that each succeeding answer has a larger scope: the physical one can envision the military one, but only the humanized one may envision all of them. The third answer is—beyond politics, but also because it incorporates humanist politics—formally and cognitively the richest one. Thus, scientific cognition relates not only to the epistemic aspect but also to the political and financial presuppositions of science as well as to its effects upon people—from which a counter-project to certain types of (today dominant) navel-gazing cognition may be inferred. I shall return to this in Section 2.

In other words, we are here faced with the necessity for a dialectics between systems and openness, in brief the necessity for open-ended systems or indeed provisional and historical totalities. The openness is both formal and historical, it pertains to viewing a subject(-matter) within different situations and by different appraisers with differing value-systems—as in the example of the atom bomb. I approach it in Suvin, „On Cognition" and "Two Cheers," but it would bear much development.

Goodman and Elgin go on to argue that one cannot know "that p" if one's belief in it, though it may happen to be true, is not connected to other propositions which "tether" it, that is, which make it part of a consistent and justifiable argument. A tether in the form of accounting and arguing for your insights there certainly must be, or no judgment will be possible, and thus no critical politics or cognition (cf. Arendt 40-41). Epistemologists divide according to the nature of this indispensable tether. "Internalists" believe the tether is purely epistemic: knowledge is anchored by justification epistemically accessible to the knower, usually as propositions in natural language, possibly buttressed by mathematics. They employ only concepts and categories, plus various operations by which they form a system. "Externalists" believe knowledge is anchored to a fact or set of facts that makes it true, and there is a debate as to the anchor, which could be arrived at inductively or deductively. From where I stand, epistemic absolutism presents the danger of wonderful closed systems of statements chasing each other's tail but with insufficient purchase upon practice; while ontological absolutism presents the danger of unjustifiable assumption of anchoring, usually some certainty of a divine kind. Bhaskar calls the former—a reduction of being to knowledge—the epistemic fallacy, and the latter—a short-circuit between knowledge and being—the ontic fallacy (*Scientific* 200ff.). I prefer a Solomonic melding: without something ontologically "out there," to be available as at least a check and an obstacle to action in any practice following from knowledge, there might be Cartesian discussions of method but there is no knowledge. But I think knowledge must pass also through epistemic justification, especially if it is to be attained within language (and is thus akin, in ways still to be elucidated, to poetry, fiction, non-fiction, and essays). A fortified city with gates in two concentric walls, maybe.

If one allows externalism or ontological realism as at least an indispensable element of knowledge, the problem of causes necessarily arises: must a belief "that *p*" necessarily be caused by "facts" or constellations from which it follows "that *p*"? It seems obvious that causal relationships are very often present: a certain type of cloudiness will as a rule (statistically) result in tempests. As Jaurès put it (and was killed for it), capitalism brings war as clouds bring tempests. But is the strong form of "must" defensible, must there always be a (however complex and mediated) cause for *p*? I am not sure of my ontological ground here, for Epicurus would say that deviations happen (cf. Suvin "Living"); but I would think that at least in human affairs causes must obtain, and that their understanding is one of the "conditions of possibility for emancipatory practices" (Bhaskar

210-11). The suspect Post-Modernist rage against causality *tout court* seems to me well foreseen by Brecht: "They could not see the causes of events, because they could not get rid of the events" (GKA 21: 307). What is well lost is a member of the family of Oneness: monocausality, the One unique or final Cause, that major sin of Hellenic *logos*.

The two major examples of monoalethism after the monotheist religions could be science-as-is and Marxism-as-was. Scientism (what I shall later call S2) was "the inheritor of the great religions by pretending to bear the truth of Being and the way of salvation, by glorifying Man as the monarch of the universe" (Morin 52). The official, stodgy, and by now dead kind of Marxism theorized economics as the scientific cause, however mediated, of all human affairs, and (since this didn't wash) practiced an arbitrary ad hoc politics. However, parallels in psychoanalysis or feminism are not difficult to imagine. The corruption of the best is indeed the worst.

Obversely, as Augustine of Hippo wrote, "When truths are reached, they renew us."

But also: When truth is sold as a commodity, its principal aim is not to convey truth. Its aim is to be sold, regardless and quite often despite any invalidating falsehood it may contain. Truth is for sharing, not for an elect caste, priests or rich. It is to be shamelessly blurted out on the streets (or on internet).

1.2. Cognition Is Constituted by and as History: Multiple Sources and Methods

> History is bunk.
>
> Henry Ford

In a remarkable passage right at the beginning of *Works and Days*, Hesiod invents the myth (maybe it's already an allegory) of the two Erises, the benign and the malign one (I: 11-26). The bad Strife favours wars and civil discords. But the firstborn is the good Strife, whom Zeus has placed at the roots of the earth, for she generates emulation: one vase-maker or poem-singer envies the other, the lazy and poor peasant imitates the industrious and richer one. This polar splitting of concepts seems to me a (perhaps the) central procedure of critical reason, dissatisfied with the present categorizations and trying to insinuate opposed meanings under the same term. While it is sometimes preferable to redefine one single term (as I did for truth), I shall adopt this Hesiodean procedure for knowledge and then science.

The principal ancestors to this endeavour may be found in Marx and to a minor degree Nietzsche. The latter seems to have hesitated between two very different meaning of truth and knowledge: the accepted one committed to an Aristotelian correspondence of knowledge to reality and therefore to an ideal of adequate description for science, and an alternate or constructivist model, where truths are instruments for given purposes. I take from him as useful what follows. First, the correspondence of intellect to thing/s is a Truth perhaps arrived at in complex ways but finally a point of rest for the weary: "simple, transparent, not contradicting itself, permanent, enduring as identical, with no crease, hidden sleight, curtain, form: a man conceives thus the world of Being as 'God' in his own image" (*Wille* 543). It is an ideal impossible to fulfil and leads to faking and skepticism. This Truth is thus a lie, and whenever erected into a system—as in religion and in Galilean science—it compels lying, always unconscious and frequently also conscious. Any cognition developed against this fixed horizon partakes for Nietzsche of a huge, finally deadly "illusion." Science can thus become a variant of asceticism, even an opiate for "suffering the lack of a great love" (*Zur Genealogie* 128). The constructivist account, on the other hand, is a creative transference of carrying across, in Greek *meta-pherein*, whence his famous hyperbolic statements about knowing being "Nothing but working with the favourite metaphors" (*Philosophy* xxxiii; on the preceding three pages the editor Breazeale gives a survey, with sources in Nietzsche's works, showing his permanent oscillation). I have argued at length elsewhere (,,On Cognition") that for Nietzsche wisdom arises out of the knowledge of nescience: "And only on this by now solid and granite basis of nescience may science have arisen, the will for knowing on the basis of a much more powerful will, the will for <u>unknowing</u>, for the uncertain, the untrue! Not as its opposite, but—as its improvement!" (*Jenseits* 24) Jumping over the monolithic Plato, Nietzsche may have derived this from the Presocratics: "Appearances are a glimpse of the invisible" (Anaxagoras, in Diels-Kranz, B21a). Careful: this "untrue" is the opposite of the illusionistic, for example of angels, gods, UFOs, Mickey Mice or the Invisible Hand of the Market as empirical existents leading to fanatical belief. It demolishes The Monolithic Truth while preserving verifiability for any given situation.

Thus Nietzsche's "philosophizing with a hammer" is most useful as destruction, with precious hints as to the direction of a reconstruction, such as his defence of multiple perspectives (*Zur Genealogie* 100-01). But it stops short of a major discovery, which can be phrased with Haraway, in the wake of theories about Possible Worlds, as "Nothing comes without its world" (*Mode*st 37; cf. Blumenberg 3 and passim). And furthermore, any such world is necessarily dynamic, it evolves in time: "Recte enim veritas temporis filia dicitur non auctoritatis" ("Truth is correctly said to be the daughter of time and not of authority"), noted Francis Bacon, fighting for a non-dogmatic truth. It must be said in Kuhn's praise that he was the first to drive home the notion that science happens in time, and is in its essence historical. But before him, much more sweepingly and "thickly" (as the anthropologists say), this was developed by Karl Marx.

Kant had a major difficulty in the *Critique of Judgment:* judgments deal with particulars, but how is one to account for any particular, notoriously contingent and as it were anarchic, for which the general concept has still to be found (cf. Rickert 150)? He sometimes finessed this by using examples, which hide a generalized allegory: the particular Achilles is the example of Courage in general (cf. Arendt 77-80); however, this doesn't always work (at other times he opted for imagination, but this raises more problems then it lays to rest). Marx's judgments applied to "thick" modern society Hegel's great insight that "truth is concrete": a paradox which means that truth must span, as a good bridge and a dialectical conceptuality do, both abstract generality and the particular or even the individual, as feedback from and possibility of intervention into the particular. Marx's concepts and the overall story they build up remove strategic insights from the static "natural" domain to social and above all <u>historical</u>—that is, dynamic—categories (cf. Aronowitz, esp. ch.s 2 and 3). His strongly developed conceptuality is "sucked into the flow of things and the pain of struggles. The uncompromisingly worldly, historical, and class character of what is being cognized becomes a property of the cognitive form itself." (Korsch 54) Capital is neither natural nor everlasting: it is a human, thisworldly, historical, and class construct.

This also means that, as long as the phenomena are integrally respected, they can be most lawfully explained in multiple ways, as Marx proposes already in his dissertation while discussing Epicurus's theory of celestial bodies: only the obviously wrong, mythically absolute unity and fixity of the superlunar sphere is to be disbarred (*Differenz* 170-71).[46] He too went in for Hesiodean splitting, opposing to dogmatic (for example, mythical) critique a "true" critique which understands the contradictions within its object as historical necessities (MEW 1: 296). Hegel's encapsulation for truth means today also that if the particular out there will vary depending on the question we put to it, then the

---

46. An excellent example of my distinction between S1 and S2 is the semantic career of the Hellenic *phainomena*. For Archimedes and the whole Hellenic science, they were perceived by interaction between subject and object. In S2, a phenomenon is an "objective" fact. See for much more the astounding Russo 440 and passim. (Marx is much impressed with Newton and paleotechnics but on the whole is to be seen as continuing the S1 of his exemplar Epicurus, as I argue in "Living".)

concreteness demands that there be no one single capital-T Truth that accounts for it. When Putnam asks "Is water necessarily H_2O?", the answer is: for some purposes—of separating H and O or reconstituting water, and all understanding pertaining to such possibilities—yes, but for other purposes no (see his whole argument in *Realism* 54-79 and 120-31, and Gendlin 39 and passim). Necessities change according to the situation, which is only understood as being such-and-such by the interests of the subject defining it. If, as argued earlier, all our judgments contain both evaluative and factual aspects (cf. also Putnam *Collapse*), though not necessarily in same admixtures; and if furthermore very many scientific accounts and all theories are not in one-to-one relation with the experiential phenomena they explain, but rather the relationship is one-to-many and many-to-one; then truth is context-dependent.

Now Marx clearly had for his explaining of capitalism as a social formation a strongly favoured red thread (arrived at after many painful attempts), and he poured his scorn on the falsities of bourgeois political economy. But his was a struggle on two fronts, for simultaneously he chastised with scorpions all attempts to subject science or cognition to "a point of view from the outside, stemming from interests outside science and alien to it" (MEW 26.2: 112). *Capital* itself is presented as a project of "free scientific research," which assumes the task to clarify the inner relationships of the phenomena it deals with without imposition from the outside and in particular against "the Furies of private interest" (MEW 23:16). His two major, consubstantial cognitive insights might be thought of as a double helix: the insight about capitalism, the labour source of value, the class conflict, and similar doctrinal tenets, which in brief reveal that societal injustices are based on exploitation of other people's living labour; and the insight that the proper way to talk about the capitalist exploitation which rules all our lives is not in the *a priori* form of dogma, a closed system, but in the *a posteriori* form of critique. The latter means that legitimate cognition is epistemically grounded in the process it describes, and strategically developed by adopting a radically deviant stance against a dominant in a given historical situation (one of the first and best of such discussions is in Marcuse, *Reason*). After Marx, it should be clear that "All modes of knowing presuppose a point of view....Therefore, the appropriate response to [this is]...the responsible acknowledgement of our own viewpoints and the use of that knowledge to look critically at our own and each other's opinions." (Levins 182; see more in Gramsci, *Selections* 427-70 and passim) The rightness of a theoretical assertion depends on evidence as interpreted by the assertor's always socio-historical needs, interests, and values.

All of this argues strongly in favour of allowing many other epistemologically sound sources of understanding or cognition beside institutionalized science's shibboleth for fully analytic and fully fragmented knowledge, today quite out of date when faced, for example, with dissipative structures. The list of more or less equivalent participants in the passion of cognition is long, for it includes not only "knowing-that" but also "knowing-how" (Anscombe). The latter is centred in bodily practices and subject to the pull of what Aristotle called "aim as cause" (*causa finalis*), so that "because" in it means "in order that" rather than merely "was caused by": Husserl spoke of "ways in which the future pulls us towards it," and Whitehead of "the lure of form as yet unrealized" (in Grene 245). To this clearly belong all arts, but also many other practices not readily expressible in conceptual form (the Greeks called most of them *tekhnè*, cf. Vernant, and it was connected with *phronesis*, practical wisdom), and finally also certain facets of emotion or feeling. An important connection is established when Aristotle in *Nicomachean Ethics* 6, though he downgrades ungentlemanly work, assigns precisely to such wisdom how virtue in political communities functions through right choices—that is, through freedom (cf. Carr 154).

I cannot enter here into any properly historical discussion, which would reveal that, even after tribal formations, there have been many civilizations either without an institutionalized science (such as the ancient Roman one) or with science based on radically different presuppositions (such as the Chinese and Arabic ones), and—most important—that all scientific paradigms are temporally finite: the "modes of production, enunciation, and application of knowledge" begin and end in function of interests within their societies (Lévy-Leblond 33). The logical structure of the present scientific method is enabled at the price of systematically limiting its investigation to the homogeneous and the quantifiable. Changeable and metamorphic history would immediately burst its bounds: science-as-is knows only a history of errors (cf. Castoriadis 164 and passim). Nonetheless, though repressed into a not further discussed "intuition," factors such as suppositions of relevance and plausibility, selection of problems recognized as valid, concepts of "projectability" of facts and theories, and so on, play a major role in it (cf. Einstein). I shall discuss here only one usually backgrounded cognitive practice, the "tacit knowledge" as explained by Michael Polanyi.

This starts "from the fact that we know more than we can tell" (4): for example, how we recognize a human face, or any other physiognomy that cannot be fully described by words—diseases, rocks, plants, animals. This also holds for bodily skills, such as swimming, skiing, and many professional gestures of using tools: "we keep expanding our body into the world by assimilating to it sets of particulars which we integrate into reasonable entities" (29). As Merleau-Ponty put it in his discussion of perception, path-breaking for us Europeans since we don't understand Buddhism and Daoism well, "thought... [can be] ahead of itself...[and] at home everywhere" (371). But beyond everything that is learned through practice and observation, often from a master, tacit knowledge intervenes crucially in formalized science too, as the experience of seeing a hitherto unknown problem through an intimation of unity or form or *Gestalt* from a few particulars: in all knowledge there is an element of inferring. No pursuit of truth can be wholly explicit: if we differentiate between focal and subsidiary awareness, Polanyi points out no knowledge can be wholly focal. When we do not know in the focal sense what we are looking for, we rely on clues to its nature, which flow also out of our own attitude, skills, real or crypto-memories, hunches (see more on this in Gendlin, and Suvin "On Cognition"). Our focal core of consciousness is carried by that tacit acceptance of things not explicit, which bind us to and within our world.

Of course, it should be added to his argument that tacit knowledge can turn out to be mistaken as often as the formalized one. However, its acknowledgement "restores knower and known [to]...the Cartesian-Newtonian world...without life," Polanyi's pupil Grene concludes (14). This means that knowledge always begins and ends in the personal; the impersonal knowledge is the collective mediation and validation on that route (23-25) and is itself codetermined by a not wholly formalizable consensus of professional opinion. Finally, the knowing mind and our ultimate beliefs are always tied to our psychophysiological orientation, stance or bearing (for more see Suvin "*Haltung*" and essay 1 in this book). We can thus use also those epistemologically indispensable constituents of knowledge that cannot be stated as a proposition or argument, including our central personal commitment which "can never be...exhaustively stated in a non-committal form" (Grene 204). Such unspecifiable elements are from Kant's *Critique of Judgment* on often called esthetical, as in Dirac's comment that the Theory of Relativity was accepted for two reasons: the agreement with experiment and the "beautiful mathematical theory [that is, "simple mathematical concepts that fit together in an elegant way"] underlying it, which gives it a strong emotional appeal" (205). The pattern may also be statistical, or an analogical model as Darwin's transfer of pigeon- and stockbreeding to the origin of all species (cf. on analogy Angenot, Hesse *Models*, Gross, Haraway *Primate*, Squier 25ff. and 54ff., and Suvin "On Cognitive" with further bibliography). In all cases it is a sense of relevance or rightness. Since today science does not deal in substances but in events (for example an experimental situation), this sense of pertinence, impossible to detach from the tacit base of knowledge, is particularly important.

Last not least, as argued earlier, all understanding is by default <u>pluralistic</u> (cf. Marglin 233-36). First, scientific theories are "underdetermined" by facts: "Many, indeed infinitely many, different sets of hypotheses can be found from which statements describing the known facts can be deduced..." (Harré 87). But second, more radically, the "facts" of scientific theories are not fully determined and univocal but always already conceptually elaborated (this also puts paid to Popperian falsification as an overriding criterion), and furthermore it is quite unclear how univocal are the prevailing philosophical categories used in science (cf. Castoriadis 175-77, 218-19, and passim). As a whole current of philosophers has maintained since Gassendi, theories are not true or false but good or bad instruments for research. Reality is in principle prior to human thought, yet it is co-created by human understanding, in a never-ending feedback.

If cognition is not only open-ended but also codetermined by the social subject and societal interests looking for it, its multiple horizons are unavoidable. The object of any praxis can only be "seen as" that particular kind of object (Wittgenstein) from a subject-driven—but also subject-modifying—standpoint and bearing. The choice which cluster of data (or problems) to begin with in any research, which to look for next, and so forth, is already a never-ending series of interpretations. True, in all developed knowledge there must be hierarchies, but there should be no pretence to a deductive unity, a watertight closed system of concepts, as the only and sometimes not even as the most important component of knowledge. The more modest inductions and analogies, that is, analogue spreads instead of the digital 0 or 1, should be stripped of their lower status. The reality described by quantum mechanics is "composed of many worlds" (Castoriadis 161). In several of its branches "a whole battery of models" is regularly used, and "no one thinks that one of these is the whole truth, and they may be mutually inconsistent" (Hacking 37):

The best kind of evidence for the reality of a postulated or inferred entity is that we can begin to measure it or otherwise understand its causal powers. The best evidence, in turn, that we have this understanding is that we can set out...to build machines that will work fairly reliably, taking advantage of this or that causal nexus. Hence, engineering, not theorizing, is the best proof of scientific realism about entities. My attack on scientific anti-realism is analogous to Marx's onslaught on the idealism of his day. Both say the point is not to understand the world but to change it. (Hacking 274).

The post-Einsteinian science is thus harking back, after centuries of the Baconian and Galileian quantified unicity, to the science of Hipparchus and Archimedes, which also dealt with a polyphony of hypotheses possible for explaining a given result (Serres 118 and passim; and cf. Russo). Such science—I shall discuss it as S1 in 2.1—becomes again, as in them or in many Asian analogues, a complex evaluation of open models (see more in Suvin, "Living").

Finally, as soon as we deal—as we must—with models, which can obviously be used only for those groups of phenomena which they are modelling, monoalethism is dead and buried (except on TV and for the politicians of capitalist domination, outside and inside science). <u>Truth has acquired a history.</u> But then, what kind of plurality within what kind of necessarily unitary horizon should we strive for in present-day technoscience, if humanity is to survive?

2. On Technoscience as Politics

Since we come by airplane to our conventions, let us not announce there that science is a mere construction.
E. T. Gendlin, 1997

Addition to above: Though every time I land, I say "we've made it once more."

DS, 1964 to the present

2.1. Life-Destroying or Life-preserving?: Science as Is vs. Science as It Has To Be[47]

...in the end, for millions and millions of people on the landmasses around us [Africa and Asia, DS], the West meant only this—science and tanks and guns and bombs.

Amitav Ghosh, 1992

I am in this section not attempting to say anything which has not been said, from Marx and Nietzsche through Simmel, Marcuse, and Benjamin to others cited below, but simply to summarize for myself and my readers, within a Babylonian confusion of interested languages, a life-affirming red thread about science—the privileged cognitive horizon for our age, to which I too am committed.

From this stance, science as it really exists gradually became after Galileo and Newton a matter of salaried professionals socialized by rigorous and hierarchical training into refusing any discussion as to their profession's presuppositions: it was delimited as sober "factuality," and whoever speculated too much about alternative horizons was read out of it (cf. Hagstrom 9 and Haberer passim). It grew into a powerful institution, an alternate Church popularized by means "of saints' (the geniuses') lives, their miracles (discoveries), and holy sites (laboratories and similar)" (Traweek 141). True-blue "scientism" believes that science possesses a universal validity which is in principle independent of the people, society, and interests

47. This section is a reworking of much milder propositions I wrote in 1987 for a gathering of the Royal Society of Canada members at McGill University. The eminent conveners of the gathering opined the discussion would not be of interest—thus confirming my diagnosis.

among which it happens to have sprung up, so that sciences are merely systems of formal propositions and procedures for the construction and corroboration of theories. This scientism eliminates the knowing subject, individual and collective, in favour of an artfully posited "objectivity": "There is nothing about human beings mentioned anywhere in this [Objectivist] account—neither their capacity to understand nor their imaginative activity nor their nature as functioning organisms..." (Johnson x; cf. for a wide-ranging introduction Aronowitz). As Eddington put it, the ideal scientist must eliminate all of his senses, except "part of an eye that he might observe" (22). Human relationships of production, consumption, and existence—from which after all science proceeds and into which it returns—are no longer its system of reference, but its accidental breeding soil. Instead of such historical relationships, institutional science-as-is adopted for its reference-system logic and mathematics as self-sufficient formal methods. This also means an orientation not simply to quantification, but to a reified quantification without qualities, as part and parcel of the capitalist orientation to exchange-value instead of use-value. This is life-denying in the strictest sense: leading to mass hunger, wars, and devastation of the planet.

True, new approaches have in the last 40 years finally taken into consideration the Einsteinian epistemological revolution by adopting a variety of methods not only as between distinct subfields but often within them. However, this has been subordinated to a counter-tendency building on the fact-value split and locked into militarization and the profit motive, which have made for highly restricted access, first, "to scientific knowledge... funding, positions, publication, conferences"; second, "to tacit knowledge—the crucial craft knowledge that is never written into articles"; and third, "to the groups that define present and future priorities for problems, methods, research equipment...." In consequence, first, the hierarchic structure of who decides what is important (or a fact) has been much reinforced, and second, scientific writing has increasingly downgraded narration, including reference to the authors' agency: "[I]t would be almost impossible to reproduce an experiment based upon the information provided in scientific articles....The[ir] purpose... is to announce findings and to lay claim to a discovery...[in] a succinct and formulaic literary economy...." (Traweek 143) In fact, the most capital-intensive research is rarely replicated, it is corroborated by differently designed experiments. But "the proof race is so expensive that only a few, people, nations, institutions or professions are able to sustain it..."; technoscience is developed in relatively few places "that garner disproportionate amounts of resources" (Latour 179, and cf. his whole ch. 4). Quite contrary to a sanitizing distance from values and politics, "[t]he definition of science is made by those who are empowered to offer resources" (Traweek 144; cf. also Castoriadis 221-24, Penley and Ross eds., Pickering ed.). This extends to imperial concentration of such "research power" in a small "North Atlantic" area of the world, which drains brains and profitable information from other areas and disallows traditional knowledge (cf. Hountondji, Shiva, and Mies and Shiva). In the era of capitalist technoscience, this means that the periphery will forever remain such, since it can only copy commodity products, not the matrix that produces them (cf. Oliveira, esp. 48-51).

The huge limitation that defines this pursuit is that, outside focussed manipulation, science is life-blind. In Tolstoy's words, "science is meaningless because it does not answer >what shall we do and how shall we live<" (cited in Weber 322; Nietzsche said similar things). Even the Nazi fellow-traveller Heisenberg had to concede that natural science "is in some ways the attempt to describe the world insofar as it is possible to abstract from ourselves, our thinking and our activity" (95). While a certain degree of indispensable abstraction enters into any name and concept, science-as-is practices that kind of extreme abstraction which Kierkegaard characterized as "the thought without the thinker" (7: 287). The horizons of such a science have been indifferent to destruction of people and the planet, and its results increasingly deadly, as testified by Belsen, Hiroshima,

Chernobyl, ecocide, and so indefinitely on. We cannot use any longer the excuse that science is a pure maiden raped by outside powers: she is collaborating enthusiastically.

Levins calls this state of affairs science's "dual nature," springing out of "the liberal progressivist ideology" it shares with capitalism (182 and 184). He believes that the "Marxist critique attempts to see science in both its liberating and oppressing aspects, its powerful insights and militant blindnesses, as a commoditized expression of liberal European capitalist masculinist interests and ideologies organized to cope with real natural and social phenomena" (186). He is clearly attuned to the feminist critique identifying "in the denial of interaction between subject and object" as well as in the stress on domination "the intrusion of a [masculinist] self" (Keller 182-83; cf. on the openly anti-feminine character of Baconian science as mastery also Harding and Hintikka eds., Dorothy Smith, and Noble *Religion;* and Leiss on its derivation from Judeo-Christian clericalism down to Luther). Today it seems plain that the relation between scientist and nature is quite analogous to the relation of a male upper class to the indispensable but dangerous Others of women and working classes. Thus I sympathize with much of what both such critiques bravely say. And I fully agree with Levins's conclusion: "We should not pretend or aspire to a bland neutrality but proclaim as our working hypothesis: all theories are wrong which promote, justify or tolerate injustice" (191). But I submit that by now, a dozen years and untold horrors later, including a full subsumption of science as institution under destructive rather than liberal capitalism, a better strategy is the Hesiodean procedure of splitting the institutionalized horizons of science-as-is fully off from those of a potentially humanized science-as-wisdom, which would count its dead as precisely as the US armed forces. I wish I could call the latter science and the former something else, perhaps technoscience, but I do not want to give up either on science or on technology. I shall provisionally call the firstborn, good science "Science 1" (S1) and the present one, whose results are mixed but seem to be increasingly steeped in the blood and misery of millions of people, "Science 2" (S2). Medieval theologians such as Aquinas would have called them *sapientia* vs. *scientia,* though in those early days they optimistically believed the latter could be tamed by the former, by knowledge as the highest intellectual virtue.

These are ideal types only, intermixed in any actual effort in most varied proportions: also, the beginnings of S2 are in S1, and it retains certain of its liberatory birthmarks—centrally, the method of hypothesis plus verification—to the present day. For example, "[i]n this tradition a self-conscious effort has been made to identify sources and kinds of errors and to correct for capricious biases. It has often been successful...." Nonetheless, the fixation on <u>domination</u> and the consubstantial <u>occultation of the knowing subject</u> in S2 "is a particular moment in the division of labor." The avoidance of capricious errors "does [not] protect the scientific enterprise as a whole from the shared biases of its practitioners." Science is highly normative, concluded Aronowitz, in its theory and method, the form of the result, the choice of field of inquiry, and the constitution of the scientific object (320). In sum, "The pattern of knowledge in science is...structured by interest and belief....Theories, supported by megalibraries of data, often are systematically and dogmatically obfuscating." It is not by chance, I would argue, that "major technical efforts based on science have [led] to disastrous outcomes: pesticides increase pests; hospitals are foci of infection; antibiotics give rise to new pathogens; flood control increases flood damage; and economic development increases poverty" (Levins 180, 183, and 181)—not to mention that Einsteinian physics produces the A and H bombs, and so on and on.

The bourgeois civilization's main way of coping with the unknown is aberrant, said Nietzsche, because it transmutes nature into concepts with the aim of mastering it: that is, it turns nature <u>only</u> into concepts and furthermore makes a more or less closed system out of concepts. It is not that the means get out of hand but that the mastery—the wrong end—<u>requires</u> consubstantially wrong means of aggressive manipulation. If you want to be Master of your Domain, you have to treat profit-making concepts as raw material on the same footing as profit-making laborers and iron ore. The problem lies not in the Sorcerer's Apprentice but in the Master Wizard. In Marcuse's summary, S2 has "by virtue of its own method and concepts," projected and promoted a universe in which the domination of nature was indissolubly linked to and intertwined with the domination of a ruling class over the majority of people. To the contrary (in S1),

> sever[ing] this fatal link would also affect the very structure of science....Its hypotheses, without losing their rational character, would develop in an essentially different experimental context (that is a pacified world); consequently, science would arrive at essentially different concepts of nature and establish essentially different facts. (*One-Dimensional* 166-67)

I conclude that S2 is not only a cultural revolution but also a latent or patent political upheaval. This clearly presupposes nature and its knowledge as a zero-sum game, a finite domain allowing for asymptotical progress to a final solution. The scientific, finally, is the political. S2 is, finally, in the sense of Marx's epigraph to this essay, based on a falsehood.

There are strong analogies and probably causal relations between this "search for truth, proclaimed as the cornerstone of progress" and "the maintenance of a hierarchical, unequal social structure," within which capitalist rationalization has created the large stratum of "administrators, technicians, scientists, educators" it needed (Wallerstein, *Historical* 82-83). In particular, it created the whole new class of managers. As Braverman's pathbreaking book pointed out, "to manage" (from *manus*, hand) originally meant to train a horse in his paces, in the manège (67). F.W. Taylor did exactly this—he broke "the men," calling in his *Shop Management* for "a planning department to do the thinking for the men" (Braverman 128). Later, since "machinery faces workers as <u>capitalized</u> domination over work, and the same happens for science" (Marx, *Theorien* 355), control was built into the new technologies. During the nineteenth century, "science, as a generalized social property" (S1) was replaced by "science as a capitalist property at the very center of production"; this is "the scientifico-technical revolution" (Braverman 156), while technoscientific ideology becomes, as Jameson notes, "a blind behind which the more embarrassing logic of the commodity form and the market can operate" (*Singular* 154). Already by the early 1960s, 3/4 of scientific R&D in the USA was corporate; it was financed directly or through tax write-offs by the Federal government, that is, by money taken from tax-payers, while profits went to corporations (164-66). For almost a century now, scientific research has been mainly determined by expected profits to the detriment of S1 (cf. at least Kapp 208ff.), where it is not neglected for purely financial speculation. Technoscience increasingly has no goals of its own but is pushed by political economics from behind; correspondingly the technoscientist also does not know what he is working for, "and generally he doesn't much care. He works because he has instruments allowing him...to succeed in a new operation." (Ellul 272)

The resulting "scientific culture" (S2) "became also a means of class cohesion for the upper stratum [of cadres]....The great emphasis on the rationality of scientific activity was the mask of the irrationality of endless accumulation." (Wallerstein, *Historical* 84-85) The presupposition that science does not deal in values, which began to be widely doubted only after the Second World War, had as "its actual function to protect two systems of values: the professional values of the scientists, and the predominant [status quo] values of society as they existed at that moment...." (Graham 9, and cf. 28-29, also Kuhn). What Putnam has passionately dubbed "The Philosophers' of Science Evasion of Values" (title of his chapter 8), not only hides that—as he agrees with Dewey—"Value judgments are essential to the practice itself" (*Collapse* 135), and that "Knowledge of facts presupposes knowledge of values....justifying factual claims presupposes value judgments" (137). Further, this evasion reveals how, instead of clarifying and further developing common experience, S2 strove for, and largely achieved, a monopoly of "expert knowers"; and the more specialized a field of expertise got, the greater became the likelihood that new skills would be invented—which then seek application, useful or not. As Bauman summarizes it, since the 19th Century it is "not the plain man who knows where it hurts but...the professional expert who 'knows best' what is good for him"; and furthermore, "the state of 'being hurt' is itself expert-defined," whether the patient likes it or not. This medical experience can stand also as a metaphor for all other fields where "the self-declared servants turn into managers," not to say dictators (212-14).

The stances of "objectivity" and erasure of subject lent themselves to the treatment of people (workers, women, patients, consumers) as objects to be manipulated, for were they not a part of nature? As a hierarchical institution devoted to manipulation, S2 was easily usable for "human resources" too: the Nazi doctors' genocidal experiments were only an extremely overt and acute form of such *Herrschaftswissen* (knowledge used for domination—cf. Müller-Hill and Leiss 101-18). This may present itself innocuously as "scientific management," but it comports centrally "the progressive alienation of the process of production from the worker" (Braverman 37-38, and his book relates this to transformation of all aspects of life within monopoly capitalism). What began with the great invention of factories in order to centralize and intensify ("rationalize") the exploitation of labour for profitable productivity (cf. Noble *Forces*, Marglin 220-23) has been preserved in updated forms as the building block of both industrial and post-industrial society. In the formulation of Max Scheler, "To conceive the world as bereft of value predicates is a task taken up precisely because of a value: the vital value of domination and power over matters" (cited in Leiss 106).

Michael L. Smith has identified as "commodity scientism" a systematic fusion of a select technology and image-creation in the service of a politico-ideological project, so that

> the products of a market-aimed technology are mistaken for the scientific process, and those products, like science, become invested with the inexorable, magical qualities of an unseen social force. For the consumer, the rise of commodity scientism has meant the eclipse of technological literacy by an endless procession of miracle-promising experts and products. For advertisers and governments, it has meant the capacity to recontextualize technology, to assign to its products social attributes that are largely independent of the products' technical design or function [that is, of their use-value] (179)

"Progress" is here identified with science, science with technology, and technology with new products supposedly enriching life but largely disregarding the products' technical capacities or function, that is their use-value, enriching the financiers while brainwashing the taxpayers (Smith 182). Under such hegemony, we must ruefully accept, with due updating, Gandhi's harsh verdict about science: "Your laboratories are diabolic unless you put them at the service of the rural poor" (Gandhigram). S2 is Power (over people), S1 is Creativity. S1 would be able to take a historical and pragmatic approach, well formulated by Gramsci—halfway between Marx and Hacking—as:

> ...what interests science is not so much the objectivity of reality but people, who elaborate research methods, who continually rectify the material instruments that reinforce their sensory organs and logical instruments for discrimination and verification—that is, culture, that is, world-view, that is, the relationship between

people and reality mediated by technology. In science too, looking for reality outside people, in a religious or metaphysical sense, is merely a paradox. (*Quaderni* II: 1457)

That does not at all mean there is nothing outside the human brain, as Orwell's O'Brien—the power freak—puts it. It means that the observer is part of the system even outside of atomic physics. In this view science is a usable and misusable ensemble of cognitions, not an absolute truth (which we sinful people can of course only approach asymptotically, that is, without ever fully reaching it). It does not pretend, as S2, to be a pure methodology, an organon with its formal propositions and procedures for the construction and verification of theories, principally a "how"; while including "how," S1 is principally a "by whom" and "for what"—an "impure" productive relationship between (for example) workers, scientists, financiers, and other power-holders, as well as an institutional network with different effects upon all such different societal groups, which can and must become less death-oriented.

Furthermore, the adversarial methodology of S2 is directly opposed to the "communal" (Merton's coy synonym for communist) nature of S1, to the truths all of its practitioners hold in common, as any true cognition does. Cognition or understanding is necessarily non-exclusive, shareable outside a conflictual stance and incompatible with a zero-sum game. True, even in the most disalienated economy of efforts, priorities have to be determined, and in that sense a confrontation between opposed interests will be with us forever. But this is perverted when conflictuality or adversariness, the antagonistic and warlike subspecies of confrontation or opposition, is posited as the central methodology (cf. Suvin, "Conflitto" and "Revelation"). To "have" an idea, an approach or technique, a software or any other byte of knowledge means others can share it without my losing it, indeed I can thereby gain enrichment, stimulus, perhaps even fame. Cognition cannot be fenced in like a piece of land or a financial share locked away in a safe.

S1 should be based on holistic <u>understanding</u>, which would encompass and steer analytical knowledge (Goodman and Elgin 161-64), always on the lookout for inevitable bifurcations which lead to benign and malign Prigoginian catastrophes. It would not at all lose its impressive status as institution, with exacting (only now further expanded) criteria for rightness and an always situationally delimited, or situated (Haraway), truth. On the contrary, S1 would finally be as truly liberating, both for its creators and its users, as its best announcers have, from Bacon to Wiener and Gould, claimed it should be. It could at last embark not only on the highly important damage control but also on a full incorporation of aims for acting, which would justify Nietzsche's rhapsodic expectation: "An experimenting would then become proper that would find place for every kind of heroism, a centuries-long experimenting, which could put to shame all the great works and sacrifices of past history" (*Fröhliche* 39)—truly, a joyous science. It would have to ask, looking at our parlous state of natural and psychic ecology, both of which are a "direct result of the externalization of costs by capitalist entrepreneurs" (Wallerstein, *Historical* 130), what questions have not been asked in the last 400 years, and for whose profit. The "long wave of Cartesian inheritance" in scientific method has been shown by Licata and Morin (in my paraphrase) as based, among others, on the propositions that the accumulation of knowledge is inversely proportional to the remainder of ignorance, and that to solve a complex problem it should be subdivided in soluble sub-problems (Licata 63). S2 is thus wedded both to monoalethism and to its dynamic adaptation to a fenced-in, solid world of private property over matters that concern everybody. To the contrary, S1 is wedded to an open world of fluxes where Being is constantly being reborn from (and dying into) Non-Being, where verbs (processes) are more important than nouns (congealed states). Its atoms and interstellar places are built on hollows, thresholds, minima, momentarily stable equilibriums, turbulences, swerves (cf.

Serres 79, 30-34, and passim).

Noble points out how the S1-S2 dichotomy can be followed in the diverging of von Neumann and Wiener paths from the 1940s. Von Neumann's "mathematical axiomatic approach reflected his affinity for military authority and power," while "Wiener insisted upon the indeterminacy of systems and a statistical, probabilistic understanding of their function...[T]he 'steersman' [of his cybernetics] was human in social systems and thus moved not by formal logic but by skill, experience, and purpose....[He] urged 'a constant feedback that would allow an individual to intervene and call a halt to a process initiated, thus permitting him...second thoughts in response to unexpected effects and the opportunity to recast wishes'." He protested military secrecy, accurately seeing "it will lead to the total irresponsibility of the scientist, and, ultimately, to the death of science" (the good one, S1). As is well known, he was ignored by a solid wall of scientifico-military bureaucracy, and decided to stop further work in militarily usable cybernetics "to kill civilians indiscriminately." He turned his attention to the development of prosthetic devices in medicine and co-operation with trade unions (Noble, *Forces* 71-74; see Wiener's 1946 "open letter" in Haberer 316-17).

Last not least, a Wienerian responsible science, co-directed by other community members, would reopen, as he did, the totally forgotten question of its democratic accessibility and accountability, definitely lost since the atom bomb, with a return to full transparency, to a "cognitive democracy" (Morin 166-69). This would also mean reorganizing fully education, from top to bottom, to befit citizens for such an understanding.

2.2. Whither Now?

> From halls of learning
> Emerge the butchers.
>
> Hugging their children tightly,
> Mothers scan with horror the skies
> For the inventions of the scientists.
> Brecht, "1940"

In 1932, sensing the worse to come (which has since, in long duration terms, not ceased coming), Brecht asked:

> Faced with all these machines and technical arts, with which humanity could be at the beginning of a long, rich day, shouldn't it feel the rosy dawn and the fresh wind which signify the beginning of blessed centuries? Why is it so grey all around, and why blows first that uncanny dusk wind at the coming of which, as they say, the dying ones die? (GKA 21: 588)

He went on for the rest of his life to worry at this image of false dawn through the example of Galileo. His final judgment was that Galileo (reason, science, the intellectuals) failed, and helped the night along, by not allying himself with a political dawn-bringer. But then, we might ask today (and I did, in "Heavenly"), where was he to find a revolutionary class who wanted such an ally in his spacetime, and where indeed was Brecht to find it after 1932 (see his poem in epigraph, after the pustule had broken)?

What would an updated, sophisticated S1 mean? Many things, to be properly developed in feedback from its mass practice. In brief, in order for our (and many other) species to survive, we need to limit human interventions on this planet flowing out of the profit principle, centrally by limiting the increase in population in poorer countries and the consumption of energy in richer ones. This necessity has become ineluctable and urgent in the last 30 years. Yet our rulers do not deign even to discuss them, and those who do are small minorities. Therefore, our <u>first necessity</u> is radical social justice, so that rethinking would get a chance. I cannot speak here about this founding presupposition, but only venture to suggest a few quite preliminary, methodological guidelines, which would flow out of the epistemological insights discussed in section 1.

This begins by noting that multiplicity entails choice. If science is a human and societal institution with a history, traversed by often intense class struggles, then our Archimedean point necessarily takes a stand on the side of humanity or against it, using all the good insights we can muster from practice, science, art or elsewhere.

We may need a modified version of the felicific calculus. I take my cue from the path-breaking work of Georgescu-Roegen, who pleads for a "maximum of life quantity," which "requires the minimum rate of natural resource depletion" (20-21; cf. Schrödinger and Lindsay 440ff.). He starts in the proper scientific way by identifying life as a struggle against entropic degradation of matter, bought at the expense of degradation of the "neighboring universe" or total system—for example Terra. The inevitable price to be paid for any life-enhancing activity reintroduces, as against classical physics' narrowing of causality to the efficient cause of manipulating matter and its disregard of the time sequence, the importance of <u>purpose</u>, Aristotle's final cause (192-95) discussed above, reinforced by Lenin's *cui bono*, a choice "for the sake of what" (in whose interest or for whom) is that activity undertaken. As Prigoginian theory puts it, there is never such a full reversibility so that time (history) could be left out as a factor: matter has memory (cf. Wallerstein, *End* 164-66).

Georgescu-Roegen explains "life quantity" as the sum of all the years lived by all humans, present and future. I differ from him by finding this first useful step still too benthamite in its disregard for quality (see for more Essay 10 in this book). True, we can neither properly specify a positive life-quality nor legislate for the horizons of future generations. But we know at least what is to be avoided as bad quality of life: lives traumatized by direct violence, hunger, mostly evitable diseases, and also by anxiety and aimlessness. And I think we know enough to say, first, what major financial orientations, and second, what major productive orientations are not to be pursued. As to the first orientation, his main continuator and updater, Herman Daly, points out that even in classical economics it is accepted "that in accounting income we must deduct for depreciation of capital in order to keep productive capacity intact. This principle...needs only to be extended to natural capital..." (16). This means that environmental costs must be internalized into prices "so that the polluter and the depleter pay", through tax measures. (15) Faced with uncertain effects of new technologies or substances, "an assurance bond in the amount of possible damage [should be required], to be posed up front and then returned over time as experience reduces the uncertainty about damage" (16). Thus we could approach a Steady-State Economy, which is not defined by the capitalist instrument of GNP but by "ecological sustainability of the throughput", which is NOT registered by market prices. (32) "[T]he maximand is life, measured in cumulative person-years ever to be lived at a standard of resource-use sufficient for a good life" (32—Daly acknowledges this standard is vague, but vagueness to be worked out in practice is much better than total disregard as in the GNP). Such a Steady-State Economy would also do better for preservation of all other species.

As to the second orientation, according to Georgescu-Roegen's "thermodynamic calculus," only pursuits as minimally entropic as possible can be allowed if civilization is not to collapse. This is directly opposed to the pursuit of unnecessary quantity: "'bigger & better' washing machines, automobiles and superjets must lead to 'bigger & better' pollution" (19).

But it is fully consonant with the post-Einsteinian concept of nature, from quantum physics to the catastrophe theory (cf. also Collingwood 13, and Grene ch. 9 on "Time & Teleology"). His approach can thus be usefully continued by using the notion developed by Nussbaum of "central human capabilities" to be used in order to establish "a basic social minimum" (70-71) for a life of human dignity. Her list of capabilities which also constitute entitlements is rich, and I shall mention from it only what seem to me two central groups and one precondition. The two groups are entitlements to life, bodily integrity and health, and then to a development of sense, imagination, thoughts, and emotions. The precondition is what I would rephrase as control over the relationship between people and the environment, which could be expanded to encompass all the inextricable political and economic means to the above ends (cf. 76-77). These entitlements as rights supply a "rich set of goals...in place of 'the wealth and poverty of the economists,' as Marx so nicely put it" (284).

Further, our technical competence, based on an irresponsible S2 yoked to the profit and militarism that finance it, vastly exceeds our understanding of its huge dangers for hundreds of millions of people and indeed for the survival of vertebrate ecosphere (cockroaches and tube worms may survive). For humanity to survive, we imperatively have to establish and enforce a graduated system of risk assessment and damage control based on the negentropic welfare of the human community and its ecosystem (which includes the fauna and flora) as an absolutely overriding criterion. This means retaining, and indeed following consistently through, Merton's famous four basic norms of science—universalism, skepticism, public communism, and personal disinterestedness (cf. also Collingridge 77-85 and 99ff.)—or Kuhn's five internal criteria—accuracy, scope, fruitfulness, consistency, and simplicity—as well as strict scientific accountability in the sense of both not falsifying findings and accounting for them. However, it means also practicing science from the word go (say, from its teaching) as most intimately co-shaped by the overriding concerns what and who is such an activity for, and thus why would it be worth supporting or indeed allowing by the community: "A stronger, more adequate notion of objectivity would require methods for systematically examining all the social values shaping a particular research process..." (Haraway, *Modest* 36, building on Harding; cf. also Wallerstein, *End* 164-67, 238-41, and 264-65, and Cini). All theories can today be seen to have powerful biases, the goodness or badness of which must be treated in each case on its epistemologico-political merits.

A lot of discussion has already ensued, from the heyday of the Welfare State on, how to fairly assess such risks, and in the USA the International Association of Machinists, spurred by automation, has even formulated a "Technology Bill of Rights" (Noble, *Forces* 350-51). I can only present here some partial and (fortunately) highly biased summaries of what appears to me a clear and present necessity. The prevention of irreparable damage would have to move through clearly delimited stages, all of them subject to review boards with various mixtures of science and community representatives, at various levels from the basic research unit to international bodies. A first step is initial screening, calling a halt to what can be reasonably demonstrated as serious dangers in our situation, where decision-making about the future of novelties must largely be based on ignorance. A second step is imposition of strict rules about a testing of consequences, which must be temporally as protracted as necessary before a full development, costly and perhaps impossible to reverse, is embarked upon. A third step is continuous and rigorous monitoring of all important products and processes in use. Though lip-service is paid to these steps now, they are always secondary to profit-making or military considerations (for an example, cf. the discussion on the wrong presuppositions of "dominating nature" within the Human Genome Project in Casalino-Keller and Lewontin); therefore, techniques for all of them are still in their infancies. Still, however difficult this may be, they can and must be developed by efforts similar in size to the US Manhattan Project for the atomic bomb, only geared to survival rather than destruction and ongoing for many targets. This will be costly, but less so than not insisting upon them, allowing the killing damages.

To specify a bit: decision-making under ignorance means "to place a premium on highly corrigible options," so that mistakes can be eliminated both relatively quickly and cheaply (Collingridge 32). Monitoring requires adversary confrontation of factual evidence from different axiological points of view, that is, who is it good for, when, how much:

> [R]eliable scientific knowledge was won for mankind [by subjecting one opinion and decision to the criticism of others]. The control of advanced technical projects on behalf of society must depend on the same principle....This is what we call monitoring technology,...a range of institutions and social techniques enabling the critical scrutiny of corporate decisions and actions, by and on behalf of competent and concerned opinion at every level. ([U.K.] Council for Science and Society 27, cited in Collingridge 147)

This means that, first, in proportion to their importance, cost, and potential irreversibility, major scientific projects should not be allowed to become "in house" *faits accomplis* without a public debate that follows the juridic norm of hearing more than one side *(audiatur et altera pars)*. Second, recognizing that "[e]very decision involves the selection among an agenda of alternative images of the future, a selection that is guided by some system of values" (Boulding 423), all individuals involved in screening, testing, and monitoring should provide the "bias statement" demanded already a third of a century ago by the American Academy of Sciences: a list of all previous major research funding, occupations, investments, public stands on political issues, and similar (cited in Collingridge 186, with disfavour); clearly, this applies *a fortiori* to the biases of collective or legal bodies, and no private bodies can be exempted.

But probably even this is not enough. We are today irreversibly steeped in technoscience: very little technology is to be had apart from the science that produced them, very little science is to be had apart of complex technology. It is a time not only of particle physics and molecular genetics but also nanotechnology and untold further possibilities of highly risky forays. We therefore have to draw on, encourage, and discuss all suggestions for limiting risks, such as the one by Kourilsky and Viney on precautionary steps before prevention, and many other debates for a "University of Disaster" (Virilio). Yet furthermore, we have to pick up the suggestion by Denis Noble "that there is an obligation on the part of creators of this stockpile of knowledge to work out how to disarm its ability to destroy" (184). "First of all, do not harm": this old Hippocratic oath must be amplified by adding, "Whatever else you do, put up barriers against destruction." These would be still recognizably scientific debates (cf. Collingridge 189-94), only enhanced by the wider horizon of a life-oriented S1, where the opponents are transparently honest and explicit about their presuppositions, and thus allow both an understanding how rival interpretations of data may be arrived at and, where necessary, a questioning of the presuppositions (for example, not where to build a highway and how to build a nuclear power-station but also whether). As mentioned above, this profile of decision-making should be, after the original decision, preserved for needed corrections as consequences unfold.

I do not pretend the above is more than a first orientation. Among its huge gaps is, for example, lack of discussion on who should establish and administer such reviews and controls, and how to prevent an unnecessarily cumbersome bureaucracy to take root. These are however not beyond human ingenuity, if transparency and accountability are achieved. What ought to be stressed is that today science (S2) is fully accountable to and strictly steered by capitalist interests, while pretending to be technical and apolitical. It has therefore grown ecocidal and genocidal (for the genus homo), with almost all scientists as "craftsmen of power" (Haberer 303), "barbarian experts" (C.P. Snow), and today willing mini-entrepreneurs of destruction. We need a science for survival (S1), which would look anew at its reason for being by openly acknowledging its civic political responsibility, and be steered—probably, in the long run, less tightly than today—by the interests of community and species survival.

Finally, I wish to point out, how strangely, richly, and intimately the opposition S1-S2 is interfused with the question of bodily freedom for one and for all, for our bodies personal and bodies politic. Democritus's atoms fell in a straight line from above to below; they come from a place of power not subject to human will, of whimsical Gods or blind Nature, and may break in upon any of us (cf. Derrida 22-24). To this picture Marx preferred in his dissertation Epicurus (*Texte* 59ff., 99-103, 142, and 148-58), who scoffed at the anthropomorphic idea that in the infinite there is an up and down: the fixed destination of Destiny may be disturbed and deviated by some action. In Lucrece's great philosophical poem, the atoms swerve and break the chains of Fate, which sanctions "the free will of people living in the world /...By which we move wherever pleasure leads each of us" (II: 254-58; cf. Suvin, "Living"). It opens a space for choice, for Being born from Non-Being, a surplus of Being.

If we really wanted to follow the Epicurean science of Lucrece, we'd have to embrace his metaphor of High Venus, mother of gods and humans. Its erotic contract with nature and human society is opposed to the hatred of Subject, and the hatred of the human body as a feeling embodiment (just see how the geneticists look at it, or how patriarchy has always looked at women!)—a contract of violent domination which is at its clearest in the service of Mars. S2 relates to S1 as warfare maiming of bodies by bombs or napalm and maiming of psyches by anxiety and terror, both characteristics of late capitalism, relates to the caress of friendly sympathy.

Works Cited

Angenot, Marc. "Dialectique et topique," in his *La Parole pamphlétaire*. Paris: Payot, 1982, 145-233.

Anscombe, G.E.M. *Intention*. London: Blackwell, 1979.

Arendt, Hannah. *Kant's Political Philosophy*. Chicago: U of Chicago P, 1989.

Aronowitz, Stanley. *Science as Power*. Minneapolis: U of Minnesota P, 1988.

Barnes, Barry, and David Edge eds. *Science in Context*. Cambridge MA: MIT P, 1982.

Bauman, Zygmunt. *Modernity and Ambivalence*. Cambridge: Polity P, 1991.

Bhaskar, Roy. *Scientific Realism and Human Emancipation*. London: Verso, 1986.

Blumenberg, Hans. *Wirklichkeiten, in denen wir leben*. Stuttgart: Reclam, 1986.

Boulding, Kenneth. "Truth or Power." *Science* 190 (1975): 423.

Braverman, Harry. *Labor and Monopoly Capital: The Degradation of Work in the Twentieth Century*. New York & London: Monthly RP, 1974.

Brecht, Bertolt. *Werke*. Grosse Kommentierte Berliner und Frankfurter Ausgabe. Frankfurt & Berlin: Suhrkamp & Aufbau V., 1988-98. [as GKA]

Bruner, Jerome. *Actual Minds, Possible Worlds*. Cambridge MA: Harvard UP, 1986.

Carr, David. "Thought and Action in the Art of Dance." *British J. of Aesthetics* 27.4 (1987): 345-57.

Casalino, Larry [, and Evelyn Fox Keller]. "Decoding the Human Genome Project." *Socialist R.* 91.2 (1992): 117-25.

Castoriadis, Cornelius. *Crossroads in the Labyrinth*. Transl. K. Soper and M.H. Ryle. Brighton: Harvester, 1984.

Cini, Marcello. "Norme e valori nella costruzione della scienza." *Giano* no. 1 (1989): 51-64.

Collingridge, David. *Social Control of Technology.* London: Pinter, & New York: St. Martin's P, 1980.

Collingwood, R.G. *The Idea of Nature.* Oxford: Clarendon P, 1945.

Daly, Herman E. *Beyond Growth.* Boston: Beacon P, 1996.

Derrida, Jacques. "Mes chances : Au rendez-vous de quelques stéréophonies épicuriennes." *Confrontation* (printemps 1988): 19-45.

Diels, Hermann, and Walther Kranz eds. *Die Fragmente der Vorsokratiker.* Berlin: Weidmann, 1951.

Eddington, A.S. *New Pathways in Science.* Cambridge: Cambridge UP, 1935.

Einstein, Albert. "Consideration Concerning Fundamentals of Theoretical Physics." *Science* 91 (1940): 487-92

Elgin, Catherine Z. *With Reference to Reference.* Indianapolis: Hackett, 1982.

Ellul, Jacques. *Technological System.* Transl. J. Neugroschel. New York: Continuum, 1980.

[Gandhigram Rural University]. www.gandhigram.org.

Gendlin, E.T. "The Responsive Order." *Man and World* 30 (1997): 383-411.

Georgescu-Roegen, Nicholas. *The Entropy Law and the Economic Process.* New York: toExcel, 1999 [rpt. of Harvard UP 1971 edn.].

Goodman, Nelson, and Catherine Z. Elgin. *Reconceptions in Philosophy and Other Arts and Sciences.* Indianapolis: Hackett, 1988.

Graham, Loren R. *Between Science and Values.* NY: Columbia UP, 1981.

Gramsci, Antonio. *Quaderni del carcere.* Ed. critica a cura di V. Gerratana. Torino: Einaudi, 1975.

—. *Selections from the Prison Notebooks.* Transl. and ed. Q. Hoare and G. Nowell Smith. New York: International. Publ. 1971.

Grene, Marjorie. *The Knower and the Known.* London: Faber & Faber, 1966.

Gross, Alan G. *The Rhetoric of Science.* Cambridge MA: Harvard UP, 1990.

Haberer, Joseph. *Politics and the Community of Science.* New York: Van Nostrand, 1969.

Hacking, Ian. *Representing and Intervening.* Cambridge: Cambridge UP, 1983.

Hagstrom, Warren O. *The Scientific Community.* NY: Basic Books, 1965.

Haraway, Donna. *Modest_Witness@Second_Millennium.* New York & London: Routledge, 1997.

—-. *Primate Visions.* New York & London: Routledge, 1990.

—-. "Situated Knowledge." *Feminist Studies* 14.3 (1988): 575-99.

Harding, Sandra. *Whose Science? Whose Knowledge?* Ithaca: Cornell UP, & Milton Keynes, Open UP, 1991.

—-, and Merrill Hintikka eds. *Discovering Reality.* Dordrecht: Reidel, 1983.

Harré, R[om]. *The Philosophies of Science.* London: Oxford UP, 1972.

Heisenberg, Werner. *Wandlungen in den Grundlagen der Naturwissenschaft.* Stuttgart: Hirzel, 1959.

[Hesiod. *Erga kai hemerai.*] Esiodo. *Le opere e i giorni* [bilingual]. Milano: Rizzoli, 1998.

Hesse, Mary B. *Models and Analogies in Science.* Notre Dame: U of Notre Dame P, 1966.

—-. *Revolutions and Reconstructions in the Philosophy of Science.* Bloomington: Indiana UP, 1980.

Hountondji, Paulin J. "Recapturing," in V.Y. Mudimbe ed., *"Présence Africaine" and the Politics of Otherness 1947-1987.* Chicago: U of Chicago P, 1992, 238-48.

Jameson, Fredric. *A Singular Modernity.* London: Verso, 2002.

Johnson, Mark. *The Body in the Mind.* Chicago: U of Chicago P, 1990.

Kapp, K. William. *The Social Costs of Private Enterprise.* Cambridge MA: Harvard UP, 1950.

Keller, Evelyn Fox. "Feminism and Science," in A. Garry and M. Pearsall, *Women, Knowledge, and Reality.* New York & London: Routledge, 1992, 175-88.

Kierkegaard, Sören. *Samlede Vaerker.* Kjöbenhavn: Gyldendal, 1920-36.

Korsch, Karl. *Karl Marx.* Frankfurt: Europäische V.sanstalt, 1975.

Kourilsky, Philippe, and Geneviève Viney. *Le principe de précaution.* Paris : O. Jacob, 2000.

Kuhn, Thomas "Objectivity, Value Judgment, and Theory Choice," in his *The Fruitful Tension.* Chicago: U of Chicago P, 1977, 320-39.

Latour, Bruno. *Science in Action.* Cambridge MA: Harvard UP, 1997.

Laugstien, Thomas. "Erkenntnistheorie," entry in *Historisch-kritisches Wörterbuch des Marxismus,* Vol. 3. Hamburg: Argument, 1997, col. 744-62.

Leiss, William. *Science and Domination.* New York: Braziller, 1972 (cited from his *Scienza e dominio.* Transl. P. Rossi. Milano: Longanesi, 1976).

Levins, Richard. "Ten Propositions on Science and Antiscience," in Andrew Ross ed., *Science Wars.* London & Durham: Duke UP, 1996, 180-91.

Lévy-Leblond, Jean-Marc. "La science est-elle universelle?" *Le Monde diplomatique* (May 2006): 32-33.

Lewontin, Richard. *It Ain't Necessarily So: The Dream of the Human Genome and Other Illusions.* New York: New York R. of Books, 2000.

Licata, Ignazio. "Complessità come apertura logica." *Dedalus* no. 2-3 (2007): 63-68.

Lindsay, R.B. "Physics, Ethics, and the Thermodynamic Imperative," in B. Baumrin ed., *Philosophy of Science: The Delaware Seminar,* Vol. 2: 1962-1963. New York: Interscience Publ., [1963], 411-48.

Longino, Helen E. *Science as Social Knowledge.* Princeton: Princeton UP, 1990.

[Lucretius Carus, Titus]—Lucrezio. *La natura delle cose— De rerum natura* [bilingual]. Ed. G. Milanese. Milano: A. Mondadori, 2000.

Marcuse, Herbert. *One-Dimensional Man.* Boston: Beacon P, 1964.

—-. *Reason and Revolution.* Boston: Beacon P, 1960.

Marglin, Stephen A. "Losing Touch," in Frédérique Apffel Marglin and idem, *Dominating Knowledge.* Oxford: Clarendon P, 1990, 217-82.

Marx, Karl. *Differenz der epikureischen und demokritischen Naturphilosophie* (1841), in his *Texte zu Methode und Praxis I.* Reinbek: Rowohlt, 1969, 131-89.

—-. *Theorien über den Mehrwert I.* Berlin [DDR]: Dietz V., 1956.

—-[and Friedrich Engels.] *Werke.* [*MEW*] Berlin [DDR]: Dietz V., 1962ff.

Merleau-Ponty, Maurice. *Phenomenology of Perception.* Tr. C. Amith. London: Routledge, 1962.

Merton, Robert K. *Social Theory and Social Structure.* Rev. edn. New York: Free P, 1957.

Mies, Maria, and Vandana Shiva. *Ecofeminism.* London: Zed Books, 1993.

Morin, Edgar. *Introduction à une politique de l'homme.* Nouvelle éd. Paris: Seuil, 1999.

Müller-Hill, Benno. *Murderous Science.* Transl. G.R. Fraser. Oxford: Oxford UP, 1988.

Nietzsche, Friedrich. *Die fröhliche Wissenschaft.* München: Goldmann, s.d.

—-. *Philosophy and Truth: Selections from Nietzsche's Notebooks of the Early 1870's.* Transl., ed., and introduced by D. Breazeale. S.l.: Humanities P, 1979.

—-. *Werke.* Leipzig: Naumann, 1900-13.

—-. *Zur Genealogie der Moral.* Ed. W.D. Williams. Oxford: Blackwell, 1972.

Noble, David F. *Forces of Production.* New York & Oxford: Oxford UP, 1986.

—-. *Religion of Technology.* London: Penguin, 1999.

Noble, Denis. "Academic Integrity," in A. Montefiore and D. Vines eds., *Integrity in the Public and Private Domains.* London & New York: Routledge, 1999.

Nussbaum, Martha C. *Frontiers of Justice.* Cambridge MA: Belknap P, 2006.

Oliveira, Francisco de. "The Duckbilled Platypus." *New Left R* no. 24 (2003): 40-58.

Penley, Constance, and Andrew Ross eds. *Technoculture.* New York: Routledge, 1991.

Pickering, Andrew ed. *Science as Practice and Culture.* Chicago: U of Chicago P, 1992.

Polanyi, Michael. *The Tacit Dimension.* L: Routledge & Kegan Paul, 1967.

Putnam, Hilary. *The Collapse of the Fact/ Value Dichotomy and Other Essays.* Cambridge MA: Harvard UP, 2002.

—-. *Realism with a Human Face.* Cambridge MA: Harvard UP, 1990.

Rickert, Heinrich. *Die Grenzen der naturwissenschaftlichen Begriffsbildung.* Tübingen: Mohr, 1921.

Rorty, Richard. *Philosophy and the Mirror of Nature.* Princeton: Princeton UP, 1980.

Russo, Lucio. *La rivoluzione dimenticata.* Milano: Feltrinelli, 2003.

Schrödinger, Erwin. *What Is Life.* New York: Macmillan, 1945.

Serres, Michel, *La Naissance de la physique dans le texte de Lucrèce.* Paris: Minuit, 1977.

Shiva, Vandana. *Biopiracy.* Boston: South End P, 1997.

Smith, Dorothy E. *The Everyday World as Problematic.* Toronto: U of Toronto P, 1987.

Smith, Michael L. "Selling the Moon," in *The Culture of Consumption.* Eds. R.W. Fox and T.J.J. Lears. New York: Pantheon Books, 1983, 175-209 and 233-36.

Squier, Susan Merrill. *Babies in Bottles.* Brunswick NJ: Rutgers UP, 1994.

Storer, H.W. *The Social System of Science.* NY: Holt, Rinehart, 1966.

Suchting, Wal A. "Epistemologie" entry in *Historisch-kritisches Wörterbuch des Marxismus*, Vol. 3. Hamburg: Argument, 1997, col. 637-58.

Suvin, Darko. „On Cognition as Art and Politics: Reflections For A Toolkit," in his *Defined by a Hollow.* London: P. Lang, 2010, 269-319.

—. "On Cognitive Emotions and Topological Imagination." *Versus* no. 68-69 (1994): 165-201.

—. "Conflitto, conflitto *über alles*?: Conflitto opposto a rivelazione come poetiche di narrazione scenica e paradigmi," in G. Manetti et al. ed. *Guerre di segni: Semiotica delle situazioni conflittuali.* Torino: Centro Scientifico, 2005, 373-91.

—. "*Haltung* (Bearing) and Emotions: Brecht's Refunctioning of Conservative Metaphors for Agency," in T. Jung ed., *Zweifel - Fragen - Vorschläge.* Frankfurt a.M.: Lang V, 1999, 43-58.

—. "Heavenly Food Denied: *Life of Galileo*," in P. Thomson and G. Sacks eds., *The Cambridge Companion to Brecht.* Cambridge: Cambridge UP, 1994, 139-52.

—. "Living Labour and the Labour of Living: A Little Tractate for Looking Forward in the 21st Century," in his *Defined by a Hollow.* London: P. Lang, 2010, 419-71.

—. "Revelation vs. Conflict: A Lesson from Nô Plays for a Comparative Dramaturgy." *Theatre J.* 46.4 (1994): 523-38.

—. "Two Cheers for Essentialism & Totality." *Rethinking Marxism* 10.1 (1998): 66-82 [chapter 2 of this book].

Traweek, Sharon. "Unity, Dyads, Triads, Quads, and Complexity," in Andrew Ross ed., *Science Wars.* London & Durham: Duke UP, 1996, 139-50.

[U.K.] Council for Science and Society. *Superstar Technologies.* [London]: Rose, 1976.

Vernant, Jean-Pierre. *Mythe et pensée chez les Grecs.* Paris: Maspero, 1982.

Virilio, Paul. *L'Université du désastre.* Paris : Galilée, 2007.

Wallerstein, Immanuel. *The End of the World as We Know It.*

Minneapolis: U of Minnesota P, 1999.

—-. *Historical Capitalism [, with] Capitalist Civilization.* London: Verso, 1996.

Weber, Max. "Vom inneren Beruf zur Wissenschaft," in his *Soziologie—Weltgeschichtliche Analysen—Politik.* Stuttgart: Kröner, 1964, 311-39 ("Science as a Vocation," in *From Max Weber.* Eds. H.H. Geerth and C.W. Mills. New York: Oxford UP, 1946).

9. DEATH INTO LIFE: FOR A POETICS OF ANTI-CAPITALIST ALTERNATIVE (2009)

—For Srećko Horvat—

> Things could be otherwise.
> —Raymond Ruyer, defining utopia

1.1. In the Ice Age
(A Counter-Project to Xiung Xi-ling)

> All that we feel is the freezing storm
> But who is there to grieve for the warmth?
> As you're leaving, bequeath this wish:
> Everybody should afford happiness!

1.2. ON CATASTROPHIC CAPITALISM TODAY

The present deep economic crisis has only brought to the surface some permanent trends of capitalism, largely occulted in the foregoing decades. There is no dearth of mortal sins to be laid at the door of capitalism. I shall suggest what I see as the most important ones.

The capitalist mode of production is always centrally shaped by the irreconcilable conflict between the capitalist urge for profits and the working people's need for a humanly decent life. The urge was somewhat curbed by the fear of revolt after the Russian Revolution and the Great Depression, which led to a modest but real "security floor" conceded to the middle and working classes, largely at the expense of the global "South" and the natural environment. With the waning of any consistently radical horizons as of the mid-1970s, capitalist corporations engaged in a large-scale offensive to depress wages per unit of production and boost profits from huge to monstrous. Using the slogans of free trade and globalization, the rich organized bundles of radical interventions by major States and the "roof" organizations of international capitalism (GATT, then WTO, IMF, and World Bank) to make themselves vastly richer, while multiplying the poor in their nations, eviscerating the middle class prosperity based on stable employment, and upping the income gap between rich and poor countries from 10:1 to 90:1. A large class of chronically poor was created, politically neutralized by creating fear of even poorer immigrants. The asset bubbles bursting now are the consequence of this class warfare from above: masses of people in the North had not only to work much more and exhaust their savings but also to borrow against their homes and other investments—the total 2008 debt in the US has been estimated at $48 trillion (Murphy, Turner, Magnus).

Facing the few thousand billionaires, possibly nearly 3,000 million struggle today to survive, falling fast, while more than half of them live in the most abject poverty, more or less quickly dying of hunger and attendant diseases (Pogge); so that the hundred million dead and several hundred million other casualties of warfare in the 20th century seem puny in comparison (though their terror and suffering is not). It has been calculated that a 1% increase in US unemployment correlates with 37,000 deaths (650 of which homicides) and a 4,000 increase in mental hospital population, but the hidden psychic toll is surely greater. Economic "growth" benefits only the richest, at the expense of everybody else, especially the poor and the powerless in this generation and future ones (Ayres, Rogers, Barnet & Cavanagh).

The purpose of capitalist economy, profit, entails mass dying and unhappiness. For billions of people it leads to shorter and more painful lives, for everybody except maybe the upper 2-5% in the world to gnawing stress, want and often despair. Technosciences could have finally made this planet habitable; but, dominated as they are by profit, they provide enormous quantities of shoddy commodities without regard to quality or duration of life. Indeed the poor could sing, "I have plenty of nothing,/ And nothing is plenty for me" (Gershwin Brothers). To this systematic, long-duration exploitation by capitalist power, aggravating factors are being added: the effect of the burst debt bubble, the recent sharp increase of prices for food-stuffs in the world—the list could go on. Hundreds of millions of the poorest and of those at the brink have begun to engage in "hunger revolts", in China, south Asia, west Africa and some Islamic countries but also in eastern Europe. The wonder is that more and stronger revolts have not yet happened: but there are no guarantees.

What are the prospects of this rotting mode of production? The Marxist and then the Leninist diagnosis has always been that capitalism finally would not work; this was much too sanguine in its time-horizons, but the case is today stronger than ever. The capitalist economy is, now globally, pursuing a cheap-labour economy on the one hand and the search for new consumer markets on the other; the former undermines the latter. It does not work for the great majority of people, the workers who live from their physical and intellectual work. It does not work for our ecological balance, severely threatened by over-consumption of energy, while to prevent collapse we need a steady-state economy, with growth resulting from efficiency (Chossudovsky, Daly, Cobb, Townsend—I shall return to this).

In sum, the Keynesian capitalist reform finally succeeded only in tandem with "military Keynesianism"—the heavy rear-mament that initially primed the pump of business upswing and remained its constant precondition—and its price was the Nazi regime, High Stalinism, and the 2nd World War. War expenses under the Bush II administration were 1,000 million dollars per year (Custers, Johnson). Though today Keynesian measures are touted by the most "progressive" Obamites, Obama's Af-Pak bog is already having the same effect on such stopgaps as Johnson's Vietnam had on his "War on Poverty": it will kill civil in favour of military Keynesianism. As for fascism, in barely refurbished guises it is doing very well almost everywhere, thank you. If radically anti-capitalist and anti-authoritarian perspectives of exiting from this predicament are not found, the dilemma of "Socialism or Barbarism" will have only one issue: wars in the South (including Northern ghettos), fascism in the North.

2.1. IMAGINE A FISH

Imagine a fish living out of water

The water is
The air is
The fish is

He has some water in his bladder
He flops along gravelly roads

Up to her eyes coated with dust
How does she see desiccated the world
Imagine

Sometimes it flops up a stump
And attempts to sing
The birds are in the water

(Imagine)

2.2. TWO UNHEEDED SIGNALS OF DANGER: WAR AND MIGRATION

War as Capitalism's Doomsday Weapon

I define war as a coherent sequence of conflicts, involving physical combats between large organized groups of people that include the armed forces of at least one state, with the aim of political and economic control over a given territory. Other aims may be securing advantages for coming conflicts (for example dominion over air, sea or oil resources), the destruction of commodities and people, and evading inner class tension. The ratio of military to civilian casualties in wars during the 20th century has "progressed" from 8:1 to 1:8 (eight civilians killed for each combatant), and the fighters diversified from regular armies into paramilitary groups, police forces, mercenaries, local warlords and purely criminal gangs. The mass casualties have been mainly people marginal to "White" patriarchal capitalism: the poor, the uppity "middle" States, the "coloured," women (Kaldor, George, Suvin "Capitalism"). Of course, theological hatred using weapons of mass destruction scarcely allows for neat discrimination.

War is more than a Hobbesian metaphor for bourgeois human relationships. It is securely based in antagonistic competition, the "essential locomotive force" of bourgeois economy and "generally the mode in which capital secures the victory of its mode of production" (Marx *Grundrisse*). Continuous warfare has <u>never</u> ceased under capitalism: around 160 wars have raged between 1945 and 1993 killing more people than in World War II; we know what has continued since. Capitalism came about in plunder wars; war financing set up its modern bureaucracy and central national banks; and there is no evidence it could climb out of economic depressions without huge military spending, a war mega-dividend. The political fallout is the spread of military rule that subordinates the civil society to its barbarity even in times of official peace—as today (Anderson, Amin, Pannekoek, Virilio).

Weapons commodities are since World War II not only the source of greatest extra-profit but a system-pillar of capitalism. The yearly money value of the international armament trade oscillated in the last 30 years, according to the available faulty statistics, between 20 and over 30 billion dollars, and today it is more. The capitalist market systematically favours armaments commodities because of their uniquely high value-added price, their specially rapid rate of obsolescence and turnover, the monopoly or semi-monopoly position of their manufacturers, and the large-scale and secure financing of military research, production and massive cost overruns—all taken from public taxation. By the time of the First Gulf War, world spending for military purposes was nearly a trillion US$ annually or between 2 and 2.5 billion dollars daily, more than half of it attributable to the USA; and today it is way past this. This most profitable part of global trade is the strongest factor of both international violence and the colonization of life-worlds and eco-systems by commodity economy. The tens of millions of dead in the two World Wars brought about tens of trillions of profitable investments in the huge reconstructions of destroyed homes and industries and ongoing rearmament: a million dollars or more per dead body. No capitalism without increasingly destructive weapons and wars which might still destroy the world: the marvellous technoscientific progress means that one nuclear submarine can destroy the peoples of an entire continent, yet eight new US nuclear submarines have been made since the fall of the USSR. One-quarter of the public monies which are expended on weapons commodities would eradicate poverty, homelessness and illiteracy, as well as pay for the cleanup of all our major environmental pollution...(Baran-Sweezy, Kolko, McMurtry, the Tofflers, Marx *Kapital*, Luxemburg)

For a politics wishing to consecrate life, the profits of war are a main pillar of Death.

Migrants and Justice

I have expatiated elsewhere (having, alas, some firsthand knowledge) upon the untold miseries and stupidities of especially Europe's immigration policy. Here I shall present only my conclusions as axioms for a future stance:

—the right to people's displacement across any and all borders is a central human right; this entails also duties of respecting the target communities.
—each political community should foster the maximum of economically and politically possible human rights for all its inhabitants, by giving them the maximum of economically and politically possible citizen rights—say, a local vote after one year of paying taxes and citizenship after three.
—our value focus ought to be on the life of immigrants, which supplies criteria for any acceptable outline of immigrant policy (regulating the flux of immigrants).
—"one person, one vote" and "no taxation without representation".

True, any society has the right to defend itself by means of penal law; yet unless we are to slide toward a permanent state of emergency with unchecked police powers, each case is to be examined on its merits, whether the accused is a migrant or not. Migration may only be normalized through a "co-development" between the global North and South (Balibar). The politico-economical precondition for this is no Northern engagement in wars (except in defence to a clear *and present* aggression). Wars are not only a major source of immiseration and therefore migration, they also cheapen the price of people and favour despotism, subjection and slavery. The alternative to co-development is violent racism, as today in Europe, and finally apartheid, possibly solidified as genetic castes. This leads to a society not worth living in.

If any such development towards horizons of global justice

comes about, primarily through the Northern economies' reduction of energy consumption, then we shall have to recognize and approach cracking the hard nut of population control. Marx was in his time rightly scathing about Malthus, but today the problem is different. I shall argue this within a discussion of ecology.

3.1. Question

when he was singing
the nightingale of times past
did he sing well?

when he was singing
the nightingale of times past
was his song heard?

3. 2. What Classical Marxist Positions Remain Valid?

The work of Karl Marx is indispensable to any attempt at avoiding catastrophe. His "categorical imperative" is still non-negotiable: "to overthrow all conditions in which man is a degraded, enslaved, forsaken, contemptible being" (MEW 1). Here is a brief sketch of what it means for people like me today, which neither can nor should pretend to a "full truth" (more in Suvin, "Living Labour").

I approach Marx's insights as a fusion of three horizons: cognition or systematic understanding, permitting better consciousness of and intervention into practice, liberty or radical democracy, and pleasure. This is accompanied by a set of regulative principles (such as dialectic, measure or justice, and deviation), and a focus identifying the underlying factor of capitalist and any post-capitalist life, the knot in which all else converges: living labour. The mortification of living labour, trading creativity for alienation, leads to mass personal and collective death. It must be radically refused.

I have discussed these domains in the essay adduced. Each of them qualifies, delimits, and throws into relief elements of the other two; each stabilizes the other two. Liberty is the precondition for a life worth living, for the pursuit of happiness or pleasure. However, liberty without cognition is blind narcissism and without pleasure it is dutiful puritanism. Cognition without pleasure is pedantry and without liberty is sterile elitist self-indulgence (as in Brecht's *Life of Galileo).* Pleasure without liberty is Sadean corruption, without cognition it is empty.

Living labour is concept arising out of a very ancient plebeian tradition of imagery, in which the immortal labouring people constitute the world's body in metabolism with the world's goods, refashioned by, in, and as their bodies (see Bakhtin's *Rabelais).* This tradition runs through Fourier's passionate attractions up to our days, if often sadly corrupted into narcissism. Marx fused it with the compatible materialist and dialectical intellectual traditions from Heraclitus to Hegel and Feuerbach. His main innovation was to alter the people's body into labour's living body, which makes out of the pre-Socratic cosmic ever-living fire a concrete, everyday matter of living labour's formative fire. This transcended the Greek vision of activity split between the *praxis* of free and wealthy citizens and the *poiesis* of the plebeian "mechanics," slaves and women. Marx not only posited that labour's undying fire was—in metabolism with nature—the sole source of all creativity, he also stressed that labour was within capitalism the realization of man "within alienation, or as alienated person" ("Economic and Philosophic Manuscripts"). He added to the plebeian defence of the consuming and hedonist body the crucial new cognition of the producing body, which both incorporated and criticized bourgeois political economy and practice.

Against these horizons, Marx's most useful insights today may be divided into propositions and methods.

I take it that some of Marx's fundamental propositions, often doubted in the Welfare State interval in the metropolitan North but today vindicated, are:

—that human societies are divided into classes based on a relationship towards and in production of life and goods, of which the two antagonistic poles are those who buy and exploit labour power (capitalists) and those who sell it (let us call them again proletarians, instead of confining this term to industrial workers); and that the "absolute general law of capitalist accumulation [is]: accumulation of wealth is at the same time accumulation of misery, agony of toil, slavery, ignorance, brutality" (*Kapital*);

—that the unceasing alienation of creative power in capitalism subjects proletarians to impoverishment; in the last generation or so the world proletariat has almost doubled, working under conditions of ever grosser exploitation and increasingly of political oppression (Harvey), so that Marx's thesis of the absolute immiseration of the proletariat as compared to 500 or 200 years ago has turned out to be correct for 90% or more of the working people in the world; and there is no doubt of the huge relative immiseration in comparison to the dominant classes and nations.

—that this immiseration, and the attendant hollowing out of all qualitative social functions and values, means that for all its technological advances capitalism as a social formation leads to a radical historical change, beneficent (as Marx mainly believed) or maleficent, that is leading to civilizational collapse.

Of methods, I shall single out: the radical critique and the social shaping of all understanding. Critique has always had the functions of exposing error and indicating the limits of a practice (Balibar): but Marx's adoption of it as his constant stance was allied with a stress on practice as its validation and with a systematic rejection of and deviation from any concept of fated class power from above (Suvin, "Living Labour"). Therefore it became also a radical and permanent labour of reassessment, of self-critique. What I call "social shaping" means that practical relationships between active agents enable and shape all understanding, thus refusing the scientistic division between looking subject and looked-at object. If there is a human "essence", it consists of a full set of people's social relationships. Thus no theory or method can be properly understood without understanding the practice of social groups to which it, in however roundabout ways, corresponds.

However, Marx held that "Truth includes not only the result but also the way.... [T]he true inquiry is the unfolded truth, whose scattered members are gathered up in the result." ("Prussian Censorship") Fruition encompasses also the—always provisional—fruits.

In sum, as opposed to production of exchange-values for profit, a vampiric dispossession of labour and its vitality, the production of use-values is a beneficent metamorphosis of life into more life. Humanized production or creativity replaces death with life: the central Marxian argument is as "simple" as this.

What then remains of Marx? Many things. Centrally: the realization that the figure of Destiny is in capitalism Political Economy. Fortune is swallowed into the Stock-market; Necessity rides on the profit-bringing and profit-enforcing bombers and missiles. Hell is the sweatshops of China and Montreal, the cubicles of solitary rooms.

Contrariwise, the main product of the hugely productive capitalist civilization is the production of destructive novums, "undermining...the springs of all wealth: the earth and the worker" by practicing "systematic robbery of the preconditions for life..., of space, air, light..." (Marx *Kapital*)—and today we could add water, silence, health in general, etc.: life and the pursuit of happiness. Death is the final horizon for a civilization of gambling, excitement, fashionable novelty (Benjamin). It is also the end-horizon of raping the planet by wars, economic exploitation and ecocide. This is not the easeful death each of us has a right to: it is the collective death of humanity.

4.1. CROSSING ON THE LEFT

> Woe to the land that wants heroes.
> Brecht, Life of Galileo

This flimsy hanging bridge frightens me badly,
I wish there were any other way out of the petrified
    desert.
If it founders, i will surely drown; yet without it
The raging river would have closed over us already.

So far i have made it, but still, looking backward,
I wonder how deep the water, stony the grounds.
Tired, i wish we had a sturdily built bridge, so
We needy travellers could feel safer on our way.

I guess if we want a more secure bridge we better
Plan to bring the planks & rebuild it ourselves
Swaying over the abyss as skyscraper workers,

Enforcedly heroic materialists, the only ones left
With a will to preserve the traffic with productive
Reason, the only way left to bring us across alive.

4.2. TO DEFEND THE COMMONS

A new Left groundswell requires organization and a grasp for power, but also autonomous, though engaged, theorization— in other words, a fruitful tension between material action and intellectual creation. (Balibar) What new tools do we need after the failure of "State socialism"? I cannot provide anything like a full list. The negative experiences of degeneration after Lenin's, Tito's or Mao's revolutions, as well as their initial huge achievements, shall be present in my proposals. I also accept the positive side of "western" Marxism, its disjunction of long-term theory from politics legitimating a State.

We have to start from where we today unsafely stand. First, Marx himself was unable to emerge fully into his own novelty, leaving us to recognize where it was that he was going (Hobsbawm). Second, much of importance has changed since Marx's insights. A vital updating must use, wherever useful, new currents of understanding.

This also means starting from the most pressing threats, for we know what they are, though not, I fear, their full extent. I shall group them as somatics and environment, while recognizing that this neglects important areas, for one example the "knowledge economy" (say trademarks, patents and copyrights even on language, regulating internet, etc.) and its influence on the debates about ideology, fetishism, subjectivity or the intelligentsia. Wars and the swelling migrations have been foregrounded earlier.

Somatics: This is what I would call a cluster of problems centring materialistically upon humanity's vulnerable personal and collective bodies. The feminist and gay movements have broached some of them (sex/gender orientation, birth/abortion, care/caress). A full discussion of both drugging and prostitution is still to be done, for like Marx's relation of worker to exploited production each of these involves "the whole of human servitude" ("Economic and Philosophic Manuscripts"). By rights war and other overt violence, these mega-lesions of personal integrity, should be included here. And breathless turbocapitalism, racing headlong into Death, has already presented us with new supertechnological means of ruthless intervention— for example biogenetics (in use) and nanophysics (coming fast).

Ecology: When our environment is poisoned, we die—of cancer, lung diseases, heart overload, and a thousand other preventable ills. It is being poisoned by capitalist industry and squandering, which has by now plundered the hydrocarbon fossil fuels to proximate extinction, caused global warming (with consequences that might include tens of millions of "climate refugees" from low-lying areas such as Bangladesh and hundreds of billions in expenses to refurbish the world's ports), and on and on. Mammalian life on this planet itself is now at risk: as Wells and Sartre foresaw, and as Don Marquis's Archy wished upon us, crabs and ants (and, undoubtedly, cockroaches) may inherit the Earth.

The nonsensical capitalist dogma of infinite growth, modelled on personal enrichment, collides with the elementary fact that any physical system of a finite Earth must itself also eventually become non-growing. There can and must be sustainable development in the sense of qualitative improvement but without quantitative growth beyond the point where the ecosystem can regenerate. (Georgescu-Roegen, Daly-Cobb, Greider) Production can only be optimized by raising the productivity of its scarcest element—today, natural resources. This is possible to achieve only if the real social costs of using air, water, soil and labour are figured in (Kapp), while unproductive activities extraneous to use-values (most marketing and PR, useless innovations, artificial obsolescence, unceasing turnover of fashion trends) are rigorously taxed. Crucially, the total consumption of energy must be strongly, if reasonably, curbed. This means fighting both population growth in the South and per capita consumption in the richer countries and classes of the North. The only fair and efficient way to curb population growth is, of course, making the poor richer—and (a corollary) emancipating women. (More on this in the following essay.)

Since a given amount of low entropy can be used by us only once, the economic process is entropic. Thus the importance of purpose—what something is done for—becomes overwhelming. Aristotle's final cause and the old Roman query *cui bono?* (in whose interest?) are rehabilitated as against scientism's narrow concentration on the efficient cause, how to manipulate matter. The economic process always generates irrevocable waste or pollution and forecloses some future options (as oil after it has been burned). Since, however, labour and knowledge in the economic process allow life and all of its possibilities, we must become careful stewards, on constant lookout for minimizing entropy. "The only possible freedom is that...the associated producers rationally regulate their metabolism with nature by spending the minimum of forces and in a way most conformable to human nature" (Marx *Kapital* III).

4.3. In Sum: Radical Democracy

The right to survive by minimizing unnecessary lesion of our bodies, unnecessary rise of entropy, and unnecessary barriers to free displacement in Terran space, all of these are humanity's "commons". Our answers to all these problems have to be a defence of commons against enclosures, always a source of pauperization. They could reassign meaning to "communism" (More, Badiou, Žižek) as radical humanism. All these threats arise out of the inhuman essence of capitalism, fitting people into the profit system regardless of how much they are broken and deadened. Capitalism jettisons humanity in all its senses: civilized relations, interests of people, even their bodies. Our immiseration is not simply economical, it seamlessly extends to political disempowerment in relation to established class authority and "religious" disempowerment in relation to the universe.

The orientation toward a maximum of use-values compatible with a low rise of entropy is diametrically opposed to the globalization based on the sole goal of profit, causally crucial for the planetary ecological disaster. Thus we need to reassert political governance—national and international—over capital. An old-fashioned and entirely legal way of beginning to do this is by taxing the worst corporate entropy-mongers more and restoring purchasing power to the middle and lower classes by taxing them less.

True, capitalist corporations will spend half of their ill-gotten hundreds of billions to prevent democratic governance. A case in point is their rejection of a simple and minimal step—the "Tobin Tax", a small exit-and-entry toll at major foreign-exchange centres, which would greatly reduce the unproductive daily speculation in money values and yield hundreds of billions of dollars for good purposes. Another necessary prerequisite is abandoning the fake instrument of GNP and reformulating the meaning of growth in all our public statistics. (Daly) Therefore, our defence of humanity must issue into social control of means for survival from below, a new kind of politics.

For, last not at all least, a radical communist humanism, putting our commons and communities over profitable commodities, means radical democracy. In it production would be organized upon cooperative democratic bodies, so that in any unit the labourers become their own board of directors. A refashioned parliamentary apex, with judicious right of recalling representatives, would be based upon direct "town meetings" or councils from below, at all intermediate levels, and would include economic guarantees for fair access to media.

If profit or surplus value—the overwhelming cause for wars and exploitation, the overwhelming cause for private property over means of survival—can be strongly curbed and eventually banished, the State apparatus, including centralized police, will have no reason to exist.

Only an approach of this kind can supply us with criteria for dealing with the present financial and generally economic crash, for money and credit are also our commons—that is, potentially useful tools for prudent production of use-values. However, the methods of our response have to be cleansed. Dogmatic deduction from older positions often fails in accelerating times. Marx's work gave us an excellent example for method implicitly, and in places explicitly—for example opposing a meta-morphically fluid model to a rock-solid one (see more in "Two Cheers," chapter 2 of this book). The enraged search for the One Full Truth is monotheistic and must be scrapped in favour of exploring sheaves of possibilities opening up in qualitatively specific times (Bloch). Already in Marx it was clear that all modes of knowing presuppose a point of view. We have to acknowledge our own viewpoints and look critically at our own and each others' opinions. (Brecht, Lefebvre, Levins)

5.1. LISTENING TO SAIGYÔ

That reality
is bounded by reality
seems dubious
why should it then be assumed
that dreams are bounded by dreams?

5.2. IN CONCLUSION

Even if we agree that most of what I argue above is desirable, many will say it's impossible, "utopia" in the bad sense of no place. But what is the alternative? Utopia is also the good place—though we have learned there will always be conflicts over priorities. Our choice is either eco-political communism, "an association where the free development of each is the precondition for the free development of all" (Marx), or unending wars and unbridled barbarity. It is utopia or oblivion.

Only use-values can stand up to capitalist unequal exchange. This holds in spades for the present economy, predominantly operating on "brain labour". Ancient designations for these use-values were compassion, indignation, and love: that is, today, communism and poetry. We need to realize that there is for us no poetry without communism, and no communism without poetry. All poets know this, often in fantastic metamorphoses; few communists have allowed their suspicion to flower. When sundered, what we get are caricatures which degrade the potential horizon of either.

Poetry and communism allow no a priori rules, only a

poetics of looking backward and forward, lessons from experience against a constant horizon. A project:

"The whole business of Man is the Arts, and all things, common" (William Blake)

DOCTRINE (after Heine)

Drummer, drum on & have no fear
and kiss the bare-breast Liberty!
This is the whole of science & art
The sum of all philosophy.

Drum & inveigle the drowsy people
Send the snake's hiss & roar of lions,
One step in front, ready to die,
This is the sum of art & science.

This is old Karl's dialectics
Of all philosophy it is the Summa.
I've understood it by steadily looking,
& seeing the Revolution one Summer.

Note

This essay was an attempt to put into 5,000 words the upshot of my investigation into political epistemology during the last dozen years. It necessarily paraphrases or indeed repeats parts of them. Foregrounding my denial of conceptual monopoly, it also interleaves such texts with poems.

I attempt here also, as is proper, to stand upon the shoulders of very many wiser prose works from Marx, Polanyi, Benjamin, Gramsci, and Baran on, as well as many poets, from Lucretius and Blake on; Milton and Brecht unite the two. Many formulations are more or less taken from such works. For ease of reading, I have opted against notes and quotation marks (except in the case of Marx), but have compromised with my scholarly conscience by putting at the end of each argument a parenthesis with names of authors for the data and some formulations used, to be found in the bibliography below.

Nine friends read and criticized, sometimes vigorously, the drafts. I thank Marcelline Krafchick, Dick Ohmann, K.S. Robinson, and especially Ursula K. Le Guin and Rich Erlich. The responsibility remains mine.

Works Mentioned

Amin, Samir. *Capitalism in the Age of Globalization.* London: Zed Books, 1997.

Anderson, Perry. *Lineages of the Absolutist State.* London: Verso, 1979.

Ayres, R[obert] U. *Limits to the Growth Paradigm.* Centre for the Management of Environmental Resources, Working Paper 96/18/EPS. Amsterdam: Elsevier Science, 1996.

Badiou, Alain. *L'Hypothèse communiste.* S.l.: Lignes, 2009.

Bakhtin, M.M. *Rabelais and His World.* Transl. H. Iswolsky. Cambridge: MIT P, 1968.

Balibar, Etienne. *La philosophie de Marx.* Paris: La Découverte, 1993.

Baran, Paul, and Paul Sweezy. *Monopoly Capital.* New York: Monthly R P, 1966.

Barnet, Richard, and John Cavanagh. *Global Dreams: Imperial Corporations and the New World Order.* New York: Simon & Schuster, 1994.

Benjamin, Walter. *Gesammelte Schriften.* Frankfurt: Suhrkamp, 1980-87.

Bloch, Ernst. *Gesamtausgabe*, 16 Vols. Frankfurt: Suhrkamp, 1959ff.

Brecht, Bertolt. *Werke.* Grosse Kommentierte Berliner und Frankfurter Ausgabe. Suhrkamp & Aufbau V., 1988-2000.

Chossudovsky, Michel. *The Globalization of Poverty:*

Impacts of IMF and World Bank Reforms. London: Zed Books, 1997.

Custers, Peter. *Questioning Globalized Militarism: Nuclear and Military Production and Critical Economy.* London: Merlin P, 2007.

Daly, Herman E. *Beyond Growth.* Boston: Beacon Press, 1996.

––. *Steady-State Economics.* 2nd ed. Washington DC/ Covelo: Island P, 1991.

––, and John B. Cobb, Jr. *For the Common Good.* rev. ed. Boston: Beacon P, 1994.

––, and Kenneth Townsend. *Valuing the Earth: Economics, Ecology, Ethics.* Cambridge: MIT P, 1993.

[George, Susan.] *The Lugano Report.* London: Pluto P, 1999.

Georgescu-Roegen, Nicholas. *The Entropy Law and the Economic Process.* New York: toExcel, 1999.

Greider, William. *One World, Ready or Not: The Manic Logic of Global Capitalism.* New York: Simon & Schuster, 1997.

Harvey, David. *Justice, Nature and the Geography of Difference.* Oxford: Blackwell, 1996.

––. *The Limits to Capital.* London & New York: Verso, 1999.

Hobsbawm, E.R. *Revolutionaries.* London: Little, Brown, 2007.

Johnson, Chalmers. "The Economic Disaster That Is Military Keynesianism." www.mondediplo.com/2008/02/05military

Kaldor, Mary. *New and Old Wars.* Cambridge: Polity P, 1999.

Kapp, Karl W. *The Social Costs of Private Enterprise.* Cambridge: Harvard UP, 1950

Kolko, Gabriel. *Century of War.* New York: New Press, 1994.

Lefebvre, Henri. *The Production of Space.* Transl. D. Nicholson-Smith. Oxford: Blackwell, 1997.

Levins, Richard. "Ten Propositions on Science and Antiscience," in Andrew Ross ed., *Science Wars.* Durham: Duke UP, 1996, 180-91.

Luxemburg, Rosa. *The Accumulation of Capital.* Transl. A. Schwarzschild. New York: Modern Reader, 1968.

Magnus, George. "Important to Curb Destructive Power of Deleveraging." *Financial Times* Sept. 30, 2008.

Marx, Karl. "Comments on the Latest Prussian Censorship Instruction", in *The Writings of the Young Marx on Philosophy and Society*. Eds. and transl. L.D. Easton & K.H. Guddat. Garden City NY: Doubleday, 1967, 67-92. [cited as "Prussian Censorship"]

——. "Economic and Philosophic Manuscripts (1844)," in *Writings*, see "Comments" above, 283-337.

——. *Grundrisse*. Transl. M. Nicolaus. London & New York: Penguin-Vintage, 1974.

——. Das *Kapital*, Vols. I and III. *MEW* Bd. 23 and 25. Berlin: Dietz V., 1993 and 1979.

——. "Speech at the Anniversary of the *People's Paper*," in *The Marx-Engels Reader*. Ed. R.C. Tucker. New York: Norton, 427-28.

——, and Friedrich Engels. *Werke*. [as *MEW*]. Vol. 1. Berlin: Dietz V., 1962ff.

McMurtry, John. *The Cancer Stage of Capitalism*. London: Pluto P, 1999.

Murphy, R. Taggart. "Bubblenomics." *New Left R* no. 57 (2009): 149-60.

Pannekoek, Anton. *Workers' Councils*. Oakland & Edinburgh: AK P, 2003.

Pogge, Thomas. "Reframing Economic Security and Justice," in D. Held and A. McGrew eds., *Globalization Theory*, Cambridge: Polity P, 2007, 207-24.

Rogers, Paul. *Losing Control: Global Security in the Twenty-first Century*. 2nd edn., London: Pluto Press, 2002.

Suvin, Darko. "Capitalism Means/Needs War" [essay 3 in this book].

——. "Immigration in Europe Today: Apartheid or Civil Cohabitation?" *Critical Quarterly* 50. 1-2 (2008): 206-33 [essay 6 in this book].

——. "Introductory Pointers toward an Economics of Physical and Political Negentropy." [essay 10 in this book].

—. "Living Labour and the Labour of Living (2004)," now in his *Defined by a Hollow.* Oxford: Peter Lang, 2010, 419-69.

Toffler, Alvin, and Heidi Toffler. *War and Anti-War.* Boston: Little, Brown, 1993.

Turner, Graham. *The Credit Crunch.* London: Pluto P, 2008.

Virilio, Paul. *Speed and Politics.* Transl. M. Polizzotti. New York: Semiotext(e): 1977.

Žižek, Slavoj. "How to Begin from the Beginning." *New Left R* no. 57 (2009): 43-55.

10. INTRODUCTORY POINTERS TOWARD AN ECONOMICS OF PHYSICAL AND POLITICAL NEGENTROPY (2009)[48]

—For Nadia Valavani, in Crete and Athens—

<u>0.</u> Dozens of weighty tomes have been written, after Marx and Karl Polanyi, about the hugely destructive effects of our rotting capitalism, so I can here only summarize a few most salient arguments about political economy, entropy, and our prospects today. When labour, nature, finally even money, bodies, and the future, are turned into commodities, then people are alienated and humiliated, the planet's resources recklessly squandered, and money subsumed under financial speculation. Human life has become extremely cheap: around 2,000 million people live today in the most abject poverty, which means more or less slowly dying of hunger and attendant diseases, facing the few thousand billionaires—so that the hundred million dead and several hundred million other casualties of capitalist warfare in the twentieth century seem puny in comparison (though their terror and suffering is not). The purpose of the economy is profit, only profit, and nothing but profit: we see it bring about

---

48. My thanks for bibliographic indications in this new continent go to the Inkrit group headed by Wolf F. and Frigga Haug, and Joyce Goggin.

mass dying and unhappiness, shorter and much uglier lives, in order to achieve social pacification for the upper third of the Northern metropolis of global capitalism. The purpose of the economy clearly ought to be the survival of the human species and other species ecologically linked to us. Our run-away sciences, which could have finally made (as Brecht put it after 1945) this planet habitable, have been turned into providers of enormous quantities of commodities without regard to quality of life. Economic growth benefits "only the richest people alive now, at the expense of nearly everybody else, especially the poor and the powerless in this and future generations....Life on planet Earth itself is now at risk." (Ayres 2) The "higher growth" of all our fake economical statistics is largely synonymous with more pollution, resource plunder, environmental and community destruction.

I shall deal in this paper with discussions about the relation of official income to actual well-being, continue with an indication of the entropy calculus as a basis for any future program of human survival, and conclude with some practical measures and difficulties of one such program.

1. On Political Economy: The Fake Instrument of GNP/GDP

1.1. One indispensable way to start is "the accounting assumptions at the very heart of industrial capitalism, the statistic known as the Gross National Product" (Greider 452), further GNP. It measures the yearly monetary transactions involved in the production of goods and services, the flow of money paid out by producers for all their costs: wages, rents, interests, and profits, also depreciation and excise taxes. It is founded on defining "capital" as the manmade assets producing goods and services, assuming nature is unlimited. Thus it ignores many costs, possibly the crucial ones, such as all the entropic costs—to which I shall return—of pollution and depletion of natural assets (not to speak of surplus extraction of value from workers). It further throws into the same bag useful and murderous goods and services. For example, any known monetary transactions in arms, drugs, prostitution, and crime, any repairs after natural or manmade devastations, unnecessary lawsuits or medical interventions, all count as increase of richness. Ridiculous paradoxes ensue: if prices fall, richness is officially reduced; if family help to the sick is monetarized by hiring a nurse, or if a family member's death is followed by payment of insurance, richness grows. Finally, GNP does not at all deal with "non-monetarizable" (unpaid) exchanges of services and goods—not only the illegal "black market" of smuggling and immigrant work but also housework, leisure and volunteer activities, etc.—which some accounts estimate at almost two-thirds of total work in industrialized countries (Möller col. 67-68). Therefore, the GNP's elaborate rows of numbers purporting to prove rising richness, and trumpeted ceaselessly by all world capitalist governments and media, conceal falling well-being and destruction of nature. The happiest event for it is a multi-million-dollar hurricane or, even better, a multi-billion war. The GNP may have been a useful instrument to measure capitalist production at the beginning of the industrial age, but beyond a certain level long ago achieved by industrialized countries, it becomes simply an instrument of ideological brainwashing, a Disneyland for the economists.

Since the Second World War, the GNP (and then the GDP) became the official US government measure for policy. Nonetheless, pioneering demurrals against it were entered in the first half of twentieth century by Irving Fisher, John Hicks, and Kenneth E. Boulding, and the critique picked up steam from the 1960s on in Baran, Sametz, Nordhaus-Tobin, Economic Council of Japan, Zolotas, and culminated in various more encompassing proposals at the end of the 1980s (see for this history Leipert 55, 62-63, 68-72, and 331ff.). Most of them concluded that the GNP is not "even a reasonable approxima-tion [of economic well-being]" (Nordhaus and Tobin, cited in

Ayres 5), and proposed to modify it more or less drastically to achieve such an approximation. To the agenda of international politics this arrived only in the 1987 Brundtland Report on "sustainable development."

1.2. Systematic, reasonable, and fairly encompassing proposals for modifying the GNP by subtracting the real if hidden—and therefore difficult to estimate precisely—costs of life under capitalism began with Daly and Cobb's magnum opus *For the Common Good* (1989, rev. edn. with slightly less pessimistic calculations 1994). They proposed to effect not only a better measurement of real income but also to relate that income to what I am calling well-being[49] (welfare being by now associated with doling out). Accepting the framework of capitalism, proposals such as theirs were naively meant to sanitize its savage aspect. But insofar as they dealt with people's real well-being rather than their monetarized richness, they were more or less radical.

Daly and Cobb identify the GNP as mainly oriented toward measuring market activity but with modest adjustments in the direction of well-being, which it also claims to judge. Instruments like GNP are thus impure, a result of ideologico-political negotiation. (A good example is the Dow-Jones average, composed of 30 stocks selected secretly by *Wall Street Journal* editors!) The GNP is in de Goede's term a "contingent compilation" (89), though purporting to be based on the market, it uses for example the non-market accounting for capital depreciation (which raises the GNP: a total depreciation, the loss of all value to capital assets, would theoretically give a maximum rise to the GNP!). And since some GNP entries relate to well-being positively, some negatively, and some neutrally, Daly and Cobb

---

49. Today, the uselessness of GNP is well established in professional discourse, and there is a plethora of further instruments, surveyed in Talberth. The estimate of the Iraq invasion costs by Stieglitz is at least 3,000 billion dollars, and at least as much was pumped by the world governments into the banking system in the last two years.

concluded they can be extended to cover, say, depreciation of natural assets. By a series of such manoeuvers—subtracting 13 categories such as environmental damage and depletion or foreign debt, and adding 4 categories that estimate household labour and some services (such as public expenditure on health and education)—they arrive first at so-called Hicksian income, that is, what can be consumed without impoverishment in the future, and then at their estimate of well-being called Index of Sustainable Economic Welfare (ISEW). In order to measure consumption (well-being) rather than production (riches), they foreground the per capita amount arrived at (Table A1, 418-19). Here is their staggering difference with the GNP (all figures as US$ per capita):

OFFICIAL GNP
1950: $3,512
1973: $5,919
1986: $7,226

DALY-COBB'S ISEW
1950: $2,488
1973: $3,787
1986: $3,403

This means that the US per capita income, recalculated to measure well-being better (but still not centrally oriented to use-value) passed since 1961 through two phases: 1961-73 it did not rise (as the GNP falsely claims) 44% but did rise 26%, still a considerable achievement; 1974-86 it did not rise 24% but fell 9%! Thence, the average US well-being was in 1986 back to where it was in the mid-1960s. Today, if the pumping of hundreds of billions of dollars paid by the working people, first into the US military expenditures and then into saving rapacious banks, were also subtracted, the index of well-being would be back at the 1930s... Income inequality is back at 1929, with the top 300 thousand people earning as much as the bottom 150 million (Talberth 20)!

In 1991 the GNP was renamed GDP (Gross Domestic Product) in another politically contingent government manoeuvre. In 1995 a group including Cobb refined their counterproposal further. They proposed a refurbished Genuine Progress Indicator which includes twenty items more than GDP: it added the value of household and community work, and subtracted for a rising income gap, pollution costs or "defensive expenditures" offsetting damage by crime and other reasons. Their conclusion was, to begin with, that the GDP is mainly "three things in disguise: fixing blunders and social decay..., borrowing resources from the future or shifting functions from...household and community to monetized economy" (Cobb et al.). Furthermore, that in the later 1990s this GPI index showed a roughly 45% decline in genuine well-being as compared to 1973 and in 2004 it was $4,419 billion as compared to a quite unreal GDP of $10,760 billion (Talberth 22). This ludicrous situation prompted in 2007 even the OECD and European Commission to convene a conference called "Beyond GDP," but its results remain to be seen.

Quite beyond even the heterodox US economists' and ecologists' horizon (bar very few), subtracting from GDP the income of the upper (say) 2% would disastrously lower the per capita for the 98% that remain. Even the GPI index vastly exaggerates the well-being of between 80 and 98% of people (depending on nation).

In sum: capitalist growth since 1973—the onset of Post-Fordism—impoverishes the great majority of US people in terms of human well-being. This would hold *a fortiori* for most other countries of the North, except a few with remnants of the welfare State, while for the South, that is three quarters of mankind, the abyss of poverty for the majority grows daily larger.

This is largely to be understood as capitalist refusal to be accountable for the "social costs" of a profit economy, defined by Kapp (chapters 4-9 and 13) and added to by Leipert (89-91 and passim), as those costs caused by capitalist producers but not paid by them. They are manifest in the avoidable damages, for example to human and animal health or to natural resources. If such "costs of social consequences"—including the "societal illnesses" due to pollution such as cancer, heart and blood circulation, and breathing ways ailments—are figured in, the conclusion is that in a society based largely on "brain labour," the ability to buy more regardless of all other factors influencing life—for example, the GNP/GDP—is a poor measure of well-being. Beyond a certain medium level of industrialized mass production and an income of ca. $10,000 per head the official economic growth proves nothing: it "reflects increasingly frantic activity, especially trade, but little or no progress of human welfare in 'real' terms (health, diet, housing, education, etc.)" (Ayres 2, and cf. 2-5 passim). It is dubious also whether increase of competitiveness—the ideology of capitalist globalization—significantly contributes to well-being. "Sustainable economic growth" as defined by the capitalist roof organizations and governments is an oxymoron: growth raises the GNP but most probably damages at least as much as it improves well-being. Daly therefore rightly concluded that quantitative economic growth is ecologically not sustainable, so that total consumption must be reduced and stabilized (Daly, *Beyond* 10-11). Qualitative "growth," that is, efficiency of resource use, can and should be favoured. Even such a political babe in the woods as he concludes that the WTO-WB-IMF domination must be broken.[50]

---

50. A good initial formulation of human welfare in the sense of well-being is in Ruskin's *Unto This Last*: "There is no wealth but life. Life, including all its powers of love, of joy and of admiration. That country is the richest which nourishes the greatest number of noble and happy human beings; that man [sic] is richest who, having perfected the functions of his own life to the utmost, has also the widest helpful influence...over the lives of others." (cited in Hobson 4-5)

2. On the Entropy Calculus

<u>2.1.</u> Of course, there can and must be sustainable development in the sense of a "qualitative improvement without quantitative growth beyond the point where the ecosystem can regenerate" (Greider 455). For now we pass beyond tinkering with exploitative and destructive economics to consideration of <u>ecology and survival</u>, where the aim changes from maximum to optimum production. The ideologized commitment of the world's capitalist governments and corporations to infinite growth on a finite globe collides with the elementary fact that "[a]ny physical system of a finite and nongrowing Earth must itself also eventually become nongrowing" (Daly-Cobb 72). It follows that the major focus must be to optimize production by raising the productivity of its scarcest element—today, the natural resources. This is possible to achieve only if the real social costs of using air, water, soil, and labour are figured in, and unproductive consumption (most marketing and PR, useless innovations, artificial obsolescence, unceasing turnover of fashion trends, and other similar activities extraneous to use-values) is rigorously taxed. This means that both population growth in the poorer countries (the South) and per capita consumption in the richer countries and classes (the North) must be strongly, if reasonably, curbed. (The only fair and efficient way to curb population growth is, of course, making the poor richer—that is, meeting poverty head on rather than deepening it as the capitalist globalization does.) Their common denominator is the total consumption of energy. However, I shall vault over the intermediate discussion of energy (cf. Georgescu-Roegen, *Entropy* 138-40, and McNeill, 15 and passim), or even Einsteinian matter-energy, however eye-opening its consequences would already be, to focus on what seems to me the furthest reach of today's discussions: the management of <u>entropy</u>.

Entropy, the central term of thermodynamics, is usually explained as the inverse measure of the energy available to do work, but it is trickier than that. As Georgescu-Roegen's pioneering text from the 1960s (which I gloss in this section) points out, the Second Law of Thermodynamics means that the entropy of any isolated structure increases not only constantly, but also irreversibly (6). Since life is tied to activity, any life-bearing entity survives by sucking low entropy from the environment, and thereby accelerating the transformation of the environment toward higher entropy. The Entropy Law founds a different physics: it leads away from motion, which is in principle reversible, and opens onto irreversible qualitative change. It has no time quantification—how fast X will happen—and no particularization or specification—exactly which X will happen at any particular point (10-12 and 169). Thus, beyond being a branch of physics dealing with heat energy, thermodynamics underlies any biophysics of life and activity (including thinking).

Life is obtainable only by paying always a clear price: the degradation of the "neighboring universe" or total system—for example Earth. "[A] given amount of low entropy can be used by us only once" (278), so that "the basic nature of the economic process is entropic" (283). Since any collectively significant activity must be paid in the coin of less chance for future activity, the importance of purpose, what is something done for, becomes overwhelming. Aristotle's final cause and the old Roman tag cui bono? (in whose interest?) are rehabilitated as against scientism's narrow concentration on the efficient cause, how to manipulate matter (194-95—see an epistemological approach to scientism as inimical to life in Suvin, "Horizons"). If, as the Second Law of Thermodynamics recites, the entropy of the universe at all times tends toward a maximum, then we are in the domain of "a physics of economic value" (276). For, "low entropy is a necessary condition for a thing to be useful" (278): for example, copper in a bar has much lower entropy than copper diffused in molecules, or coal than ashes. Now, the economic process is, regardless of local fluctuations, entropically unidirectional: it will always be generating irrevocable waste or pollution, and foreclosing some future options (use of oil after it has been burned). Since, however, it also generates not only life but also all possibilities for "enjoyment of life" (281-82), we must become careful stewards, on the constant lookout for minimizing entropy or increasing negentropy.

Minimizing entropy centrally means that we must switch from the present use of terrestrial energy (oil, gas, and coal) to solar energy, which we get from outside the Earth system. The proportions in the mid-1980s were oil, gas, and coal 82%, nuclear 2% (its very dubious use depends on both safety and the entropic cost of waste disposal), renewables 16%—and today it is probably worse. This has already brought upon us the climate change only hired guns in science pretend not to notice, with economic damages on the order of untold billions of dollars which will be rising geometrically (but the foot-dragging capitalist combatting of which uses up even more energy, raising the entropy—and the GDP!). And since solar energy is huge—all terrestrial stocks of energy (low entropy) are equivalent to four days of sunlight—and practically free except for the initial cost of R&D plus installations, yet limited in its yearly rate of arrival to Earth, the preparations for the increase of its proportion in our energy consumption, which is the only alternative to a civilizational crash, should begin as soon as possible. Photosynthesis is our best bet, and if gasoline need be used for limited purposes, it should be gotten from corn instead of feeding it to cattle (cf. 304). Our wars for oil are a testimony not only to gigantic cruelty but also to gigantic imbecility and a lemming-like suicidal urge among our leaders and their brainwashed followers.

3. A Basic Prospect

So what is to be done? Again I can only mention a few general orientations towards maximizing life.

3.1. An idea by Georgescu-Roegen could be developed into a

pleasing calculus of preconditions for felicity. He pleads for a "maximum of life quantity," defined as the sum of all the years lived by all humans, present and future, and stresses it "requires the minimum rate of resource depletion" (*Entropy* 20-21). We could refine this, possibly by adding past humans too, certainly by specifying minimum conditions of dignified life, etc. Clearly the goal is <u>a maximum stock of life quality</u>, but quality presupposes a minimum quantity. Since this is an anti-entropic (negentropic) enterprise par excellence, a move toward it would have to include a shift to an economics of stewardship not ownership (cf. Brown), such as seems to have obtained before class society. The biosphere is indispensable to human physical and psychic survival, even beyond the need for photosynthesis. The flourishing of humanity is predicated on a substantial decrease of the human ecological niche as well as of the human boosting of entropy (cf. Daly-Cobb 378). This ties into the diminution and eventual elimination of dire poverty, since desperation cannot be expected to spare the environment (for example, locate farming where it does the least ecological damage). Such orientation toward a maximum of use-values compatible with a low rise of entropy must override all globalization based not only on financial speculation but also on the sole goal of profit.

Various sets of measures will be necessary for this, and have been for years now debated by some writers and in the "new global" movements.

3.2. The ecological imperative to focus on use-values instead of exchange-values brings us, finally, back to Marx's living labour (cf. Suvin, "Living"). For this is the only horizon against which a serious change of social formation can be again envisaged, if in circumstances radically different from the nineteenth and also from the early twentieth century. I shall proceed, I hope in his spirit, by indicating some medium-range necessities, some practical difficulties, and a horizon for overcoming them.

To prevent economic breakdown, indeed civilizational crash on the scale of the fall of Roman Empire seventeen centuries ago, we need to implement what Georgescu-Roegen called "a minimal bioeconomic program." He opined it would have to include "lower[ing] the population to a level that could be adequately fed only by organic agriculture" (today we'd have to add: without the OGMs) and strict regulation of energy wastage "by overheating, overcooling, overspeeding, overlighting, etc." ("Energy" 33-34). A third of a century and untold destructions later, Serge Latouche summed it up in the slogan of *décroissance*, meaning a lot of terms with "re": revaluing, reconceptualizing, restructuring, redistributing, reducing, reusing, recycling... (Latouche passim). The latest banking mega-bubble of 2007-08ff. has alerted us to the absolute necessity of mastering the "[b]usiness cycles...due to financial attributes that are essential to capitalism" (Minsky 173). Capitalism is not only a social system where all major means of production are privately owned, the key ones by a few dozen mega-corporations, but also a system of plutocratic power making a mockery out of democracy. An entity maniacally focussed on immediate profit, as any capitalist must be, is at best indifferent but usually actively opposed to public well-being. This system cannot be abolished overnight, but we have seen in the Welfare State period ca. 1940-73 that it can be up to a point controlled by a strong radical democracy. While my horizon is less radical than Samir Amin's when he states that the present crisis of misery and ecocide cannot be overcome within capitalism and yet must be overcome if we're not to fall back into barbarism (114)—or perhaps a genetic caste society—I believe he is on the right track.

Here are some possible initial policy measures which use, and modify, suggestions by Georgescu-Roegen, Minsky 287ff. and 328ff., the Tilburg Declaration, Greider, and others:

1/ Investment into production of use-values, from shoes through machines to good movies, which would strive for high productivity but not high profitability, meaning it would usefully employ the maximum possible number of willing people;

2/ Gathering means for such investments and other necessities of a radical democracy by progressive tax revenue on profits and ecological damage rather than on labour, and in favour of sustainable energy uses—for example: a tax on all built-over land, on consumption of water and minerals, and a tax on nuclear power to cover all expected costs of security and waste disposal (which would probably make their use uneconomical). This should include a large tax on incomes surpassing the legal minimum wage (say) more than tenfold, and a simultaneous reduction of taxes for the great majority of people. It is important that the taxes strongly encourage all suggestions for limiting risks by new products, for precautionary steps before prevention (Kourilsky and Viney, cf. Testart 23-25 and Suvin, essay 8? In this book).

The revenue from such taxes will have to be a multiple of the present revenues which amount to $7.5 trillion per year: "A carbon tax on coal, oil, and natural gas alone could raise roughly a trillion $ per year worldwide. That revenue could pay for a 20% cut in conventional taxes—on wages, for example." (Roodman 6-7) There are ample precedents to this; for example: "since 1991, five European countries have taken the seminal step of combining environmental tax hikes with income or payroll tax cuts" (Roodman 8, and see further illuminating examples there).

3/ To measure this, to abandon the GDP and reformulate the meaning of sustainable growth in all our public statistics is another necessary prerequisite. "[T]he GDP not only masks the breakdown of the social structure and the natural habitat...; worse, it actually portrays such breakdown as economic gain" (Cobb et al.). The use of converging indices such as Daly-Cobb's ISEW, the GPI by Cobb et al.—or the Ecological Footprint Analysis (EFA) that measures depletion of "natural capital," and at the moment indicates we would need 1.25 Earths to sustain the present rate of consumption (Talberth 24)—would educate the public as to the more realistic costs of what we do. It would also open the door for recognition and tax support of "activity by and for a collective" and a "community-oriented economy" (Möller col. 71-72): the unpaid work in the family or elsewhere taking up more time than the paid work (especially among women—cf. also Delphy, Haug, and Mies-Shiva).

4/ <u>Reduce the working time for a living wage per week to 35 hours.</u> Working time is a good rule-of-thumb measure of exploitation. In the last 35 years this has grown hugely, at the direct expense of human health and lives in tiredness, stress, disease, etc. The French Socialist Party's proposal for a 35-hours' week had the right idea but, as most social-democrats, they had no real will to defend it. This holds for the North and has to be accompanied *pari passu* with the <u>urgent alleviation of poverty in the South</u> by introducing work for a living wage and social protection there. Without an alliance between radical democracy in the North and South of our globe, in the long term both will come to nothing. The huge and hugely growing inequalities between them would remain the breeding ground of group terrorism responding to State terrorism.

One major difficulty would immediately arise. Some reformers (the Tilburg group, some ecologists) propose two simultaneous points. The first is that a radical economic reorientation for more affluent countries, including (say) the reduction by two thirds of consumption in key materials such as fossil fuels—some ecologists envisage a gradual reduction of materials and energy flow by 10 times!— "will protect us from even bigger future problems, such as health hazards, environmental degradation, a further increase in the global poverty gap, and armed conflicts and refugee movements"; I find this fully correct. The second point is that this "will not bring about a decrease in human welfare" (Tilburg 1); I believe this is correct only a/ if by welfare one means happiness (well-being) rather than financial wealth, and b/ in the long run, but not necessarily at the inception of such a reorientation. For capitalism functions by distancing the privileged Northern consumer from the true costs of production. Let me take the clearest case of energy prices in the North. As Kapp, Leipert, and others have argued, the Northern consumer buys not only the commodity "energy" but also the hidden decrease of ecological quality (deaths, diseases, costs of "defensive measures") destroyed by its production. The ecological replacement cost has to be added to the energy price, or entropy will spiral away and the sporadic crashes of our energy supply will grow systematic. Figuring in such costs was in the 1980s calculated as adding, for densely populated industrialized countries, up to two thirds of the present prices (Leipert 32-33 and 39-40, and cf. Greider 446 and passim). The case of energy can be extended, perhaps less starkly, to other instances of what William Morris called the unnecessary offers of the market.

Thus both gradual implementation and constant care of large majority support would be a necessity. As to the second, our horizon of radical democracy shall necessarily have to mix forms of representative, associational, and direct democracy (including recall of all elected representatives by proper procedures—cf. Cohen and Rogers). The Tilburg Group have rightly started thinking about "a permanent consultation organ aiming toward sustainability and solidarity" (2), which in order to be effective would have to be elected and constitutionally on a par with other parliamentary houses—let me call it an "Ecological Senate." As to gradualness, the *décroissance* must be well planned so as to avoid chaos. An example of a very simple and minimal step towards sanity was the 1980s' proposal of the "Tobin Tax," a small exit-and-entry toll at major foreign-exchange centers, which would greatly reduce the unproductive daily speculation in money values and yield hundreds of billions of dollars for good purposes (Greider 257, cf. Nordhaus and Tobin). But more important, implementing the above measures and major tasks of politically educating working people into their necessity and final superiority—such as persuading a family to pay 165 dollars or euros or pounds instead of 100 in order to save our planet—would be impossible without access to State power and thus to the mass media. This means reasserting political governance—where possible international, where need be national—over capital; an old-fashioned and entirely legal way of doing this is by taxing the worst corporate entropy-mongers more and restoring purchasing power to the middle and lower classes by taxing them less (cf. Greider passim).

One should expect huge opposition to all of this, since major corporations would spend half of the billions they fear to lose from their destruction of people and our planet to suborn efficient opposition to it, on the model of the destruction of Allende in Chile. It is not necessarily the fact that a program implementing significant ecological and societal justice measures could, as Wallerstein has remarked, "well serve as the coup de grâce to the viability of the capitalist economy" (81). Some capitalist enterprises could well and justly profit (within reason). Nonetheless one possible outcome would be a "transition beyond capitalism" as the only alternative to hugely destructive class warfare on all social levels (Amin 85). I do not think this can today be anybody's immediate program, as opposed to a coexistence with some segments of capitalists à la New Deal. But we have seen military destruction brought upon Serbia, Irak, and Afghanistan by the US government, which has taken upon itself the role of the executive committee of the world capitalist classes, when much smaller and further-off threats were perceived. I have remarked upon the political naivety of proposals such as Daly-Cobb's: this was perhaps tolerable at the time of President Carter, but is not today. In particular, Greece has had the experience of the Colonels' terror rule. Thus, in the case of active subversion, democracy will have to defend itself as best it knows, in ways we cannot foresee.

Bibliography

Ayres, R[obert] U. *Limits to the Growth Paradigm.* Centre for the Management of Environmental Resources, Working Paper 96/18/EPS. [Amsterdam?]: Elsevier Science, 1996.

Baran, Paul E. *The Political Economy of Growth.* New York: Monthly R P, 1957.

Brown, Peter G. "Why We Need an Economics of

Stewardship." *University Affairs* [Ottawa] Nov. 2000, 37 and 42.

Cobb, Clifford, Ted Halstead, and Jonathan Rowe. "If the GDP Is Up, Why Is America Down?" *Atlantic Monthly* (Oct. 1995).

Cohen, Joshua, and Joel Rogers, eds. *Associations and Democracy.* London: Verso, 1995

Daly, Herman E. *Beyond Growth.* Boston: Beacon P, 1996.

—-. *Steady-State Economics.* San Francisco: Freeman, 1977; 2nd edn. Washington DC/Covelo: Island P, 1991.

—-., and John B. Cobb, Jr. *For the Common Good.* Boston: Beacon P, 1989 (rev. edn. 1994).

Delphy, Christine. *Close to Home.* Transl. D. Leonard. Amherst: U of Massachusetts P, 1984.

[Economic Council of Japan.] *Measuring Net National Welfare of Japan: Report of the NNW Measuring Committee.* [Tokyo]: Economic Council of Japan, 1974.

Georgescu-Roegen, Nicholas. "Energy and Economic Myths" [1972], in his *Energy and Economic Myths*: ...*Essays.* New York: Pergamon P, 1976, 3-36.

—-. *The Entropy Law and the Economic Process.* Cambridge MA: Harvard UP, 1971 (rpt. New York: toExcel, 1999).

de Goede, Marieke. *Virtue, Fortune, and Faith.* Minneapolis: U of Minnesota P, 2005.

Greider, William. *One World, Ready or Not: The Manic Logic of Global Capitalism.* New York: Simon & Schuster, 1997.

Haug, Frigga. "Arbeit," in *Historisch-kritisches Wörterbuch des Marxismus*, Vol. 1. Ed. W.F. Haug. Hamburg: Argument, 1994, col. 401-22.

Hobson, J.A. *The Science of Wealth.* Rev. 4tnh edn. ed. by R.F. Harrod. London: 1950.

Kapp, Karl W. *Soziale Kosten der Marktwirtschaft.* Frankfurt: Fischer, 1979 (also as Kapp, K. William.*The Social Costs of Private Enterprise.* Cambridge MA: Harvard UP, 1950).

Kourilsky, Philippe, and Geneviève Viney. *Le principe de précaution.* Paris: O. Jacob, 2000.

Latouche, Serge. *Petit traité de décroissance sereine.* Paris:

Mille et une nuits, 2007.

Leipert, Christian. *Die heimlichen Kosten des Fortschritts: Wie Umweltzerstörung das Wirtschaftswachstum fördert.* Frankfurt: Fischer, 1989.

McNeill, John R. *Something New under the Sun: An Environmenal History of the 20th-Century World.* New York: Norton, 2001.

Mies, Maria, and Vandana Shiva. *Ecofeminism.* London: Zed Books, 1993.

Minsky, Hyman P. *Stabilizing an Unstable Economy.* New Haven: Yale UP 1986.

Möller, Carole. "Eigenarbeit," in *Historisch-kritisches Wörterbuch des Marxismus*, Vol. 4. Ed. W.F. Haug. Hamburg: Argument, 2000, col. 66-73.

Nordhaus, William D., and James Tobin. *Is Growth Obsolete?* Ann Arbor & London: University Microfilms, 1981.

Polanyi, Karl. *The Great Transformation.* Boston: Beacon P, 1957.

Roodman, David Malin. *Getting the Signals Right: Tax Reform to Protect the Environment and the Economy.* Worldwatch Paper 34. Washington DC: Worldwatch, May 1997.

Sametz, Arnold W. "Production of Goods and Services: The Measurement of Economic Growth," in E.B. Sheldon and W.E. Moore eds., *Indicators of Social Change.* New York: Russell Sage, 1968, 72ff.

Suvin, Darko. "On the Horizons of Epistemology and Science" [essay 8 in this book].

—-. "Living Labour and the Labour of Living," in his *Defined by a Hollow.* Oxford: P. Lang, 2010, 419-69.

Talberth, John. "A New Bottom Line for Progress," ch. 2 of *2008 State of the World.* [Washington DC]: Worldwatch Institute, 2008, 18-31 and 216-19.

[Tilburg Group.] *Declaration of Tilburg: A Convenient Truth.* March 2008. www.ekonomischegroei.net

Wallerstein, Immanuel. *The End of the World as We Know It.* Minneapolis: U of Minnesota P, 2001.

Zolotas, Xenophon E. *Economic Growth and Declining Social Welfare*. New York: New York UP, 1981.

11. ON THE CONCEPT OF CLASS (2011)[51]

—With thanks to Mladen Lazić,
this bastard offspring—

1. Delimitation

A working hypothesis on how to use the concept of societal class today can be derived from the discussion that begins with Marx's indications. I propose to retain from it the following six points, which seem reasonably certain and indispensable for further work:

1. After the tribal community, human societies are divided into multifarious antagonistic groups of more and more differentiated kinds. Some of these groups determine so strongly the position and behaviour of their members that they compete in importance with the overall society, and that membership in one excludes membership in other groupings on the same level (Gurvitch 105 and 116-20). Among an array of terms for such groups, such as caste, stratum or layer, and—before capitalism—estate (*Stand, état*), I shall use only "class" and "class fraction": Poulantzas (see *Pouvoir* 77-100, especially 99—cf.

---

51. This article has been written as an introduction for a study on classes in SFR Yugoslavia 1945-75, which should clarify and correct it. Unacknowledged translations are mine.

also his *Classes*) acknowledges only those two constitute a societal force, and Marx could be read that way too (Ollman, "Marx's" 576).

I shall sidestep the problem whether classes can be said to exist in a rather different form also before the rise of capitalism—and a certain bourgeoisie—though I believe that they did. I shall mention the Weberian tradition of approach to societal groups where necessary for the discussion of Yugoslavia. It will not be prominent: two major advantages of the Marxian approach seem that it relates to the economy in general (though his analytical stress was on production) while Weber relates only to distribution, and that the former can encompass the Weberian "elite" as a class fraction, while the "elite" approach as a rule tends to deal with elites plus biosociological "masses." However, it will be useful where the Marxist tradition has refused to face problems and degenerations after its own coming to power.

<u>2.</u> Classes are distinguished from other supra-local societal groups not only by their importance, multiple functions, and an inner articulation, but also by being legally *open* to anybody; in reality they are halfway closed.

<u>3.</u> As many other groups coterminous with society as a whole, classes do not exist alone but are <u>relational</u> animals, and the relation takes the form of a complex and changing process; for example, there is no bourgeoisie without aristocracy or proletariat (see Thompson, also Bensaïd, Resnick-Wolff, Ritsert, Roemer, and Wright). Each class is not only different from other ones but its interests are, especially for the Marxian tradition, often incompatible to those of other classes (Ossowski 120 and passim). Nonetheless, class differences and antagonisms, as well as their alliances may vary considerably, and their boundaries are often "[obliterated by m]iddle and intermediate strata" (Marx, *Capital* 3: 870, at /ch52.htm).

Classes practice simultaneously a certain solidarity, stimulated by common opposition against other ones, and internal competition, with frequent inner and outer conflicts (see MEW 3: 54). Thus, opposition and furthermore tensions and collisions are included into the very concept of societal class. Class conflict is a zero-sum game: for example, from what is monopolized by one dominant class is denied to the dominated classes (Lazić, *Čekajući* 47).

4. Classes are multi-functional, and insofar too compete in importance for its members with the national unit of which they are parts, or with gender. Among central factors of class unity is the individuals' common power-position in the mode of production and financial share of the societal wealth, which can be in capitalism called their economic conditions of existence, "that separate their mode of life, their interests, and their culture from those of the other classes, and put them in hostile opposition to the latter" (Marx, *18ᵗʰ Brumaire*, /ch07.htm). In the Marxian vision, classes are primarily organized around the axis of "a relationship of exploitation," that is, "appropriation of a part of the product of labour of others" (Ste. Croix, "Class" 99-100 and passim, and see his *Class Struggle*). A second factor reinforcing their class unity is professional condition. Both of these conditions, taken in the largest sense, mean that members of a class belong to the same layer of the societal pyramid. Thus, an individual's membership in a class is relatively stable, except in politically and/or economically revolutionary times, and classes themselves are relatively stable.

5. Classes are, as different from most other groups, "partially conscious and partially unconscious" of some important aspects of themselves (Gurvitch 111). In the Marxist tradition, "Class in the full sense only comes into existence when classes begin to acquire consciousness of themselves as such " (Hobsbawm 16, and see the foundational case-study by Thompson); Gramsci calls it an advance from economic to political consciousness (181). The attribution of such consciousness often led to wishful thinking, based first on revolutionary impatience and later on

dogmatism. Marx's and Engels's initial, somewhat monolithic conception of a stable class consciousness seems to me subject to conjunctural oscillations in micro-history, clearly visible in their own later writing and the tormented theory and practice after them, and brought to the clearest point by Lukács's "imputed consciousness" (126ff.). A class's consciousness is a "potential...rooted in a situation" (Ollman, *Dialectical* 157), it is constructed by various existential pressures upon existing presuppositions and inclinations, often alienated, and depends on actions: independent of concrete micro-historical situations, "it is wrong to suppose that any particular class...is subjectively and incorruptibly revolutionary *per se*...." (Hobsbawm 222). As of the rise of industrial capitalism, the degree of class consciousness clearly rises, and becomes more exclusively economic beginning with nineteenth-century western Europe (cf. Hobsbawm 17-18 and Lukács). Finally, the same class's relation to societal reality, and thus consciousness, often changes drastically, sometimes even in the short term.

In conjunction with point 3 on classes as relational, this means they are (especially before the rise of Fascism) organized only partially, in flexible and changing ways. They have many subordinated fractions, overlapping functions, and fuzzy fringes. Nonetheless, they are "powerful centers of spontaneous collective reactions " (Gurvitch 133), articulated in current ideologies and long-duration cultural artefacts. Each class shares an everyday culture, more or less estranged from the culture of other classes—in some cases, for example England, Ceylon or Haiti, speaking different dialects (Ossowski 152).

6. Polanyi supplies some important reminders of matters forgotten in the Marxist vulgate, which often envisaged practically isolated entities. First, "the relation of a class to society as a whole" (163), which defines a class's role and prospects, includes major overall factors—such as a war or climate change—that affect different classes in different ways. Second, alongside deep-seated class enmity in some cases, there exists

in other ones an irrefragable need for complementary roles, which was recognized by all theoreticians who were also practical politicians, such as Lenin or Weber; indeed, the success of any major class interest depends on alliances with other classes, and thus on the ability of formulating a common wider interest for society as a whole (159). Third, "interests" should be interpreted not only (though always also) economically but they significantly include factors like comparative status and security (161-62; cf. Hobsbawm 222).

I would opt for an operative use of following elements from Gurvitch's definition (116): Classes are really-existing, large, supra-local societal groups characterized by strong determination of their members' lives, partial openness toward new members, exclusiveness toward and opposition to other classes in the same spacetime, multi-functionality focussed on and by their members' economic plus professional condition as well as other needs of status and security, whose interests crystallize in a spread of changing class consciousnesses.

However, this needs three crucial additions. The first one, from Lenin, uses the relationship to surplus labour (though with a stress on its political aspect) and also has the pragmatic merit of being applicable to all the connotations of class in Marx and Engels (Ossowski 82). His definition of classes is "large groups of people differentiated by their position in a given historical system of societal production, by their relations (in most cases fixed and sanctioned by laws) to the means of production, by their function in the societal organization of labour, and consequently, by the way and the measure in which they enjoy the share of riches of which they dispose. Classes are groups of people of which one can appropriate the labour of the other according to the distinct place occupied in a given system of social economy." (Lenin 472)

Second, elements from Polanyi and Gramsci: As classes are fully relational entities, the obverse of 3. above means they are, especially at times of threat and rapid change, organized in hegemonically structured alliances based on the hegemon's ability to interpret society's strategic goals.

A third crucial addition has to do with an evaluation of class society today, and it is a paraphrase of the constant horizon shared by Marx and all the people and movements that claim this filiation: However, class society, especially after the full development of capitalist industrialization, is an increasingly destructive fetter stymieing not only social justice but threatening the very existence of humanity. True, that type of society eventually attained in capitalism, amid horrendous sufferings, a rise in societal wealth which can finally make exploitation and domination unnecessary for a decent life by one and all; but in the last two or three epochs, say after 1848, class societies are a root cause of psychophysical destructions, a hugely growing threat to the existence of society and indeed of the genus Homo.

The resulting overview may be too loose for a definition, but the term "class" has probably an inherently polysemic character. At any rate I need a guideline for further work:

—Synchronically, <u>classes are large, supra-local societal groups differentiated by their position in a given historical system of societal reproduction, which means their power and function in the exploitative organization of labour and their position within the repartition of the fruits of production, including for the upper and middle classes the appropriation of labour from the lower ones. Classes are characterized by strong determination of their members' lives, partial openness toward new members, exclusiveness toward and opposition to other classes in the same spacetime, multi-functionality focussed on and by the individuals' economic plus professional conditions as well as other needs of status and security, and a spread of changing class consciousnesses.</u>

—Diachronically, <u>classes are as a rule, especially at times of threat and rapid change, organized in hegemonically structured alliances based on the hegemon's ability to interpret society's strategic goals. However, class society, especially after the full development of capitalist industrialization, is an increasingly</u>

destructive fetter stymieing not only social justice but threatening the very existence of humanity.

2. Discussion

For individuals, the above delimitations mean that class is a
grouping to which members do not belong by birth (as in caste)
nor by explicit choice (as in voluntary associations) nor by any
command of a precise societal power. On the other hand, the
members' overriding common interests make for a tendency
toward attaining class consciousness, especially in situations
that threaten the whole class (as was the case with the bourgeoisie before the French Revolution or the industrial proletariat of 19th-Century Europe). Marx's category of interest,
itself based on "need" (*MEW* 3: 28) but larger, seems to me of
strategic importance, for it unites collective and personal levels,
while at the same time allowing to factor in people's material
circumstances. It is accompanied by the terms of "orientation"
and personal "motivations" (Ritsert 69-71).

The focus of Marx's opus, however, grew to be the critique of
"economics," a branch of sapience or science which arose with
capitalism and bourgeois quantification in 17th-18th Century
Britain, and in which classes are for the first time established
exclusively on the basis of ownership and/or labour, rather than
military or political-cum-religious role. In his tradition classes
are strategic nodes for understanding a society, since they are
relations between, on the one hand, the key production, circulation, and consumption of goods needed for life, and on the
other hand everything else in the human production of life.
These relations arise on the basis of unequal appropriation of
surplus labour, thus of "objective" (that is, tendentially dominant) economic and psychological interests of large groups of
people whose individual interests are decisively shaped by class
situatedness within a societal division of labour.

If we want to find some simpler common denominators for

classes as forms of interdependence between people, that is, of how some groups of people depend from other groups, the debate after Marx gives us three main criteria: dependence on basis of power, of societal function, and of economic position. The best Marxians such as Gramsci, have also retained Marx's original anthropological bent by stressing the cultural practices, in the widest sense, of the reproduction of societal life. These four criteria are not exclusive but usually combined in various ways. Further, paraphrasing what Lazić points out, the reproduction of classes is not exclusively economical, but tied to human productivity in the domains of material production, of societal control, and of the symbolic imagination, three different forms of praxis themselves differently integrated in different societal formations and concrete societies (*Čekajući* 47).

From times immemorial, the dominant metaphor of spatial opposition in politics was based on heaviness or labour of those below and lightness or privilege of those above, often mediated by metaphors from engineering construction (basis and superstructure) and by geology (strata). This can be used in a binary (digital) or gradual (analog) way, resulting in the opposition of only two or of more (usually 4 to 8) classes. The first way is the sturdy plebeian or popular cognition of "us" vs. "them" (oppressed/oppressor, powerless/powerful, the have-nots/haves); Marx uses it in his didactic overviews such as *The Communist Manifesto,* modifying the last opposition after his work on *Capital* into exploited/exploiters, and adding to this a "middle" class oscillating between the upper and lower one. The second one is the scholar's work on an actual society; Marx uses it in his historical investigations such as *The 18th Brumaire*, and Lenin at various points from *The Development of Capitalism in Russia* to his characterization of early Soviet society. The unresolved question of class (self-)consciousness, which has vexed the Marxian approach from Marx and Engels through Lukács and Gramsci to Lefebvre and the present day, is so difficult to resolve because it is at the crossroads of the of Marx's revolutionary didactics and scholarly punctiliousness; I shall approach this too in concrete Yugoslav discussions.

It has been pointed out that Marx's work sometimes uses the term loosely (Ollman, "Marx's" 576), and furthermore fuses three approaches to class structuring: the dichotomic one, the gradational, and the functional, while occasionally introducing a flexible but inductive fourth one, the interaction of two or more dichotomies (Ossowski 93), which became the central Marxist procedure. In sum, class was never explicitly defined by Marx or Engels but used in flexible ways, with various connotations according to the investigation at hand. Nonetheless, the nucleus of the concept of societal class, to which I have pointed above, is—together with the one of surplus labour—a kind of emblem and metonymy of Marx's doctrine and of all Marxist political programs. True, owing to the reluctance of non-Marxists to found it in exploitation of labour and to various misconceptions among Marxists, it has given rise to multiple and incompatible interpretations. Yet, Marx's theory of class is foundational: "simultaneously rich in possibilities, in some ways rather contradictory, and insufficiently worked out..." (Gurvitch 6).

Works Cited

Gramsci, Antonio. *Selections from the Prison Notebooks.* Ed. and transl. Q. Hoare and G. Nowell-Smith. New York: International Publ., 1975.

Gurvitch, Georges. *Le Concept des classes sociales de Marx à nos jours.* Les Cours de la Sorbonne. Paris: CDU, 1954.

Hobsbawm, E.J. *Worlds of Labour.* London: Weidenfeld & Nicolson, 1984.

Lazić, Mladen. *Čekajući kapitalizam.* Beograd: Službeni glasnik, 2011.

Lenin, V.I. *Izbrannye proizvedeniia v dvukh tomakh*, Vol. 2. Moscow: Gosizdat politicheskoi literatury, 1946.

Lukács, Georg. *Geschichte und Klassenbewusstsein.* Neuwied & Berlin: Luchterhand, 1971.

Marx, Karl. *Capital*, Vol. III. www.marxists.org/archive/marx/works/1894-c3.

—-. *The 18ᵗʰ Brumaire of Louis Bonaparte*, at www.marxists.org/archive/marx/works/1852/18th-brumaire.

—-. and Friedrich Engels. *Werke.* Berlin: Dietz, 1962ff. [cited as MEW].

Ollman, Bertell. *Dialectical Investigations.* New York & London: Routledge, 1993.

—-. "Marx's Use of 'Class'." *The American J of Sociology* 73 (1967-68): 573-80.

Ossowski, Stanisław. *Struktura klasowa v społecznej świadomości.* Wròcław: Ossolineum,1963 (cited from *Struttura di classe e coscienza sociale*. Transl. B. Bravo. Torino: Einaudi, 1966).

Polanyi, Karl. *The Great Transformation.* Boston: Beacon P, 2006 [original 1944].

Poulantzas, Nikos. *Classes in Contemporary Capitalism.* London: New Left Books, 1975.

—-. *Pouvoir politique et classes sociales*, Vol. 1. Paris: Maspero, 1978.

Resnick, Stephen, and Richard Wolff. *Knowledge and Class.* Chicago: U of Chicago P, 1987.

Ritsert, Jürgen. *Soziale Klassen.* Münster: Westfälisches Dampfboot, 1998.

Roemer, John. *A General Theory of Exploitation and Classes.* Cambridge MA: Harvard UP, 1983.

Ste. Croix, Geoffrey de. "Class in Marx's Conception of History, Ancient and Modern. " *New Left R.* no. 146 (1984): 94-111.

—-. *The Class Struggle in the Ancient Greek World..* London : Duckworth, 1983

Suvin, Darko. "Living Labour and the Labour of Living," in his *Defined by a Hollow.* Oxford: P. Lang, 2010, 419-69.

Thompson, E.P. *The Making of the English Working Class.* Harmondsworth: Penguin, 1976.

Trotsky, Lev D. *The Revolution Betrayed.* www.marxists.

org/archive/trotsky/1936/ revbet/index.htm

Wright, Eric Olin. *Classes.* London: Verso, 1985.

ABOUT THE AUTHOR

DARKO R. SUVIN, scholar, critic and poet, born in Yugoslavia, has studied at the universities of Zagreb, Bristol, the Sorbonne, and Yale, taught in Europe and North America, is Professor Emeritus of McGill University and Fellow of The Royal Society of Canada. Was vice-president of the Union Internationale des Théâtres Universitaires (1962-65), co-editor of *Science-Fiction Studies* (1973-81), editor, *Literary Research/Recherche littéraire,* International Comparative Literary Association review organ (1986-95), vice-president, International Brecht Society (1984-88); Honorary Fellow of Clare Hall College 1973-74, University College London 1980-81, Visiting Research Fellow Tokyo University 1990-91, Rikkyo University (Tokyo) 1994; Award Fellow of Humboldt Foundation 1996-2000, visiting professor at ten universities in N. America and Europe. He retired in 2000 and lives with his wife of 50+ years in Lucca, Italy. In these last years he publishes extensively in ex-Yugoslavia and is preparing a book on its trajectory.

He has published eighteen books of essays in Political Epistemology, Comparative Literature and Dramaturgy, Theory of Literature and Theatre, European and Japanese Dramaturgy (especially Brecht), Utopian and Science Fiction, and Cultural Theory; and hundreds of articles. He received the Pilgrim Award by the Science Fiction Research Assn. for scholarly contribution to the field, his 1979 book *Metamorphoses of Science Fiction* was chosen as one of the "Outstanding Academic Books 1979" by *Choice* magazine (May 1980). Published three volumes of poetry, won poetry prizes in US and Canadian competitions. Number of entries on DS in the *Arts & Humanities Citation Index...* 1975-98: 454.

His latest books in English are *Defined by a Hollow: Essays on Utopia, Science Fiction, and Political Epistemology,* Oxford: P. Lang, 2010, xxxiii + 582pp., ISBN 978-3-03911-403-0; and *Darko Suvin: A Life in Letters,* ed. Ph.E. Wegner, Vashon Island WA 98070: Paradoxa, 2011, 366pp., ISBN 1-929512-34-8 paper. His latest article publications are "Darwinism, Left And Right: And Two S-F Probes," *Foundation* no. 109 (2010): 7-17, rpt.in C- Pagetti ed., *Darwin nel tempo,* Milano: Cisalpino, 2011, 251-64; "Bureaucracy: A Term and Concept in the Socialist Discourse About State Power (Up to 1941)," *Croatian Political Science R* 47.5 (2012): 193-214; *Memoari jednog skojevca [Memoirs of a Young Communist],* installments being published in *Gordogan* [Zagreb] no. 15-18 (2008-09): 25-54 (available on www,gordogan.com.hr/gordogan/wp-content/uploads/2011/10/2009-Gordogan-15-18-25-54-Suvin-Memoan-manji.pdf), no. 19-22 (2011): 26-92, and forthcoming in 2012.

www.ingramcontent.com/pod-product-compliance
Lightning Source LLC
Chambersburg PA
CBHW031458270326
41930CB00006B/148